CYBERSECURITY ESSENTIALS

Cybersecurity Essentials

PROTECTING INFORMATION IN A DIGITAL AGE

Dr. Hesham Mohamed Elsherif

ELDON-USA Publishing

Contents

ABOUT THE AUTHOR

Cybersecurity Essentials
Protecting Information in a Digital Age
BY
Dr. Hesham Mohamed Elsherif

Dr. Hesham Mohamed Elsherif stands at the forefront of library management and research, boasting an impressive 22-year tenure in the field. Holding dual doctoral degrees, one in Management and Organizational Leadership and the other in Information Systems and Technology, Dr. Elsherif brings a unique blend of knowledge to any intellectual endeavor.

An expert in Empirical research methodology, Dr. Elsherif specializes particularly in the Qualitative approach and Action research. This specialization has not only strengthened his research endeavors but has also allowed him to contribute invaluable insights and advancements in these areas.

Over the years, Dr. Elsherif has made significant contributions to the academic world not only as a professional researcher but also as an Adjunct Professor. This multifaceted role in the educational landscape has further solidified his reputation as a thought leader and pioneer.

Furthermore, Dr. Elsherif's expertise isn't confined to one region. He has served as a consultant to numerous educational institutions on an international scale, sharing best practices, innovative strategies, and his deep insights into the ever-evolving realms of management and technology.

Combining a passion for education with an unparalleled depth of knowledge, Dr. Elsherif continues to inspire, educate, and lead in both the library and academic communities.

PREFACE

Welcome to "Cybersecurity Essentials: Protecting Information in a Digital Age," a primer designed to guide college students through the complex and critical field of cybersecurity. As we navigate an increasingly digital world, the importance of cybersecurity becomes more evident each day. This book is a response to the growing need for accessible, comprehensive education on how to protect digital assets and information in various contexts.

Our journey into cybersecurity does not assume prior knowledge. Instead, it begins with the fundamental concepts that underpin the field, gradually moving towards more sophisticated topics. This approach ensures that all students, regardless of their background, can grasp the essentials of cybersecurity and apply them in real-world situations.

Cybersecurity is not just a technical challenge; it encompasses legal, ethical, and social dimensions. Thus, our exploration includes a holistic view, preparing readers not only to understand the mechanisms of digital defense but also to appreciate the broader implications of cybersecurity practices.

The structure of this book is designed to facilitate learning in a logical and engaging manner. Starting from the basics, we delve into the principles of cybersecurity, explore the variety of threats that exist in the digital landscape, and examine the strategies developed to combat these threats. The final sections of the book look forward to the future of cybersecurity, discussing emerging trends and the ongoing evolution of cyber threats and defenses.

Key features of this book include:

- **Clear Explanations**: Complex concepts are broken down into understandable segments.
- **Practical Exercises**: Hands-on labs and exercises to apply theoretical knowledge.
- **Case Studies**: Real-world examples to illustrate key points and encourage critical thinking.
- **Review Questions**: End-of-chapter questions to test comprehension and foster discussion.
- **Further Reading**: Curated lists of resources for students interested in exploring topics in more depth.

This book is the culmination of efforts from a diverse group of individuals, including cybersecurity professionals, academic researchers, and educators. Their contributions have been invaluable in creating a resource that is both informative and engaging. Our collective aim is to inspire a new generation of cybersecurity-aware individuals who are equipped to protect themselves and their communities in the digital age.

As you embark on this journey through "Cybersecurity Essentials," we encourage you to approach the material with curiosity and an open mind. The field of cybersecurity is dynamic and ever-changing; there is always more to learn. We hope this book serves as a solid foundation upon which you can build a lifetime of learning and exploration in cybersecurity.

Thank you for choosing to explore the fascinating world of cybersecurity with us. Let's get started.

Dr. Hesham Mohamed Elsherif

WHO SHOULD READ BOOK?

Cybersecurity Essentials: Protecting Information in a Digital Age is crafted for a wide audience, reflecting the universal importance of cybersecurity in our digital lives. Whether you're a student just starting your academic journey, a professional seeking to broaden your knowledge base, or simply a curious individual concerned about digital safety, this book has something for you. Below, we outline specific groups who will find this book particularly beneficial:

College Students and Educators

Students across disciplines interested in understanding the fundamentals of cybersecurity, how it impacts various fields, and the basics of protecting digital information. This includes those studying computer science, information technology, business, law, and any other discipline where digital data plays a crucial role.

Educators and academic instructors looking for a comprehensive resource to integrate into their curriculum, enhance their teaching materials, or provide a solid foundation for students new to the subject.

Aspiring Cybersecurity Professionals

Individuals aiming to pursue a career in cybersecurity who need a solid grounding in the essentials of the field. This book provides the foundational knowledge necessary to delve deeper into specialized areas of interest or prepare for more advanced studies and certifications in cybersecurity.

Business Professionals and Entrepreneurs

Business leaders and managers who must understand the cybersecurity landscape to protect their company's digital assets effectively. This includes small business owners, entrepreneurs, and anyone involved in decision-making processes related to digital security.

Professionals in non-technical roles within tech companies who wish to gain an understanding of cybersecurity principles to better collaborate with technical teams or manage products and services with a cybersecurity component.

Tech Enthusiasts and General Readers

Technology enthusiasts keen on staying informed about the latest trends in cybersecurity, understanding how to protect personal data, and ensuring their digital practices are secure.

General readers concerned about digital privacy and security, looking for practical advice on safeguarding personal information against common threats and vulnerabilities.

Policy Makers and Legal Professionals

Individuals involved in crafting policies or legal frameworks related to digital security, data protection, and privacy. This book provides the necessary background to understand the technical underpinnings of cybersecurity challenges and solutions.

This book is designed to be accessible, avoiding overly technical jargon without sacrificing depth. It aims to demystify cybersecurity, making it understandable and engaging for readers from all backgrounds. Whether you're reading to enhance your professional skills, to incorporate cybersecurity principles into your daily life, or to embark on a new academic or career path, **Cybersecurity Essentials** offers the knowledge and insights to achieve your goals in the digital age.

Happy Readings!

Dr. Hesham Mohamed Elsherif

WHY THIS BOOK IS AN ESSENTIAL READING

WHY THIS BOOK IS AN ESSENTIAL READING

Cybersecurity Essentials: Protecting Information in a Digital Age stands out as a pivotal resource for anyone looking to navigate the complexities of cybersecurity in our increasingly digital world. This book is not just another textbook; it's a comprehensive guide designed to bring clarity and insight into a field that affects us all, whether we're aware of it or not. Here's why making this book an essential part of your reading list will be a valuable investment:

Broad and Inclusive Approach

We've tailored this book to be as inclusive as possible, ensuring that readers from various backgrounds, with differing levels of expertise, can find value and understanding. Whether you're a student, professional, or curious mind, the foundational knowledge provided here is indispensable in today's digital-centric world.

Practical and Theoretical Balance

"Cybersecurity Essentials" strikes a perfect balance between theoretical knowledge and practical application. This approach allows readers not only to grasp the underlying principles of cybersecurity but also to apply this knowledge in real-world scenarios, enhancing their digital security posture both personally and professionally.

Real-World Relevance

In a landscape where cybersecurity threats evolve daily, understanding these challenges is crucial. This book brings forward the most current issues, technologies, and strategies in cybersecurity, providing insights into the real-world implications of security practices and how they impact our digital lives.

Clear, Accessible Language

Cybersecurity, with its technical complexities, can be daunting. We've consciously used clear, accessible language to demystify the technical jargon, making the principles of digital security understandable for everyone. This accessibility ensures that readers are not just passive recipients of information but are empowered to actively engage with the material.

Comprehensive Coverage

From the basics of information security to advanced topics in cryptography, network security, and ethical hacking, this book covers a wide range of subjects necessary for a thorough understanding of cybersecurity. It lays a solid foundation that readers can build upon as they progress in their careers or academic pursuits.

Future-Proof Skills

In our digital age, cybersecurity literacy is not just an asset; it's a necessity. The skills and knowledge imparted in this book are designed to be future-proof, preparing readers to navigate and adapt to the ever-changing landscape of digital security.

A Stepping Stone for Further Learning

For those looking to delve deeper into cybersecurity, whether through advanced studies, certifications, or career development, "Cybersecurity Essentials" serves as an ideal stepping stone. It provides the necessary groundwork that will make further exploration of specialized topics more approachable.

In essence, "Cybersecurity Essentials: Protecting Information in a Digital Age" is more than just a book; it's a comprehensive guide for living, working, and thriving in a world where digital security is paramount. By making this book essential reading, you equip yourself with the knowledge, skills, and understanding to make informed decisions about your digital life and the security of the information you hold dear.

Chapter 1: The Digital Frontier

Part I: Introduction to Cybersecurity

The digital age has ushered in unprecedented opportunities for innovation, communication, and advancement. However, it has also introduced complex challenges in protecting the information that powers this digital ecosystem. Cybersecurity, at its core, is the practice of defending computers, servers, mobile devices, electronic systems, networks, and data from malicious attacks. It encompasses a broad range of practices, technologies, and processes designed to protect data, networks, and devices from attack, damage, or unauthorized access.

The Necessity of Cybersecurity

In today's interconnected world, cybersecurity is no longer optional; it's essential. The reliance on digital technology in every aspect of our lives means that the stakes are higher than ever. Cyber threats can disrupt economies, compromise personal privacy, endanger national security, and even impact the physical safety of individuals. As such, understanding cybersecurity is not just for IT professionals but is critical for anyone who interacts with digital technology.

Understanding the Threat Landscape

The threat landscape in cybersecurity is vast and varied, constantly evolving as technology advances and as attackers become more sophisticated. Cyber threats can range from malware, such as viruses and ransomware, to more insidious attacks like phishing, social engineering, and advanced persistent threats (APTs). These threats are not limited to criminal activities but also include espionage, cyber warfare, and terrorism. Understanding these threats and the motivations behind them is the first step in developing effective defense mechanisms.

Fundamental Concepts in Cybersecurity

At the heart of cybersecurity are several fundamental concepts that form the basis of how security measures are designed and implemented. These include:

Confidentiality: Ensuring that information is accessible only to those authorized to have access.

Integrity: Protecting information from being altered by unauthorized individuals, thereby ensuring its accuracy and reliability.

Availability: Ensuring that authorized users have access to information and resources when needed.

These principles, often referred to as the CIA Triad, guide the development of security policies and practices.

Cybersecurity Domains

Cybersecurity is a multi-faceted field that includes various domains, each focusing on different aspects of security. Some of these domains include:

Network Security: Protecting network infrastructure and data transmitted over networks.

Application Security: Ensuring that software applications are free from vulnerabilities that could be exploited.

Endpoint Security: Securing individual devices (computers, phones) that connect to the network.

Data Security: Protecting data at rest, in motion, and in use.

Identity and Access Management (IAM): Ensuring that only authorized individuals can access specific resources in the network.

Cloud Security: Securing data stored in the cloud from theft, leakage, and deletion.

The Importance of a Proactive Approach

A proactive approach to cybersecurity involves anticipating potential threats and implementing measures to prevent them before they occur. This includes regular system updates, security audits, employee training, and the implementation of robust security policies and procedures. It also involves staying informed about the latest cybersecurity trends and threats.

Introduction to cybersecurity is not just about understanding the threats and technologies; it's about adopting a mindset that values vigilance, responsibility, and ongoing education. As we continue to integrate digital technology into every facet of our lives, the role of cybersecurity becomes increasingly fundamental, not just in safeguarding our digital assets but in protecting our very way of life. By embracing the principles and practices of cybersecurity, individuals and organizations can navigate the digital world with confidence and security.

The Importance of Cybersecurity:

In the modern era, where digital advancements have transformed every facet of society, the importance of cybersecurity cannot be understated. As we navigate through the digital frontier, the realms of personal, corporate, and national security are increasingly intertwined with the cyber landscape. Cybersecurity is no longer a niche area of concern; it is a fundamental aspect of living and working in the digital age.

Protecting Personal Information

One of the most immediate concerns in cybersecurity is the protection of personal information. In an age where vast amounts of sensitive data are stored online—from financial records to personal communications—the potential for abuse is significant. Identity theft, financial fraud, and privacy breaches are just some examples of what can happen when personal information is compromised. Effective cybersecurity measures ensure that individuals' data remains confidential and secure, safeguarding against unauthorized access and exploitation.

The Spectrum of Personal Information

Personal information extends beyond just names and addresses; it encompasses a wide array of data points – from financial records and social security numbers to emails, private communications, and even preferences and behavioral data collected through various online activities. Each piece of data, seemingly trivial or not, can be a piece of the puzzle for malicious actors looking to exploit identities for fraud, theft, or other cybercrimes.

Cyber Threats to Personal Information

The threats to personal information in the digital realm are as varied as they are sophisticated, including:

- **Identity Theft**: Cybercriminals use stolen personal information to impersonate individuals, accessing financial accounts, obtaining credit, or committing crimes under the guise of someone else's identity.
- **Phishing Attacks**: These involve deceptive communications, often disguised as reputable entities, designed to trick individuals into revealing sensitive information such as passwords, credit card numbers, or social security numbers.
- **Data Breaches**: Large-scale hacks into company databases can expose vast amounts of personal information, making millions vulnerable to various forms of cyber exploitation.
- **Ransomware and Malware**: Malicious software can be used to hijack personal data, holding it hostage or silently stealing information for nefarious purposes.

The Role of Cybersecurity in Protecting Personal Information

The role of cybersecurity in safeguarding personal information cannot be understated. It involves a multi-faceted approach that includes:

- **Awareness and Education**: Understanding the value of personal information and the risks associated with its exposure is the first line of defense. Cybersecurity education empowers individuals to recognize threats and adopt safer online behaviors.

- **Data Encryption**: Encrypting data, both at rest and in transit, ensures that even if data is intercepted or accessed by unauthorized individuals, it remains unreadable and secure.
- **Secure Authentication**: Implementing strong, multi-factor authentication methods adds layers of protection, making it significantly harder for attackers to gain unauthorized access to personal information.
- **Regular Updates and Patch Management**: Keeping software and systems up to date closes vulnerabilities that could be exploited to access personal data.
- **Privacy Settings and Controls**: Actively managing privacy settings across online platforms and applications can help control the amount of personal information that is exposed and to whom it is accessible.

The Collective Responsibility for Protection

Protecting personal information is a shared responsibility. Individuals must be vigilant and informed about the security of their data, but the onus is also on corporations, application developers, and service providers to implement robust cybersecurity measures and uphold high standards of data protection and privacy. Moreover, governments play a crucial role in setting regulations that protect personal information and holding violators accountable.

In the digital frontier, where personal information traverses global networks in milliseconds, cybersecurity stands as the guardian of our digital identity. It's a complex, ongoing challenge requiring continuous attention and adaptation to emerging threats. Protecting personal information is paramount, not just to prevent financial loss or identity theft, but to preserve the very essence of our privacy and freedom in the digital age. As we navigate this vast digital expanse, let us do so with a commitment to cybersecurity, ensuring that our journey is both empowering and secure.

Ensuring Business Continuity and Trust

For businesses, cybersecurity is critical to safeguarding assets, maintaining customer trust, and ensuring the continuity of operations. A single breach can result in significant financial losses, erode customer confidence, and damage a company's reputation irreparably. In certain industries, such as finance and healthcare, the implications of a cybersecurity breach can also have serious legal and regulatory ramifications. Cybersecurity strategies that include risk assessment, incident response planning, and regular security updates are essential for businesses to thrive in the digital marketplace.

Cyber Threats and Business Vulnerabilities

Businesses face a diverse array of cyber threats, including but not limited to data breaches, ransomware attacks, phishing schemes, and insider threats. These threats can disrupt operations, lead to substantial financial losses, compromise sensitive data, and irreparably damage a company's reputation. The ripple effects can extend beyond the immediate financial impact, affecting stakeholder trust and the long-term viability of the business.

Ensuring Business Continuity

Business continuity planning (BCP) is essential for minimizing the impact of cyber incidents and ensuring that critical business functions can continue during and after a cyber attack. Cybersecurity plays a pivotal role in BCP by:

- **Identifying Critical Assets and Functions**: Understanding what needs to be protected is the first step in safeguarding business continuity. This includes identifying critical data, systems, and processes that are essential for day-to-day operations.
- **Implementing Robust Defenses**: Deploying firewalls, intrusion detection systems, encryption, and other cybersecurity measures to protect against unauthorized access and data breaches.
- **Regularly Updating and Patching Systems**: Keeping software and systems up to date to mitigate vulnerabilities that could be exploited by cybercriminals.

- **Developing and Testing Incident Response Plans**: Having a clear, actionable plan in place for responding to cybersecurity incidents can significantly reduce recovery time and costs.

Fostering Trust Through Cybersecurity

Trust is the currency of the digital economy. Customers, clients, and partners need to have confidence that their information is being handled securely and responsibly. Cybersecurity is at the heart of building and maintaining this trust by:

- **Protecting Customer Data**: Demonstrating a commitment to data protection through comprehensive cybersecurity measures reassures customers that their personal and financial information is secure.
- **Transparency and Communication**: Being transparent about cybersecurity policies, and proactive in communicating about and responding to cyber incidents, can help maintain trust even when things go wrong.
- **Compliance with Regulations**: Adhering to industry standards and regulations, such as GDPR, HIPAA, or PCI DSS, not only ensures legal compliance but also signals to stakeholders that the business takes data protection seriously.
- **Building a Culture of Security**: Fostering a workplace environment where cybersecurity is a shared responsibility enhances overall security posture and demonstrates to customers and partners that the business prioritizes security at all levels.

In the digital frontier, cybersecurity is not just a technical necessity; it is a strategic business imperative. Ensuring business continuity and building trust are fundamental to the success and sustainability of any business operating in the digital domain. By investing in cybersecurity, businesses not only protect themselves against immediate threats but also secure their future in an increasingly interconnected and digitalized world. The commitment to cybersecurity is a commitment to the resilience, reliability, and reputation of the business, underscoring its importance in the digital age.

National Security and Critical Infrastructure

At the national level, cybersecurity is intrinsically linked to security and sovereignty. State-sponsored cyber attacks, espionage, and cyber terrorism represent growing threats to national security. Furthermore, the cybersecurity of critical infrastructure—such as power grids, water supply systems, and communication networks—is vital for the functioning of society. Disruptions to these systems can have catastrophic consequences, highlighting the need for robust national cybersecurity policies and practices.

Cyber Threats to National Security

The threat landscape impacting national security and critical infrastructure is diverse, involving state-sponsored actors, terrorist groups, and cybercriminals. These actors can launch sophisticated cyberattacks aimed at disrupting, degrading, or gaining unauthorized access to critical systems. These systems include power grids, water treatment facilities, transportation networks, and healthcare systems. The potential impact of such attacks ranges from economic disruption and environmental damage to loss of life and national emergencies.

Enhancing the Resilience of Critical Infrastructure

The resilience of critical infrastructure against cyber threats is essential for maintaining national security and public safety. This resilience is achieved through a multifaceted approach that includes:

- **Risk Assessment and Management**: Identifying and evaluating the cyber risks facing critical infrastructure, followed by the implementation of strategies to manage and mitigate these risks.
- **Robust Cybersecurity Frameworks**: Adopting comprehensive cybersecurity frameworks that encompass threat detection, prevention, response, and recovery processes tailored to the specific needs of critical infrastructure sectors.

- **Information Sharing and Collaboration**: Facilitating information sharing and collaboration between government agencies, private sector entities, and international partners to enhance situational awareness and coordinate responses to cyber threats.
- **Incident Response Planning**: Developing and regularly updating incident response plans to ensure that agencies and organizations can quickly and effectively respond to cybersecurity incidents, minimize damage, and restore services.

The Role of Government in Cybersecurity

Governments play a crucial role in enhancing national security and protecting critical infrastructure from cyber threats. This role encompasses regulatory, operational, and strategic dimensions, including:

- **Setting Standards and Regulations**: Implementing regulations and standards that mandate cybersecurity practices for critical infrastructure sectors, ensuring a baseline level of protection across the board.
- **Investing in Cybersecurity Capabilities**: Allocating resources to develop advanced cybersecurity capabilities, including research and development in cyber defense technologies and workforce development to address the cybersecurity skills gap.
- **International Cooperation**: Engaging in international cooperation to combat cyber threats that cross national boundaries, including diplomatic efforts to establish norms and agreements on responsible state behavior in cyberspace.

The Importance of a Whole-of-Society Approach

Protecting national security and critical infrastructure in the digital age requires a whole-of-society approach. This approach recognizes that cybersecurity is not solely the responsibility of governments or specific sectors but is a shared concern that affects all citizens. Public awareness, private sector engagement, and academic contributions to cybersecurity research and education are all vital components of a comprehensive national cybersecurity strategy.

The importance of cybersecurity in the context of national security and critical infrastructure cannot be overstated. In the digital frontier, the stakes are high, and the potential impacts of cyberattacks on societal functions are profound. By prioritizing cybersecurity, nations can not only defend against immediate threats but also build a resilient framework capable of withstanding the evolving challenges of the digital age. Ensuring the security of critical infrastructure and national assets in cyberspace is fundamental to preserving peace, security, and stability in the modern world.

The Evolution of Cyber Threats

The digital frontier is constantly expanding, and with it, the complexity and sophistication of cyber threats evolve. Cybercriminals, hacktivists, and state actors employ increasingly advanced techniques to exploit vulnerabilities. Ransomware, phishing, deepfakes, and AI-driven attacks are examples of the evolving threat landscape. The dynamic nature of these threats necessitates that individuals and organizations adopt a proactive, informed approach to cybersecurity.

Historical Context

The history of cyber threats reveals a trajectory of increasing complexity and sophistication. Early forms of cyber attacks were often limited in scope and impact, primarily involving basic viruses and worms that spread through floppy disks or early networks. However, as the digital infrastructure expanded and became integral to both economic and social activities, the nature and scope of cyber threats grew correspondingly. Today, cyber threats encompass a wide range of malicious activities, including state-sponsored cyber espionage, financially motivated data breaches, and ideologically driven cyber attacks.

The Nature of Modern Cyber Threats

Modern cyber threats are characterized by their sophistication, stealth, and the speed at which they can spread across global networks. These threats leverage advanced techniques, including artificial intelligence (AI) and machine learning, to bypass traditional security measures. Some of the most prominent threats include:

- **Ransomware**: Malicious software that encrypts a victim's files, with the attacker demanding a ransom to restore access. Ransomware attacks have targeted individuals, corporations, and even municipal governments, causing significant financial and operational disruptions.
- **Phishing and Spear Phishing**: Deceptive practices that trick individuals into revealing sensitive information. Spear phishing, in particular, targets specific individuals or organizations and is often the first step in sophisticated cyber espionage or data breach campaigns.
- **Advanced Persistent Threats (APTs)**: Prolonged and targeted cyberattacks in which an attacker gains access to a network and remains undetected for an extended period. APTs are often state-sponsored and aimed at stealing information or surveilling critical infrastructure.
- **Supply Chain Attacks**: Attacks that target less-secure elements in the supply chain to gain access to secure or sensitive environments. The rise of these attacks highlights the interconnected nature of cybersecurity risks.

Adaptive and Proactive Cybersecurity Measures
The evolution of cyber threats necessitates an adaptive and proactive approach to cybersecurity. Traditional reactive measures are no longer sufficient; instead, organizations and individuals must anticipate potential threats and implement strategies to prevent them. This includes:

- **Continuous Monitoring and Threat Intelligence**: Utilizing advanced tools and techniques to monitor digital systems continuously for signs of malicious activity and staying informed about the latest cyber threat intelligence.

- **Security by Design**: Integrating security considerations into the design and development of digital systems, rather than treating security as an afterthought.
- **Cyber Hygiene and User Education**: Promoting good cyber hygiene practices among users and providing ongoing education about the latest threats and how to avoid them.
- **Collaboration and Information Sharing**: Engaging in partnerships and information-sharing networks to enhance collective defense against cyber threats.

The evolution of cyber threats in the digital frontier presents an ongoing challenge to cybersecurity efforts. As the complexity and sophistication of these threats continue to grow, so too does the importance of cybersecurity in protecting against them. By understanding the nature of modern cyber threats and adopting an adaptive, proactive approach to cybersecurity, organizations and individuals can better safeguard their digital assets, personal information, and the critical systems upon which our society relies. This dynamic battle in the digital frontier underscores the need for vigilance, innovation, and collaboration in the face of evolving cyber threats.

The Role of Education and Awareness

Understanding cybersecurity is not solely the domain of IT professionals. As digital technologies permeate all areas of life, a basic knowledge of cybersecurity principles is essential for everyone. Education and awareness are key to fostering a culture of security. By educating citizens and employees about the risks and best practices, we can collectively enhance our defense against cyber threats.

Empowering Individuals through Cybersecurity Education

The first line of defense against cyber threats is often not a piece of sophisticated software, but an informed user. Cybersecurity education aims to equip individuals with the knowledge and skills needed to recognize and respond to cyber threats effectively. This includes understanding the basics of digital hygiene, such as creating strong passwords, recognizing phishing attempts, and ensuring that personal and professional devices are appropriately secured. Education programs can significantly reduce the risk of successful cyber attacks by turning potential victims into active defenders against cyber threats.

Cybersecurity Awareness in Organizations

For organizations, cybersecurity awareness is integral to protecting sensitive data, maintaining customer trust, and ensuring business continuity. Employees must understand the role they play in safeguarding their organization's digital assets. Regular training sessions, security drills, and awareness campaigns can help instill a culture of security within the organization. By making employees aware of the latest cyber threats and teaching them how to avoid common pitfalls, organizations can significantly reduce their vulnerability to cyber attacks.

The Evolving Cyber Threat Landscape

The digital frontier is constantly expanding, and with it, the cyber threat landscape continues to evolve. Education and awareness programs must, therefore, be dynamic and adaptive, reflecting the latest developments in cyber threats and cybersecurity technologies. This includes educating individuals and organizations about new forms of malware, emerging techniques used in social engineering attacks, and the importance of security in emerging technologies such as the Internet of Things (IoT) and artificial intelligence (AI).

The Role of Educational Institutions

Educational institutions play a critical role in shaping the future of cybersecurity. By integrating cybersecurity into the curriculum, schools and universities can prepare the next generation of cybersecurity professionals to meet the challenges of the digital age. This includes not only technical training but also courses on the ethical, legal, and social implications of cybersecurity. Furthermore, educational institutions can serve as centers for cybersecurity research, contributing to the development of innovative solutions to emerging cyber threats.

Public Awareness Campaigns

Governments and non-profit organizations also contribute to cybersecurity awareness through public campaigns. These campaigns aim to educate the general public about cyber threats and promote safe online practices. By raising awareness at the national or even global level, these campaigns play a vital role in creating a more secure digital environment for all users.

In the digital frontier, where cyber threats loom large, the role of education and awareness in cybersecurity cannot be overstated. It is a vital component of a comprehensive cybersecurity strategy, empowering individuals and organizations to protect themselves against the myriad of cyber threats they face. Through ongoing education and awareness efforts, we can build a more secure digital world, one in which users are not only aware of the risks but are also equipped to counter them effectively.

A Collective Responsibility

Cybersecurity is a collective responsibility that extends beyond individual actions or organizational policies. It involves cooperation between governments, businesses, and individuals to create a secure digital ecosystem. Public-private partnerships, information sharing, and collaborative efforts to develop and enforce cybersecurity standards are crucial in this endeavor.

Bridging the Knowledge Gap

A significant challenge in combating cyber threats is the knowledge gap that exists among the general population. Many users of digital technology are unaware of the potential risks or the basic steps they can take to protect themselves online. Public awareness campaigns aim to bridge this gap by disseminating crucial information in an accessible and engaging manner. By raising the baseline level of cybersecurity knowledge, these campaigns can significantly reduce the number of successful cyber attacks.

Empowering Individuals and Communities

Public awareness campaigns empower individuals and communities by providing them with the knowledge and tools they need to protect themselves in the digital world. This empowerment goes beyond merely avoiding risks; it encompasses understanding how to respond to and recover from cyber incidents. Campaigns often highlight practical steps such as regular software updates, the use of strong passwords, and the importance of backing up data. By empowering individuals, these campaigns foster a more resilient digital community capable of withstanding and responding to cyber threats.

Shaping Cyber Hygiene Practices

Just as personal hygiene practices are vital for public health, cyber hygiene practices are crucial for maintaining digital health and security. Public awareness campaigns play a significant role in shaping these practices. Through consistent messaging about the importance of regular updates, cautious clicking, and secure browsing, these campaigns help to instill habits that significantly reduce the risk of cyber infections and breaches. Over time, these practices can become ingrained in the digital culture, leading to a more secure digital environment for all users.

Encouraging Proactive Behaviors

One of the key objectives of public awareness campaigns is to encourage proactive behaviors among internet users. This includes staying informed about the latest cyber threats, using cybersecurity tools, and adopting a questioning attitude towards unsolicited or suspicious online content. By promoting a proactive approach, these campaigns help individuals and organizations to stay one step ahead of cybercriminals.

Fostering a Culture of Security

Ultimately, the aim of public awareness campaigns is to foster a culture of security where cybersecurity is recognized as a shared responsibility. These campaigns stress that cybersecurity is not solely the domain of IT professionals but is a concern for everyone in the digital age. By cultivating a culture of security, public awareness campaigns contribute to the creation of a more secure digital ecosystem where users are aware of the risks and are equipped to protect themselves and others.

In the vast and often perilous digital frontier, public awareness campaigns stand as beacons of information and empowerment. Their role in the fight against cyber threats is indispensable, providing the first line of defense by educating the public and promoting safe online practices. As the digital landscape continues to evolve, the importance of these campaigns will only grow. By enhancing public awareness and fostering a culture of security, we can collectively work towards a safer, more secure digital world for future generations.

Basic Concepts and Terminology:

In navigating the vast and complex landscape of the digital frontier, understanding the basic concepts and terminology of cybersecurity is fundamental. This foundational knowledge not only demystifies the field but also equips individuals with the necessary tools to recognize and protect against cyber threats. Let's delve into some of the essential concepts and terms that form the backbone of cybersecurity discourse.

Cybersecurity

Cybersecurity refers to the practice of protecting computers, servers, mobile devices, electronic systems, networks, and data from malicious attacks. It encompasses a range of techniques and strategies designed to safeguard information technology and data from unauthorized access, damage, or theft.

The CIA Triad

The **CIA Triad** is a widely respected model that outlines the three main objectives of cybersecurity: Confidentiality, Integrity, and Availability.

- **Confidentiality**: Ensures that sensitive information is accessed only by authorized individuals and remains private or secret.
- **Integrity**: Guarantees that the information is trustworthy and accurate, and has not been tampered with or altered by unauthorized individuals.

- **Availability**: Ensures that information and resources are accessible to authorized users when needed, maintaining the functionality and efficiency of systems.

Malware

Malware, short for malicious software, is any software intentionally designed to cause damage to a computer, server, client, or computer network. Types of malware include viruses, worms, Trojan horses, and ransomware.

- **Viruses** are malicious programs that attach themselves to clean files and infect other clean files. They can spread uncontrollably, damaging a system's core functionality and deleting or corrupting files.
- **Worms** are standalone malware that replicate themselves to spread to other computers, often without any human action or knowledge.
- **Trojan Horses** are malicious programs that disguise themselves as legitimate software. Users are tricked into loading and executing the Trojans on their systems, at which point they are executed to cause harm or steal data.
- **Ransomware** locks or encrypts the victim's data, demanding a ransom to restore access to it.

Phishing

Phishing is a cyberattack that uses disguised email as a weapon. The goal is to trick the email recipient into believing that the message is something they want or need — for example, a request from their bank or a note from someone in their company — and to click a link or download an attachment.

Encryption

Encryption is the process of converting information or data into a code, especially to prevent unauthorized access. This secure coding ensures that only authorized parties can access the information, making it a cornerstone of data confidentiality.

Firewall

A **firewall** is a network security device that monitors and controls incoming and outgoing network traffic based on predetermined security rules. A firewall typically establishes a barrier between a trusted internal network and untrusted external network, such as the Internet.

VPN

A **Virtual Private Network (VPN)** extends a private network across a public network, enabling users to send and receive data across shared or public networks as if their computing devices were directly connected to the private network. This provides online privacy and anonymity by creating a private network from a public internet connection.

Incident Response

Incident Response is an organized approach to addressing and managing the aftermath of a security breach or cyberattack. The goal is to handle the situation in a way that limits damage and reduces recovery time and costs.

Understanding these fundamental concepts and terminology is crucial in the digital age, where cybersecurity threats loom large. Armed with this basic knowledge, individuals and organizations can better navigate the digital frontier, making informed decisions to protect their digital assets in an increasingly interconnected world.

Conclusion

The importance of cybersecurity in the digital frontier cannot be overstated. As we continue to explore and expand into digital spaces, the need to protect our information, infrastructure, and way of life from cyber threats becomes increasingly critical. Cybersecurity is not just about preventing attacks; it's about ensuring the resilience and integrity of our digital world. By prioritizing cybersecurity, we safeguard not only our personal and financial well-being but also the foundational structures of our society.

Chapter 2: Historical Overview of Cybersecurity

The journey of cybersecurity is a fascinating chronicle that mirrors the rapid evolution of digital technology and the internet. From its nascent stages in the early days of computing to its current status as a cornerstone of global security, the history of cybersecurity is marked by a continuous arms race between cyber defenders and attackers. This overview highlights key milestones and shifts in the landscape of cybersecurity, providing insight into how past challenges and responses shape today's strategies.

The Dawn of Cybersecurity:

The origins of cybersecurity can be traced back to the 1970s, with the advent of the first computer viruses and the realization that software could be exploited for malicious purposes. One of the earliest recorded instances of a computer virus was the Creeper virus in 1971, which affected ARPANET, the precursor to the internet. Creeper was an experimental self-replicating program that moved between systems, leaving a message: "I'm the creeper, catch me if you can!" This led to the creation of the Reaper program, which could be considered the first antivirus software designed to delete Creeper.

The dawn of cybersecurity traces back to an era when the concept of digital security was virtually nonexistent, primarily because the proliferation of personal computers and the internet was still on the horizon. This early phase in cybersecurity history set the groundwork for the complex and multifaceted domain it has become today

The Origins of Cybersecurity

Cybersecurity's infancy can be directly linked to the advent of the first computer systems and networks. As these systems became more integral to military, academic, and business operations, the potential impact of their compromise became apparent. The creation of ARPANET in 1969, a precursor to the modern internet, marked a pivotal moment in the history of computing and, by extension, cybersecurity (Leiner et al., 2009).

One of the earliest known cybersecurity threats was the Creeper virus, emerging in 1971. Creeper was an experimental, self-replicating program designed to test the limits of ARPANET's connectivity. It displayed a simple message: "I'm the creeper, catch me if you can!" (Thomas, 2003). This benign virus necessitated the creation of Reaper, a program designed to seek out and remove Creeper, representing an early form of antivirus software.

Recognizing the Need for Cybersecurity

The realization that computer systems could be exploited maliciously led to the development of strategies and technologies aimed at protecting these systems. The 1970s and 1980s saw the emergence of more sophisticated threats, including malware and computer viruses, which were distributed via floppy disks, demonstrating the need for systemic cybersecurity measures (Kaspersky, 2021).

One of the significant milestones in the history of cybersecurity was the recognition of network vulnerabilities. The Morris Worm of 1988 was a watershed moment, as it exploited weaknesses in UNIX systems and caused considerable disruption to thousands of computers connected to the internet, leading to the realization that connected systems could be vulnerable to widespread attacks (Spafford, 1989).

The Institutional Response

The fallout from the Morris Worm led to the establishment of the first Computer Emergency Response Team (CERT) at Carnegie Mellon University, funded by the Defense Advanced Research Projects Agency (DARPA). This initiative marked the beginning of organized efforts to address cybersecurity threats and underscored the need for continuous monitoring, threat analysis, and coordinated response mechanisms to protect digital infrastructure (West-Brown et al., 2003).

The dawn of cybersecurity was characterized by a transition from curiosity-driven exploration of computer networks to a growing awareness of the potential for malicious exploitation. The early incidents of cyber threats highlighted the need for protective measures and spurred the development of the cybersecurity industry. This period laid the foundation for the complex and ever-evolving field of cybersecurity, emphasizing the importance of anticipation, innovation, and collaboration in combating cyber threats.

The Rise of the Internet and Cyber Threats

As the internet grew in the late 1980s and early 1990s, so did the potential for cyber threats. The Morris Worm of 1988 was one of the first worms to gain significant attention, exploiting vulnerabilities in UNIX systems and causing considerable disruption. This incident highlighted the need for cybersecurity measures and prompted the formation of the Computer Emergency Response Team (CERT), setting a precedent for future cybersecurity efforts.

The rise of the internet marked a pivotal era in the development of cybersecurity. As the digital network expanded, connecting millions of computers and users around the world, the landscape of cyber threats evolved correspondingly, becoming more sophisticated and widespread. This period of rapid technological advancement highlighted the growing need for robust cybersecurity measures to protect against an array of emerging digital threats.

The Expansion of the Internet

The transition from the ARPANET to the modern internet in the late 1980s and early 1990s facilitated unprecedented levels of connectivity and data exchange. This expansion was not only a technological breakthrough but also a turning point for cybersecurity (Leiner et al., 2009). The internet's open nature, designed to foster communication and information sharing, inadvertently introduced vulnerabilities that could be exploited for malicious purposes.

Emergence of Cyber Threats

With the internet's growth, the early 1990s witnessed a surge in cyber threats, ranging from viruses and worms to more sophisticated hacking attempts. One of the most significant early internet worms was the Morris Worm of 1988, which exploited vulnerabilities in UNIX systems, causing widespread disruption and highlighting the fragility of networked environments (Spafford, 1989). This incident underscored the need for vigilant cybersecurity practices and the development of mechanisms to protect interconnected computer systems.

The Response to Growing Threats

The response to the increasing cyber threats of the early internet era was multifaceted, involving both technological innovations and policy initiatives. The establishment of the first Computer Emergency Response Team (CERT) at Carnegie Mellon University represented a foundational step in organizing a coordinated response to cybersecurity incidents (West-Brown et al., 2003). Furthermore, the development of antivirus software and firewalls became critical components of individual and organizational cybersecurity strategies.

The Evolution of Cybersecurity Measures

As cyber threats continued to evolve, so did the strategies and technologies designed to combat them. The late 1990s and early 2000s saw the introduction of more advanced cybersecurity measures, including intrusion detection systems (IDS) and encryption protocols, aimed at securing data transmission over the internet (Stallings, 1995). These developments reflected a growing recognition of the internet's dual role as a facilitator of global connectivity and a vector for cyber threats.

The Role of Legislation

The rise of the internet and the corresponding increase in cyber threats also prompted legislative action aimed at addressing cybersecurity challenges. Laws and regulations, such as the Computer Fraud and Abuse Act (CFAA) in the United States, were enacted to criminalize unauthorized access to computer systems and data, marking the beginning of legal frameworks governing cybersecurity (United States Department of Justice, n.d.).

The rise of the internet and the concurrent emergence of cyber threats marked a critical period in the history of cybersecurity. This era underscored the complex relationship between technological advancement and cybersecurity, highlighting the continuous need for adaptive strategies and measures to protect digital infrastructure and information. As the internet continues to evolve, so too does the landscape of cyber threats, necessitating ongoing vigilance and innovation in cybersecurity practices.

Cybersecurity in the Digital Age

The proliferation of personal computers in the 1990s and the expansion of the internet ushered in a new era of cybersecurity challenges. Viruses and malware became more sophisticated, targeting not just institutions but individual users. The ILOVEYOU virus in 2000 was a notable example, demonstrating the potential for massive disruption on a global scale. As e-commerce and online banking grew, so did the incentives for cybercrime, leading to an increase in attacks aimed at stealing financial information and identity theft.

As we transitioned into the digital age, marked by the proliferation of internet usage, mobile computing, and the advent of e-commerce, the field of cybersecurity entered a new era of complexity and importance. This period is characterized by an exponential increase in cyber threats, alongside the rapid advancement of technology. Cybersecurity strategies and mechanisms had to evolve quickly to address the sophisticated and varied nature of attacks that emerged with the digital revolution.

The Proliferation of Internet Usage

The late 1990s and early 2000s witnessed a dramatic increase in internet accessibility and usage, fundamentally altering how societies operate, communicate, and transact. This digital revolution, while bringing about significant benefits, also introduced new vulnerabilities and attack vectors for cybercriminals. As internet usage became ubiquitous, the potential impact of cyberattacks expanded, affecting individuals, businesses, and governments on an unprecedented scale (Castells, 2001).

The Rise of E-Commerce and Digital Transactions

The advent of e-commerce and the widespread adoption of digital transactions introduced financial incentives for cybercriminals, leading to an increase in cyber theft, fraud, and espionage. The security of online transactions became a critical concern, necessitating the development of secure electronic payment systems and the implementation of encryption protocols to protect sensitive financial data during transmission (Schneier, 2000).

Advanced Persistent Threats and State-Sponsored Cyberattacks

The digital age also saw the emergence of Advanced Persistent Threats (APTs) and state-sponsored cyberattacks. These sophisticated attacks are characterized by their long-term engagement, significant resources, and high levels of stealth, often targeting sensitive national security information, critical infrastructure, and corporate intellectual property. The revelation of cyber espionage campaigns such as Stuxnet, which targeted Iranian nuclear facilities, underscored the geopolitical dimensions of cybersecurity in the digital age (Zetter, 2014).

The Evolution of Cybersecurity Measures

In response to the evolving threat landscape, cybersecurity measures became more sophisticated, incorporating artificial intelligence (AI), machine learning, and big data analytics to predict and combat cyber threats. The development of cybersecurity frameworks and standards, such as the National Institute of Standards and Technology (NIST) Cybersecurity Framework, provided structured approaches for organizations to assess and improve their cybersecurity posture (National Institute of Standards and Technology, 2018).

Cybersecurity Legislation and Global Initiatives

The increasing prevalence of cyberattacks necessitated legislative and global initiatives to enhance cybersecurity and promote international cooperation. Laws such as the General Data Protection Regulation (GDPR) in the European Union were enacted to protect personal data and privacy, setting a precedent for global data protection standards. International efforts, including the Budapest Convention on Cybercrime, aimed to facilitate cross-border cooperation in the investigation and prosecution of cybercrimes (Council of Europe, 2001).

The digital age has significantly transformed the cybersecurity landscape, presenting new challenges and requiring innovative solutions. The proliferation of internet usage, the rise of e-commerce, and the emergence of sophisticated cyber threats necessitated a comprehensive and adaptive approach to cybersecurity. As technology continues to evolve, the importance of cybersecurity remains paramount, underscoring the need for ongoing vigilance, innovation, and international cooperation to protect the digital world.

Government and Corporate Response

The increasing threat posed by cyberattacks led to significant responses from both governments and corporations. In the early 2000s, cybersecurity legislation began to take shape, with laws such as the USA PATRIOT Act including provisions to combat cyber terrorism. Corporations also started to invest heavily in cybersecurity measures, recognizing the critical importance of protecting customer data and maintaining trust.

The escalation of cyber threats over the past few decades has elicited significant responses from both governmental bodies and corporate entities worldwide. As the digital age advanced, the necessity for robust cybersecurity measures became undeniable, leading to the development of comprehensive strategies, regulations, and technologies designed to protect digital infrastructure, sensitive information, and maintain public trust.

Government Response

Governments around the globe have recognized the critical importance of cybersecurity in protecting national security, economic interests, and citizens' privacy. This acknowledgment has led to the establishment of national cybersecurity strategies, dedicated cybersecurity agencies, and the enactment of cybersecurity legislation.

National Cybersecurity Strategies

Countries have developed national cybersecurity strategies to provide a structured framework for protecting against cyber threats. These strategies typically outline the government's approach to securing critical infrastructure, combating cybercrime, and fostering collaboration between the public and private sectors (Bada, Sasse, & Nurse, 2019).

Cybersecurity Agencies

Many governments have established dedicated agencies responsible for coordinating national cybersecurity efforts. For instance, the United States formed the Cybersecurity and Infrastructure Security Agency (CISA) to enhance the security and resilience of the nation's critical infrastructure (U.S. Department of Homeland Security, 2018).

Cybersecurity Legislation

Legislation plays a crucial role in the government's cybersecurity response. Laws such as the General Data Protection Regulation (GDPR) in the European Union and the Cybersecurity Information Sharing Act (CISA) in the United States have been enacted to protect personal data, promote information sharing between government and private entities, and enhance overall cybersecurity (European Parliament and Council, 2016; U.S. Congress, 2015).

Corporate Response

As cyber threats increasingly target the private sector, corporations have also ramped up their cybersecurity efforts. The protection of customer data, intellectual property, and corporate reputation has driven businesses to invest significantly in cybersecurity measures.

Investment in Cybersecurity Technologies

Corporations have significantly increased their investment in cybersecurity technologies, including advanced threat detection systems, encryption technologies, and secure cloud services. These investments are aimed at protecting corporate networks and data from cyberattacks and ensuring the continuity of business operations (Morgan, 2020).

Cybersecurity Governance

Corporate governance now often includes a focus on cybersecurity, with many companies establishing dedicated cybersecurity governance structures. This includes the creation of Chief Information Security Officer (CISO) positions and cybersecurity teams tasked with overseeing the organization's cybersecurity posture (Gordon, Loeb, Lucyshyn, & Zhou, 2015).

Collaboration and Information Sharing

Recognizing that cybersecurity is a shared challenge, corporations have engaged in greater collaboration and information sharing with each other and with government agencies. Initiatives such as the Global Cyber Alliance and Information Sharing and Analysis Centers (ISACs) facilitate the exchange of cyber threat intelligence and best practices among stakeholders (Global Cyber Alliance, n.d.).

The government and corporate responses to the evolving cybersecurity landscape underscore the critical importance of cybersecurity in the digital age. Through the development of national strategies, legislation, dedicated agencies, and significant investments in cybersecurity technologies, both sectors aim to protect against the myriad of cyber threats that jeopardize digital security and privacy. As cyber threats continue to evolve, ongoing adaptation and collaboration between the public and private sectors will be essential to safeguard the digital frontier.

The Modern Era of Cybersecurity

Today, cybersecurity is a multi-faceted field that encompasses a broad range of disciplines, including network security, application security, information security, and operational security. The threats have evolved to include sophisticated state-sponsored cyber espionage, cyber warfare, and ransomware attacks that target individuals, corporations, and governments alike. In response, cybersecurity strategies have become more sophisticated, leveraging artificial intelligence, machine learning, and blockchain technology to defend against attacks.

The modern era of cybersecurity is characterized by an unprecedented scale of digital connectivity, with the proliferation of internet-enabled devices, the advent of cloud computing, and the increasing digitization of critical infrastructure. This era is marked by the sophistication and diversity of cyber threats, necessitating equally advanced cybersecurity measures. As we navigate through this era, cybersecurity has evolved from a niche IT concern to a strategic priority at the highest levels of government and corporate leadership.

Evolution of Cyber Threats

In the modern era, cyber threats have become more sophisticated, leveraging advanced techniques such as artificial intelligence (AI) and machine learning to bypass traditional security measures. Ransomware attacks have seen a significant rise, targeting businesses, healthcare institutions, and municipal systems, demanding payments to unlock encrypted data (Özment & Schechter, 2011). Additionally, the Internet of Things (IoT) has expanded the attack surface, introducing vulnerabilities in everyday connected devices, from smart home systems to industrial control systems.

Cybersecurity Strategies and Technologies

To combat these evolving threats, cybersecurity strategies and technologies have also advanced. The use of AI and machine learning in cybersecurity tools has become more prevalent, enabling proactive identification and mitigation of threats before they can cause harm. Blockchain technology has been explored for its potential to enhance data integrity and security, particularly in securing transactions and supply chains (Feng, Zhang, & Zhang, 2019).

The Role of Legislation and Compliance

The modern era has also seen an increase in cybersecurity legislation and compliance requirements, aimed at protecting personal data and ensuring the security of digital systems. The General Data Protection Regulation (GDPR) in the European Union and the California Consumer Privacy Act (CCPA) in the United States are prime examples of legal frameworks designed to enhance data protection and privacy (European Parliament and Council, 2016; State of California, 2018).

Public-Private Partnerships

Recognizing the complexity of modern cyber threats, public-private partnerships have emerged as a critical component of cybersecurity strategies. These partnerships facilitate information sharing, collaboration on threat intelligence, and the development of best practices to enhance the collective security posture of participants. Initiatives such as the Global Cyber Alliance and the Cyber Threat Alliance exemplify the collaborative efforts between government agencies, private sector entities, and non-profit organizations (Global Cyber Alliance, n.d.; Cyber Threat Alliance, n.d.).

Cybersecurity Education and Workforce Development

The modern era has underscored the importance of cybersecurity *education and workforce development to address the growing skills gap* in the field. Universities, industry, and governments have launched initiatives to expand cybersecurity education and training programs, aiming to prepare the next generation of cybersecurity professionals (Newhouse, Keith, Scribner, & Witte, 2017).

The modern era of cybersecurity is defined by the dynamic interplay between advancing cyber threats and the development of sophisticated cybersecurity measures. As digital technologies continue to evolve, the importance of adaptive cybersecurity strategies, robust legislation, public-private collaboration, and workforce development has become increasingly clear. The future of cybersecurity will likely continue to be shaped by technological innovations, necessitating ongoing vigilance, collaboration, and innovation to protect the digital world.

The establishment of international frameworks and cooperation, such as the Budapest Convention on Cybercrime, reflects the global nature of cyber threats and the need for a coordinated response. Cybersecurity is now recognized as a critical component of national security, economic policy, and individual privacy.

Milestones in Cybersecurity History:

Cybersecurity has evolved significantly from its early days, adapting to the rapidly changing landscape of technology and the sophistication of cyber threats. This evolution is marked by several key milestones that have shaped the field of cybersecurity, impacting how personal, corporate, and national security is managed in the digital age. These milestones not only highlight the progression of cyber threats but also the innovative responses developed to protect against these threats.

The Creation of the Morris Worm (1988)

One of the most significant early events in the history of cyber-security was the creation and release of the Morris Worm in 1988. Designed by Robert T. Morris, the worm was intended to gauge the size of the internet. However, due to a programming error, it replicated excessively, slowing down computers to the point of unusefulness and affecting approximately 10% of all internet-connected computers at the time, thereby revealing the vulnerability of networked systems to malicious software (Spafford, 1989).

The creation of the Morris Worm in 1988 stands as a pivotal moment in cybersecurity history, marking one of the first instances where the vulnerability of networked computer systems was exposed on a large scale. This event not only highlighted the potential for digital systems to be exploited maliciously but also catalyzed the development of the cybersecurity industry and the establishment of protocols and practices aimed at protecting digital infrastructure.

The Morris Worm Incident

On November 2, 1988, a computer worm was released by Robert Tappan Morris, a graduate student at Cornell University, ostensibly to gauge the size of the internet. The worm exploited vulnerabilities in UNIX systems, specifically targeting the sendmail program, the finger daemon, and weak rsh/trust authentication. Unlike a virus, the worm did not need to attach itself to an existing program but could replicate and spread independently across networks (Spafford, 1989).

The worm's replication mechanism was flawed, causing it to infect machines multiple times and significantly slowing down or completely halting affected systems. An estimated 6,000 to 10,000 machines were affected, which represented a significant portion of the internet-connected computers at the time. This led to substantial disruption and the realization of the need for enhanced cybersecurity measures (Eichin & Rochlis, 1989).

Impact and Response

The Morris Worm incident had a profound impact on the nascent internet community, leading to widespread recognition of the need for cybersecurity. In response to this event, the first Computer Emergency Response Team (CERT) was established at Carnegie Mellon University with funding from the Defense Advanced Research Projects Agency (DARPA). CERT's formation marked the beginning of organized efforts to address and mitigate cybersecurity threats and vulnerabilities (West-Brown et al., 2003).

Legal and Ethical Implications

The incident also raised significant legal and ethical questions regarding computer security and the responsibilities of network users and administrators. Robert Tappan Morris became the first individual convicted under the Computer Fraud and Abuse Act (CFAA) of 1986, highlighting the legal implications of exploiting software vulnerabilities and causing widespread damage (United States v. Morris, 1991).

Lessons Learned and Future Directions

The Morris Worm served as a catalyst for the cybersecurity industry, underscoring the importance of securing networked computer systems against unauthorized access and exploitation. It led to increased research and development in cybersecurity technologies and practices, including the creation of antivirus software, the implementation of more rigorous network security protocols, and the establishment of ethical guidelines for network research.

The incident also emphasized the importance of vulnerability disclosure and patch management processes, as the vulnerabilities exploited by the worm were known but not widely addressed at the time. This has informed current practices around responsible vulnerability disclosure and the critical need for regular software updates and patches to protect against known threats.

The creation of the Morris Worm in 1988 stands as a seminal event in the history of cybersecurity, highlighting the vulnerabilities inherent in networked computer systems and catalyzing the development of the cybersecurity field. Its legacy is evident in the robust cybersecurity measures, legal frameworks, and ethical standards that have been developed in response to this and subsequent cyber threats, shaping the ongoing effort to secure digital infrastructure and protect against cyber attacks.

The Establishment of the Computer Emergency Response Team (CERT) (1988)

In response to the Morris Worm incident, the first Computer Emergency Response Team (CERT) was established at Carnegie Mellon University, with funding from the Defense Advanced Research Projects Agency (DARPA). This marked the beginning of organized efforts to address cybersecurity threats and underscored the need for continuous monitoring, threat analysis, and coordinated response mechanisms to protect digital infrastructure (West-Brown et al., 2003).

The establishment of the Computer Emergency Response Team (CERT) in 1988 represents a foundational milestone in the history of cybersecurity. This development marked the inception of a formalized approach to cyber threat response and management, setting a precedent for the creation of similar entities worldwide. The formation of CERT was a direct response to the proliferation of internet connectivity and the emerging threats that accompanied it, most notably highlighted by the Morris Worm incident.

The Genesis of CERT

In the aftermath of the Morris Worm incident, which revealed significant vulnerabilities in the connected infrastructure of the internet, there was a clear and immediate need for an organized approach to addressing cybersecurity threats. The Defense Advanced Research Projects Agency (DARPA), recognizing this need, funded the creation of the first CERT at Carnegie Mellon University's Software Engineering Institute (SEI) (West-Brown et al., 2003). This team was tasked with coordinating responses to cyber incidents, developing best practices for internet security, and conducting research to enhance the security of networked systems.

Role and Responsibilities

The primary role of CERT was to serve as a central agency that could respond to cybersecurity incidents, analyze the threats, and disseminate information to prevent future occurrences. Over time, the responsibilities of CERT expanded to include vulnerability disclosure, the development of security practices, and the provision of critical cybersecurity training and awareness programs. The establishment of CERT marked a paradigm shift in the approach to cybersecurity, emphasizing proactive measures and collaboration among various stakeholders in the digital ecosystem (Killcrece et al., 2003).

Impact and Expansion

The establishment of the first CERT had a profound and lasting impact on the field of cybersecurity. It not only provided a model for incident response but also underscored the importance of coordinated efforts in combating cyber threats. The success of the original CERT at Carnegie Mellon University led to the formation of national and sector-specific CERTs around the world, each dedicated to protecting against cyber threats within their respective domains.

These teams play a crucial role in the global cybersecurity infrastructure, facilitating information sharing between government entities, private sector organizations, and academic institutions. They also contribute to the development of international standards and practices for cybersecurity, enhancing the collective ability to respond to and mitigate cyber incidents (West-Brown et al., 2003).

Evolution and Legacy

The evolution of CERT over the years reflects the changing landscape of cybersecurity threats and the continuous need for innovation in cyber defense strategies. Today, CERTs operate under various names and structures, including Computer Security Incident Response Teams (CSIRTs), with a broader mandate that encompasses emerging threats in the digital age, such as cyber terrorism, espionage, and large-scale data breaches.

The legacy of CERT is evident in its enduring influence on cybersecurity policies, practices, and the establishment of similar entities worldwide. By fostering a culture of security awareness and collaboration, CERTs continue to play a pivotal role in safeguarding the digital frontier.

The establishment of the Computer Emergency Response Team (CERT) in 1988 was a landmark event in cybersecurity history, catalyzing the development of a coordinated approach to cyber threat management. The legacy of CERT is a testament to the importance of collaboration, research, and proactive measures in the ongoing battle against cyber threats. As the digital landscape continues to evolve, the principles and practices pioneered by CERT remain central to the global effort to maintain cybersecurity.

The Advent of Public Key Cryptography (1976)

The invention of public key cryptography by Whitfield Diffie and Martin Hellman in 1976 revolutionized data security, enabling secure communication over insecure channels and laying the foundation for secure internet transactions. This cryptographic method allows for the secure exchange of information and has become a cornerstone of modern cybersecurity practices (Diffie & Hellman, 1976).

The advent of public key cryptography in 1976 represents a seminal milestone in the annals of cybersecurity history, fundamentally transforming the landscape of digital communication and security. Prior to this innovation, secure communication over untrusted networks posed a significant challenge, as it relied on the secure exchange of secret keys a process fraught with vulnerabilities. The introduction of public key cryptography by Whitfield Diffie and Martin Hellman marked the dawn of a new era in cybersecurity, enabling secure communications without the need for sharing secret keys.

The Breakthrough of Public Key Cry"togr'phy

In their landmark paper, "New Directions in Cryptography," Diffie and Hellman introduced the concept of public key cryptography, a revolutionary approach that utilized two separate keys for encryption and decryption: a public key, which could be shared openly, and a private key, which was kept secret by the owner (Diffie & Hellman, 1976). This breakthrough addressed the key distribution problem, allowing individuals to encrypt messages using the recipient's public key, which could then only be decrypted by the corresponding private key.

Impact on Digital Security and Communication

The advent of public key cryptography had a profound impact on digital security and communication, providing the foundational technology for secure internet transactions, digital signatures, and the Secure Sockets Layer (SSL) protocol, among others. It enabled the secure exchange of information over the internet, laying the groundwork for the growth of e-commerce, online banking, and confidential communication across the digital domain.

Public key cryptography also introduced the concept of digital signatures, which provided a means for verifying the authenticity and integrity of digital documents and communications. This capability has become integral to establishing trust in the digital world, ensuring that messages and transactions are genuinely from their purported sources and have not been tampered with in transit.

Challenges and Further Developments

While public key cryptography represented a significant advancement, it also introduced new challenges, particularly in the realm of computational complexity and the need for robust key management practices. The security of public key cryptographic systems relies on mathematical problems that are difficult to solve without the appropriate key, such as factoring large prime numbers, which demands considerable computational resources (Boneh, 1999).

In response to these challenges, researchers and developers have continued to refine cryptographic algorithms and explore quantum-resistant cryptography to anticipate future threats that could exploit advances in computing power, including the potential development of quantum computing.

The advent of public key cryptography in 1976 fundamentally altered the course of cybersecurity, introducing a mechanism for secure, private communication over public networks and solving the critical issue of key distribution. This milestone not only enhanced the security of digital communications but also enabled the development of the modern digital economy by providing a foundation for secure online transactions. As we continue to navigate the complexities of the digital age, the principles underlying public key cryptography remain at the heart of cybersecurity efforts, embodying the perpetual challenge of balancing accessibility with security.

The Introduction of the First Antivirus Software (1987)

The emergence of computer viruses in the 1980s led to the development of the first antivirus software. In 1987, the German company G Data Software developed the first antivirus program to combat the PC-virus, marking the beginning of the antivirus industry. This milestone was crucial in the fight against malware, setting the stage for the development of comprehensive cybersecurity solutions (G Data Software, 1987).

The introduction of the first antivirus software in 1987 marks a significant milestone in the history of cybersecurity, reflecting the evolving landscape of digital threats and the beginnings of the cybersecurity industry's response to malicious software. As personal computers became more prevalent in the 1980s, so did computer viruses, leading to the necessity for protective software solutions. This era highlighted the growing awareness of cyber threats and catalyzed the development of antivirus technologies designed to detect, prevent, and remove malware.

The Emergence of Computer Viruses

The emergence of computer viruses in the early 1980s, such as the Brain virus in 1986—the first PC virus in the wild—underscored the vulnerability of digital systems to malicious attacks (Kaspersky, n.d.). These early viruses were primarily spread through floppy disks, exploiting the widespread practice of sharing software and data between computers. The impact of these viruses ranged from benign pranks to significant data loss and system malfunction, illustrating the need for dedicated security measures.

The Advent of Antivirus Software

In response to the growing threat posed by viruses, the first antivirus software was developed. In 1987, Bernd Fix developed a tool to remove the Vienna virus, marking one of the earliest examples of antivirus software. Almost simultaneously, the Czechoslovakian company G Data Software launched the "Anti-Virus Kit," the first commercial antivirus product, recognizing the need for broader protective measures against the variety of viruses beginning to circulate among computer users (G Data, n.d.).

These initial efforts in antivirus development focused on identifying and removing specific viruses based on their unique signatures—a method that involved scanning systems for patterns or sequences of bytes known to be part of malware. While effective against known viruses, this approach required regular updates to the antivirus software's database to protect against new threats.

The Evolution of Antivirus Technologies

The development of the first antivirus software set the stage for the evolution of more sophisticated technologies. As viruses became more advanced, employing techniques such as polymorphism to evade detection, antivirus solutions also advanced. Heuristic analysis, behavioral detection, and cloud-based threat intelligence became integral components of antivirus software, enhancing the ability to detect previously unknown viruses and respond more rapidly to emerging threats.

The Impact on Cybersecurity Practices

The introduction of antivirus software had a profound impact on cybersecurity practices, establishing the foundation for the ongoing development of malware detection and removal tools. It also raised awareness among computer users and organizations about the importance of cybersecurity hygiene, including regular software updates, backups, and the use of security software as part of a comprehensive cybersecurity strategy.

Moreover, the antivirus industry's growth catalyzed the broader cybersecurity sector, leading to the emergence of a range of security solutions targeting different aspects of digital security, from firewalls and intrusion detection systems to endpoint protection and beyond.

The introduction of the first antivirus software in 1987 represents a pivotal moment in cybersecurity history, signaling the commencement of an ongoing battle against malware. This milestone underscores the dynamic nature of cyber threats and the necessity for continuous innovation in cybersecurity technologies and practices. As we move forward, the principles laid down by the pioneers of antivirus software continue to guide the development of new security solutions, adapting to the ever-changing landscape of cyber threats.

The Enactment of the General Data Protection Regulation (GDPR) (2016)

The implementation of the General Data Protection Regulation (GDPR) by the European Union in 2016 represents a significant milestone in privacy and cybersecurity legislation. The GDPR has set a new global standard for data protection, emphasizing the importance of securing personal data and granting individuals greater control over their information. This regulation has had a profound impact on how organizations worldwide manage and protect user data (European Parliament and Council, 2016).

The enactment of the General Data Protection Regulation (GDPR) by the European Union in 2016 stands as a monumental milestone in the annals of cybersecurity and data protection history. This comprehensive data privacy and protection regulation, which came into effect on May 25, 2018, has had a profound impact on how organizations around the world handle and secure personal data. The GDPR not only enhanced the data protection rights of individuals within the EU but also set a new global benchmark for privacy laws, influencing similar regulations worldwide.

Background and Objectives of GDPR

The GDPR was designed to modernize laws that protect the personal information of individuals within the European Union. It aimed to give individuals more control over their personal data while simplifying the regulatory environment for international business by unifying the regulation within the EU. A key aspect of the GDPR is its broad scope; it applies to any organization operating within the EU, as well as organizations outside of the EU that offer goods or services to customers or businesses in the EU (European Parliament and Council, 2016).

Key Provisions of GDPR

The GDPR introduced several critical provisions that have significantly influenced the cybersecurity and data protection landscape, including:

- **Consent**: Organizations must obtain explicit consent from individuals before collecting, using, or sharing their personal data.
- **Right to Access**: Individuals have the right to know whether, where, and for what purpose their personal data is being processed, and to obtain a copy of their personal data.
- **Right to Be Forgotten**: Individuals have the right to demand the deletion of their personal data under certain conditions.
- **Data Portability**: Individuals have the right to receive their personal data in a structured, commonly used format, and to transfer that data to another controller.
- **Breach Notification**: Organizations must notify the relevant data protection authority of a data breach within 72 hours of becoming aware of it, and in certain cases, must also inform the individuals affected by the breach.

- **Data Protection Officers**: Organizations are required to appoint a Data Protection Officer (DPO) if they process or store large amounts of personal data.

Impact on Global Data Protection Practices

The GDPR has significantly raised the bar for data protection and privacy practices globally. Organizations worldwide have had to reassess and often overhaul their data handling and cybersecurity practices to comply with the regulation's stringent requirements. This includes implementing stronger data security measures, revising data protection policies, and ensuring transparency in data processing activities.

The regulation has also had a "ripple effect," inspiring countries outside the EU to adopt similar data protection laws. Examples include the California Consumer Privacy Act (CCPA) in the United States and the Lei Geral de Proteção de Dados (LGPD) in Brazil, reflecting a growing global consensus on the importance of protecting personal data in the digital age.

Challenges and Opportunities

The implementation of GDPR has not been without challenges for organizations, particularly small and medium-sized enterprises with limited resources. The complexity of the regulation, coupled with the potential for significant fines for non-compliance, has necessitated significant investment in cybersecurity and data protection measures.

However, the GDPR also presents opportunities by fostering a greater trust between organizations and individuals, enhancing the protection of personal data, and encouraging the development of privacy-enhancing technologies. It has underscored the critical role of cybersecurity in the digital economy and highlighted the need for a comprehensive approach to data protection that balances individual rights with the realities of the digital world.

The enactment of the GDPR represents a significant milestone in the evolution of cybersecurity and data protection, setting a high standard for privacy regulations worldwide. By prioritizing the rights of individuals over their personal data and imposing rigorous data protection requirements on organizations, the GDPR has reshaped the global conversation on privacy and cybersecurity, highlighting the necessity of robust data protection practices in the digital age.

The Stuxnet Attack (2010)

The discovery of Stuxnet in 2010 highlighted the potential for cyber weapons to target and disrupt critical infrastructure. Stuxnet, a sophisticated computer worm, was designed to sabotage Iran's nuclear program, marking the first known instance of a digitally executed attack on industrial systems. This event signaled a shift in cyber threats, demonstrating the capability for cyberattacks to have real-world physical consequences (Zetter, 2014).

The Stuxnet attack of 2010 is widely regarded as a watershed moment in the history of cybersecurity, signifying the first known use of a digitally based weapon designed to cause physical, real-world damage. Unlike previous cyber threats focused on information theft or system disruption, Stuxnet targeted industrial control systems, specifically those used in Iran's nuclear enrichment program. This sophisticated cyber-attack marked a paradigm shift in the nature of cyber threats and has had profound implications for national security, cybersecurity practices, and the development of cyber warfare strategies.

Overview of the Stuxnet Attack

Stuxnet was a highly sophisticated computer worm discovered in 2010, but believed to have been in development since at least 2005. It was designed to target Siemens industrial control systems used in Iran's nuclear enrichment facilities, with the aim of damaging centrifuges used to enrich uranium. Stuxnet operated by exploiting zero-day vulnerabilities in Windows operating systems to infect computers, then sought out specific Siemens software controlling the centrifuges. Once the target was located, Stuxnet subtly altered the speeds of the centrifuges, causing physical damage while simultaneously sending normal operating data to the control monitors to avoid detection (Langner, 2011).

Technical Sophistication and Implications

The technical sophistication of Stuxnet was unprecedented. It utilized four zero-day vulnerabilities, a remarkable feat given the rarity of such vulnerabilities. Additionally, it had the capability to spread through USB drives, enabling it to infect systems not directly connected to the internet, thereby bypassing network defenses. The complexity and precision of the attack suggested the involvement of state actors, and while no country officially claimed responsibility, it is widely attributed to a US-Israeli collaboration (Zetter, 2014).

Stuxnet's success demonstrated the potential for cyber attacks to cause physical damage to critical infrastructure, fundamentally altering perceptions of cybersecurity and national defense. It highlighted vulnerabilities in industrial control systems, many of which were designed without internet-era threat models in mind. This realization prompted a reevaluation of security practices surrounding critical infrastructure worldwide.

Cybersecurity and National Security

The Stuxnet attack had significant implications for national security, underscoring the potential for cyber operations to execute geopolitical objectives. This event signaled the emergence of cyber warfare as a tangible element of statecraft, with the power to achieve strategic objectives without traditional military engagement. Consequently, nations around the globe have since increased their focus on developing offensive and defensive cyber capabilities, recognizing the strategic importance of cybersecurity in national defense (Farwell & Rohozinski, 2011).

Regulatory and Industry Response

The revelation of Stuxnet spurred regulatory and industry efforts to enhance the security of industrial control systems and critical infrastructure. Initiatives such as the development of the NIST Cybersecurity Framework and increased collaboration between government agencies and the private sector aimed to address the vulnerabilities exposed by Stuxnet. Moreover, the attack prompted the creation of new cybersecurity standards and practices designed to protect against similar threats, including the importance of air-gapping sensitive systems and the need for rigorous software supply chain security.

The Stuxnet attack represents a pivotal moment in cybersecurity history, illustrating the evolution of cyber threats from digital espionage and disruption to the physical destruction of critical infrastructure. This event has shaped subsequent cybersecurity strategies, emphasizing the need for robust security measures in both governmental and industrial sectors. As the distinction between cyber and physical realms continues to blur, the lessons learned from Stuxnet remain critical in guiding future defenses against the ever-evolving landscape of cyber threats.

These milestones in cybersecurity history reflect the dynamic and evolving nature of cyber threats and the continuous innovation required to protect digital assets. From the early days of the Morris Worm to the regulatory advancements of the GDPR and the complexities of modern cyber warfare exemplified by Stuxnet, the field of cybersecurity has grown in importance and sophistication. As technology continues to advance, the history of cybersecurity will undoubtedly continue to expand, marked by new challenges and achievements.

Evolution Of Cyber Threats and Security Measures:

The evolution of cyber threats and security measures is a dynamic narrative that underscores the cat-and-mouse game between cyber attackers and defenders. This continuous arms race has driven the advancement of cybersecurity practices, technologies, and policies. As digital technologies have become more integrated into all aspects of society, the sophistication and scope of cyber threats have expanded, necessitating equally advanced security measures.

The Early Days of Cyber Threats

In the initial stages of computing and early internet days, cyber threats were relatively primitive, often manifesting as viruses and worms designed more for nuisance or proof of concept rather than for financial gain or espionage. The Morris Worm of 1988 is a seminal example, causing significant disruption but primarily serving as a wake-up call regarding the vulnerabilities inherent in connected systems (Spafford, 1989).

The evolution of cyber threats and security measures is a testament to the dynamic interplay between technological advancement and the ingenuity of both cyber attackers and defenders. The early days of cyber threats marked the beginning of what would become a constantly escalating arms race in the digital domain. This period set the stage for the development of cybersecurity as a discipline and underscored the necessity for ongoing vigilance and innovation in the face of evolving digital dangers.

The Genesis of Cyber Threats

The inception of cyber threats can be traced back to the advent of computing and early networks, even before the widespread use of the internet. Initially, these threats were relatively rudimentary, often created by individuals out of curiosity or for the challenge, rather than for malicious intent or financial gain. One of the earliest recorded incidents was the Creeper virus in the early 1970s, which was essentially a self-replicating program that displayed a benign message. Though not harmful, Creeper demonstrated the potential for software to spread autonomously across networked systems (Denning, 1987).

The Appearance of Malware and Viruses

As personal computers became more accessible in the 1980s, the landscape of cyber threats began to evolve with the appearance of the first computer viruses that spread outside of computer labs and research environments. The Brain virus, identified in 1986, is considered one of the first computer viruses to be released "in the wild." It targeted IBM PC computers by infecting the boot sector of floppy disks, thereby demonstrating the potential for malicious software to disrupt personal computing (Cohen, 1987).

The Response to Early Cyber Threats

The response to these early cyber threats was largely reactive, consisting of individual efforts to mitigate or remove infections. The concept of cybersecurity, as it is understood today, was still in its infancy, and formalized security measures were not yet widespread. However, the growing prevalence of malware prompted the development of the first antivirus software in the late 1980s, representing the initial steps toward a more systematic approach to cybersecurity (Kaspersky, n.d.).

The Role of Awareness and Collaboration

The emergence of early cyber threats also highlighted the importance of awareness and collaboration among the burgeoning computer user community. Bulletin board systems (BBS) and later, online forums, became crucial for sharing information about threats and remedies. This period underscored the necessity for collective vigilance and the sharing of knowledge and resources as foundational principles for combating cyber threats.

The Evolution of Cybersecurity Measures

The response to the initial wave of cyber threats laid the groundwork for the cybersecurity measures that would follow. The creation of the first antivirus software heralded the beginning of an industry dedicated to protecting digital assets and information. Moreover, these early challenges prompted the development of more sophisticated security protocols and practices, eventually leading to the establishment of dedicated cybersecurity teams and organizations.

The early days of cyber threats were marked by a pioneering spirit, both on the part of those creating the threats and those responding to them. This period was crucial in shaping the understanding of digital vulnerabilities and the need for security measures to protect against them. The lessons learned from the initial encounters with malware and viruses continue to inform the strategies and technologies deployed in the ongoing battle against cyber threats.

The Rise of Financially Motivated Cybercrime

As the internet became more commercialized in the late 1990s and early 2000s, the motivation behind cyber-attacks shifted significantly towards financial gain. This era saw the proliferation of malware designed to steal credit card information, personal identification details, and later, banking credentials. The advent of phishing attacks, where attackers trick victims into divulging sensitive information, became a common tactic (Jagatic, Johnson, Jakobsson, & Menczer, 2007).

The evolution of cyber threats has been significantly marked by the rise of financially motivated cybercrime, transitioning from the early exploratory phases of hacking into a highly organized, profit-driven industry. This shift has fundamentally altered the cybersecurity landscape, introducing new challenges and necessitating the development of sophisticated security measures to protect against an ever-expanding array of cyber threats aimed at financial gain.

The Shift to Financially Motivated Cybercrime

In the late 1990s and early 2000s, as the internet became more integral to commerce and daily life, cybercriminals began to exploit the online ecosystem for financial gain. This era saw the emergence of various forms of financially motivated cybercrime, including identity theft, phishing scams, and the proliferation of malware designed to steal financial information (Anderson, Barton, Böhme, Clayton, Van Eeten, Levi, Moore, & Savage, 2012).

One of the most significant developments during this period was the creation of botnets—networks of infected computers used to carry out a range of malicious tasks, from sending spam emails to conducting distributed denial-of-service (DDoS) attacks. Cybercriminals often used these botnets to extort money from businesses by threatening or executing attacks that could cripple their online operations (Manky, 2013).

The Emergence of Ransomware

Ransomware emerged as a particularly lucrative form of financially motivated cybercrime, with attackers encrypting the victim's data or locking users out of their systems and demanding payment for the decryption key. One of the first widespread ransomware attacks was the AIDS Trojan in 1989, which encrypted file names on the infected computer and demanded payment for recovery instructions. However, it was not until the mid-2000s that ransomware became a common threat, with sophisticated variants like CryptoLocker setting the stage for the modern ransomware epidemic (Hypponen, 2016).

The Evolution of Cybersecurity Measures

The rise of financially motivated cybercrime has driven significant advancements in cybersecurity measures. Financial institutions and online retailers, prime targets for cybercriminals, have been at the forefront of adopting multi-factor authentication, encryption, and secure socket layer (SSL) technologies to protect user data and transactions. The development of advanced threat detection systems, incorporating machine learning and behavioral analytics, has become critical for identifying and mitigating attacks before they can cause harm.

Cybersecurity Legislation and Financial Regulations

The financial sector's vulnerability to cybercrime has also prompted regulatory responses aimed at strengthening the cybersecurity posture of financial institutions. Regulations such as the Payment Card Industry Data Security Standard (PCI DSS) were established to enforce stringent security controls around cardholder data to reduce credit card fraud. Additionally, legislations like the European Union's General Data Protection Regulation (GDPR) have imposed heavy penalties for data breaches, incentivizing organizations to prioritize cybersecurity (European Parliament and Council, 2016).

The rise of financially motivated cybercrime has profoundly impacted the cybersecurity landscape, introducing complex challenges that require dynamic and sophisticated responses. As cybercriminals continue to develop new methods for exploiting digital systems for financial gain, the evolution of cybersecurity measures remains an ongoing imperative. The collaboration between industry, government, and cybersecurity professionals is crucial for staying ahead of threats and safeguarding the digital economy against the financial motivations driving modern cybercrime.

Advanced Persistent Threats (APTs) and State-Sponsored Attacks

The mid-2000s to the present day has been characterized by the emergence of Advanced Persistent Threats (APTs), where highly skilled attackers, often state-sponsored, engage in prolonged and targeted attacks to steal information or sabotage systems. Notably, the discovery of Stuxnet in 2010 marked a significant milestone in cyber threats, demonstrating the capability to cause physical damage through digital means (Zetter, 2014).

The landscape of cybersecurity has been significantly reshaped by the emergence of Advanced Persistent Threats (APTs) and state-sponsored attacks. These sophisticated cyber operations, often conducted over extended periods, have introduced a new level of complexity to cybersecurity, blending traditional espionage tactics with cutting-edge cyber techniques. The evolution of APTs and state-sponsored attacks reflects a shift towards strategic, long-term objectives, such as intelligence gathering, sabotage, and influence operations, which go beyond mere financial gain or disruption.

Advanced Persistent Threats (APTs)

APTs are characterized by their stealth, persistence, and significant resources, typically attributed to nation-states or state-sponsored actors. These threats are designed to infiltrate networks undetected, maintain a prolonged presence within the target's infrastructure, and exfiltrate data without triggering alarms. One of the hallmarks of APTs is their use of sophisticated techniques, including zero-day vulnerabilities and custom malware, to achieve their objectives (Alperovitch, 2011).

A notable example of an APT is the discovery of Stuxnet in 2010, a highly sophisticated worm designed to sabotage Iran's nuclear program. Stuxnet demonstrated the potential for cyber operations to cause physical damage and highlighted the strategic use of cyber tools in achieving geopolitical objectives (Zetter, 2014).

State-Sponsored Attacks

State-sponsored attacks often involve APTs but can also encompass a broader range of cyber operations, including disinformation campaigns, cyber espionage, and attacks on critical infrastructure. These operations are typically aimed at advancing a nation's strategic interests, destabilizing adversaries, or gaining a competitive advantage. The attribution of these attacks to specific nation-states can be challenging due to the anonymity of cyberspace and the use of proxy actors, complicating international relations and cybersecurity diplomacy.

The 2014 attack on Sony Pictures Entertainment, attributed to North Korean hackers, exemplifies the use of cyber operations to achieve political objectives. The attack, which involved data theft and the public release of sensitive information, was reportedly in retaliation for the planned release of a film that depicted the fictional assassination of North Korea's leader (Borger & Hern, 2014).

Evolution of Cybersecurity Measures

The rise of APTs and state-sponsored attacks has necessitated the development of advanced cybersecurity measures. Organizations and governments have had to augment traditional security practices with advanced threat detection and response capabilities, including:

- **Threat Intelligence**: Leveraging detailed knowledge of adversaries, including their tactics, techniques, and procedures (TTPs), to anticipate and defend against APTs.
- **Segmentation and Zero Trust**: Implementing network segmentation and adopting a zero-trust security model to minimize the attack surface and prevent lateral movement within networks.
- **Incident Response and Forensics**: Developing robust incident response plans and forensic capabilities to quickly respond to breaches and understand attack methodologies for future defense.

Policy and International Cooperation

The threat posed by APTs and state-sponsored attacks has also underscored the importance of policy initiatives and international cooperation in cybersecurity. Efforts such as the Budapest Convention on Cybercrime and the United Nations Group of Governmental Experts on Developments in the Field of Information and Telecommunications in the Context of International Security (UNGGE) aim to foster global collaboration in combating cyber threats and establishing norms for responsible state behavior in cyberspace.

The evolution of cyber threats to include APTs and state-sponsored attacks represents a significant challenge in the field of cybersecurity. These sophisticated and strategically motivated operations have prompted a corresponding evolution in security measures, emphasizing the need for advanced detection, intelligence, and international collaboration. As cyber operations continue to play a central role in international relations and national security, the ability to defend against and respond to such threats will remain a critical priority.

Evolution of Cybersecurity Measures

In response to evolving threats, cybersecurity measures have become more sophisticated. The development and implementation of encryption technologies, such as SSL/TLS for secure internet communications, became standard practice. Furthermore, the use of multifactor authentication (MFA) has been widely adopted to provide an additional layer of security beyond passwords.

The evolution of cybersecurity measures has been a direct response to the ever-changing landscape of cyber threats. From the earliest days of computing to the complex digital ecosystem of today, cybersecurity measures have advanced from basic protective practices to sophisticated defense mechanisms incorporating cutting-edge technology and comprehensive strategies. This progression reflects the ongoing arms race between cyber attackers, who continuously develop new methods of exploitation, and defenders, who innovate to protect against these threats.

The Beginnings: Antivirus and Firewalls

In the early days of cybersecurity, the focus was primarily on combating viruses and malware. The introduction of the first antivirus software in the late 1980s marked the beginning of cybersecurity measures aimed at detecting and removing malicious software. Similarly, the development and implementation of firewalls provided a basic level of protection by controlling incoming and outgoing network traffic based on an applied rule set, thus preventing unauthorized access (Cheswick, Bellovin, & Rubin, 2003).

The Rise of Encryption

The advent of public key cryptography in 1976 was a significant milestone, introducing a method for secure communication over insecure channels (Diffie & Hellman, 1976). Encryption technologies have since evolved to become a cornerstone of cybersecurity, safeguarding data in transit and at rest from interception and theft. The widespread adoption of SSL/TLS protocols for secure internet communication exemplifies the importance of encryption in modern cybersecurity practices.

The Shift to Intrusion 'etection and Prevention Systems

As cyber threats became more sophisticated, relying solely on perimeter defenses like firewalls became insufficient. The development of intrusion detection systems (IDS) and intrusion prevention systems (IPS) represented a shift towards more proactive cybersecurity measures. These systems monitor network and system activities for malicious actions or policy violations, providing an additional layer of security by identifying and potentially stopping attacks in progress (Scarfone & Mell, 2007).

The Adoption of Behavioral Analytics and Machine Learning

The increasing volume and sophistication of cyber threats have necessitated the adoption of advanced technologies such as behavioral analytics and machine learning. By analyzing patterns of behavior, these technologies can identify anomalies that may indicate a cyber attack, even if the specific threat has not been previously encountered. This approach has enhanced the ability of cybersecurity measures to detect and respond to zero-day vulnerabilities and sophisticated APTs (April Tanner & Cam, 2018).

The Role of Cybersecurity Frameworks

The evolution of cybersecurity measures has also been influenced by the development of comprehensive cybersecurity frameworks, such as the National Institute of Standards and Technology (NIST) Cybersecurity Framework. These frameworks provide organizations with best practices, guidelines, and standards to manage and reduce cybersecurity risk. They have been instrumental in standardizing cybersecurity measures across different sectors and improving the overall security posture of organizations (National Institute of Standards and Technology, 2018).

The evolution of cybersecurity measures from basic antivirus software and firewalls to the use of advanced technologies like machine learning and behavioral analytics reflects the dynamic nature of the cyber threat landscape. As cyber threats continue to evolve in complexity and scale, so too must the strategies and technologies employed to defend against them. The history of cybersecurity measures underscores the necessity of continuous innovation, adaptation, and collaboration within the cybersecurity community to protect digital assets and maintain trust in the digital world.

The Role of Artificial Intelligence and Machine Learning

The latest frontier in cybersecurity defense involves the use of artificial intelligence (AI) and machine learning (ML) technologies. These technologies are being employed to predict, detect, and respond to cyber threats with greater speed and accuracy than humanly possible. AI and ML algorithms can analyze vast datasets to identify patterns indicative of cyber attacks, enhancing the ability to preemptively thwart attacks (Apruzzese et al., 2018).

The role of Artificial Intelligence (AI) and Machine Learning (ML) in the evolution of cybersecurity threats and security measures represents a pivotal chapter in the ongoing narrative of digital defense mechanisms. As cyber threats have grown in sophistication and complexity, the incorporation of AI and ML technologies into cybersecurity strategies has become increasingly vital. These technologies have transformed the cybersecurity landscape, offering both new methods for attackers and powerful tools for defenders.

Advancements in AI and ML for Cybersecurity

AI and ML have been leveraged to enhance various aspects of cybersecurity, from threat detection to incident response. One of the key advantages of ML in cybersecurity is its ability to analyze vast quantities of data at speeds and scales unattainable by human analysts. This capability allows for the identification of patterns and anomalies indicative of cyber threats, including sophisticated zero-day attacks that traditional security measures might miss (April Tanner & Cam, 2018).

ML algorithms, through their learning capabilities, continuously improve their threat detection efficacy by ingesting new data. This process enables them to adapt to evolving threats over time, making ML-based systems an essential component of modern cybersecurity defenses. Furthermore, AI-driven security tools can automate the response to detected threats, reducing the time from detection to mitigation and thereby limiting the potential damage inflicted by cyber attacks.

AI and ML in Cyber Threat Evolution

Conversely, the same technologies that bolster cybersecurity defenses are also being utilized by cyber attackers. AI and ML can be employed to develop more sophisticated malware and phishing campaigns, with algorithms designed to optimize the effectiveness of these attacks or evade detection by traditional security tools. For instance, AI can be used to automate the generation of phishing emails that are more convincing and tailored to individual targets, increasing the likelihood of successful breaches (Anderson, et al., 2016).

Moreover, AI and ML have facilitated the rise of automated attacks, including the use of bots capable of exploiting vulnerabilities at unprecedented speeds. These advancements pose significant challenges to cybersecurity professionals, necessitating the development of equally sophisticated AI and ML-driven countermeasures.

The Importance of Ethical Considerations

The dual-use nature of AI and ML in cybersecurity highlights the importance of ethical considerations. The development and deployment of AI-driven cybersecurity solutions must be guided by ethical frameworks to prevent misuse and ensure that these technologies are used responsibly to protect digital assets without infringing on privacy or individual rights (Taddeo & Floridi, 2018).

The Future of AI and ML In Cybersecurity

Looking forward, the integration of AI and ML into cybersecurity is expected to deepen, with emerging technologies such as deep learning offering even more advanced capabilities for threat detection and response. The future of cybersecurity will likely see a greater reliance on autonomous systems capable of predictive threat intelligence, proactive defense mechanisms, and self-healing networks that can mitigate threats without human intervention.

The incorporation of Artificial Intelligence and Machine Learning into cybersecurity represents a critical evolution in the fight against cyber threats. These technologies have transformed the capabilities of both cyber attackers and defenders, introducing a new era of cybersecurity that is more dynamic, adaptive, and intelligent. As we move forward, the continued advancement and ethical application of AI and ML will be paramount in shaping effective cybersecurity strategies and ensuring the security of the digital landscape.

Cybersecurity Frameworks and Legislation

The evolution of cyber threats has also influenced the development of cybersecurity frameworks and legislation aimed at enhancing organizational and national security postures. The National Institute of Standards and Technology (NIST) Cybersecurity Framework provides guidelines for managing cybersecurity risk, while laws such as the General Data Protection Regulation (GDPR) in the European Union have set new standards for data protection and privacy (National Institute of Standards and Technology, 2018; European Parliament and Council, 2016).

The evolution of cybersecurity threats and security measures has been significantly influenced by the development of cybersecurity frameworks and legislation. As digital threats have grown in complexity and scale, affecting individuals, organizations, and nations worldwide, there has been a concerted effort to establish comprehensive guidelines and legal standards to protect against these threats. Cybersecurity frameworks and legislation serve as foundational pillars in this endeavor, offering structured approaches to managing cybersecurity risk, enhancing data protection, and fostering a secure digital environment.

Cybersecurity Frameworks

Cybersecurity frameworks provide organizations with best practices, guidelines, and standards for managing and reducing cybersecurity risk. One of the most influential frameworks is the National Institute of Standards and Technology (NIST) Cybersecurity Framework. Developed in the United States in response to Executive Order 13636, "Improving Critical Infrastructure Cybersecurity," the NIST Framework offers a policy framework of computer security guidance for how private sector organizations in the United States can assess and improve their ability to prevent, detect, and respond to cyber attacks (National Institute of Standards and Technology, 2018).

The framework is structured around five core functions: Identify, Protect, Detect, Respond, and Recover. These functions provide a high-level strategic view of the lifecycle of an organization's management of cybersecurity risk. The NIST Cybersecurity Framework has been widely adopted by organizations both within and outside the United States, demonstrating its effectiveness and adaptability across different sectors and industries.

Cybersecurity Legislation

Cybersecurity legislation plays a crucial role in establishing legal standards for data protection, privacy, and the response to cyber threats. Notable examples of such legislation include the General Data Protection Regulation (GDPR) in the European Union and the California Consumer Privacy Act (CCPA) in the United States.

The GDPR, which came into effect in May 2018, represents a significant overhaul of data protection regulation in the EU. It introduces stringent data protection requirements for organizations and grants individuals greater control over their personal data. Key provisions of the GDPR include the right to access personal data, the right to be forgotten, and the requirement for organizations to report data breaches within 72 hours of discovery. The regulation applies to any organization operating within the EU, as well as organizations outside of the EU that offer goods or services to customers or businesses in the EU (European Parliament and Council, 2016).

Similarly, the CCPA, effective from January 2020, provides consumers in California with rights regarding the access to, deletion of, and sharing of their personal data collected by businesses. It represents one of the most comprehensive state data privacy laws in the United States and has prompted discussions on federal data privacy legislation (State of California Department of Justice, n.d.).

Impact and Challenges

Cybersecurity frameworks and legislation have significantly impacted how organizations approach cybersecurity, driving the adoption of more rigorous security practices and enhancing the protection of personal data. However, these frameworks and laws also present challenges, particularly for small and medium-sized enterprises that may lack the resources to fully comply with complex regulations. Additionally, the global nature of the internet poses challenges for legislation that is often confined to national borders, highlighting the need for international cooperation in cybersecurity policy.

The development of cybersecurity frameworks and legislation has been instrumental in shaping the response to evolving cyber threats. By providing structured approaches to risk management and establishing legal standards for data protection, these frameworks and laws play a crucial role in enhancing cybersecurity practices and safeguarding the digital landscape. As cyber threats continue to evolve, the ongoing refinement of these frameworks and the enactment of new legislation will be vital in addressing future cybersecurity challenges.

The evolution of cyber threats and security measures highlights the dynamic nature of cybersecurity as a field. From rudimentary viruses to complex state-sponsored cyber attacks, the escalation in cyber threats has been met with increasingly sophisticated security measures. This ongoing arms race necessitates continuous innovation and adaptation in cybersecurity practices, technologies, and policies to protect digital assets and preserve trust in the digital age.

Conclusion

The historical overview of cybersecurity reveals a dynamic field that has evolved rapidly to meet the challenges posed by technological advancements and the ingenuity of cyber attackers. From the creation of the first computer viruses to the complex cyber threats of today, the history of cybersecurity is a testament to the ongoing struggle to protect digital information and infrastructure. As we look to the future, the lessons of the past underscore the importance of vigilance, innovation, and international cooperation in safeguarding the digital frontier.

Chapter 3: Understanding Information Security

Part II: Principles of Cybersecurity

Understanding information security is fundamental in safeguarding digital assets in an era where digital transactions and communications form the backbone of both personal and professional spheres. Information security, often encapsulated in the triad of Confidentiality, Integrity, and Availability (CIA Triad), provides a structured framework for protecting information from unauthorized access, alteration, and disruption.

The CIA Triad

The CIA Triad is a model designed to guide policies for information security within an organization. It represents the three primary objectives that any information security program should strive to achieve:

Confidentiality:

Ensures that sensitive information is accessed only by authorized individuals and prevents it from being disclosed to unauthorized parties. Confidentiality measures include data encryption, access controls, and authentication mechanisms (Stallings & Brown, 2012).

Understanding the concept of confidentiality within the framework of the CIA Triad is crucial for grasping the foundational principles of information security. Confidentiality, as one of the cornerstones of this triad, focuses on ensuring that sensitive information is accessible only to those authorized to view or process it. This aspect of information security aims to protect personal or corporate data from unauthorized access and disclosure, thereby preserving privacy and preventing potential misuse.

The Essence of Confidentiality

Confidentiality revolves around the measures and protocols implemented to safeguard information from being accessed by unauthorized individuals or entities. This protection extends across various forms of data, including digital documents, personal information, corporate secrets, and communications. The primary goal is to ensure that this information remains inaccessible to anyone not authorized by the data owner or custodian (Stallings & Brown, 2012).

Mechanisms to Ensure Confidentiality

Several mechanisms and technologies are employed to uphold confidentiality in information security:

- **Encryption**: Encryption is a fundamental tool for maintaining confidentiality. It involves converting plaintext into ciphertext using algorithms and encryption keys, making the information unreadable to anyone without the decryption key. Encryption can protect data both at rest and in transit, thereby securing communications over networks and safeguarding stored data (Pfleeger & Pfleeger, 2012).
- **Access Control**: Implementing robust access control systems ensures that only authorized users can access certain information based on their permissions. Access control mechanisms include user authentication, role-based access control (RBAC), and mandatory access control (MAC), among others. These systems are critical for defining and enforcing who has the right to view, modify, or delete specific data (Sandhu & Samarati, 1994).
- **Data Classification**: Data classification involves categorizing organizational data based on its sensitivity and the level of

confidentiality required. This practice helps in applying appropriate security controls to different types of data, ensuring that highly sensitive information receives the highest level of protection (Breaux & Antón, 2008).

Challenges in Maintaining Confidentiality

Maintaining confidentiality in the digital age presents numerous challenges. The proliferation of cyber threats, including phishing attacks, malware, and advanced persistent threats (APTs), poses constant risks to data confidentiality. Moreover, the increasing complexity of IT systems and the widespread use of cloud services complicate the task of securing information across diverse platforms and environments.

Human factors also play a significant role in confidentiality breaches. User error, lack of awareness, and insider threats can lead to accidental or intentional disclosure of sensitive information, underscoring the need for continuous education and awareness programs as part of a comprehensive information security strategy (Hadnagy, 2018).

Confidentiality is a pivotal component of the CIA Triad and a fundamental aspect of information security. Protecting the privacy and integrity of data against unauthorized access is essential in today's digital world, where information is both a valuable asset and a potential liability. Employing encryption, access control, and data classification, along with addressing human factors, are key to maintaining confidentiality. As cybersecurity threats evolve, so too must the strategies and technologies used to protect confidential information, ensuring that it remains secure in an increasingly interconnected world.

Integrity:

Maintains the accuracy and reliability of data and systems by preventing unauthorized alteration. Integrity is crucial for the trustworthiness of data and involves mechanisms like checksums, digital signatures, and version controls to detect and mitigate tampering (Pfleeger & Pfleeger, 2012).

Integrity, as a fundamental component of the CIA (Confidentiality, Integrity, Availability) Triad, plays a crucial role in information security. It refers to the assurance that data is accurate, complete, and unaltered, except by authorized parties in authorized ways. The concept of integrity extends beyond just the data itself to encompass systems, processes, and communications, ensuring that every aspect of information technology operates as intended, without unauthorized modification.

The Essence of Integrity in Information Security

Integrity in information security ensures that data, once created, transmitted, or stored, remains exact and unaltered until it reaches its intended recipient or is accessed by authorized users. This aspect of the CIA Triad guards against both intentional and accidental modifications to data, which could compromise its accuracy and reliability. Integrity is vital in many contexts, including financial transactions, legal documents, and personal records, where the authenticity and accuracy of information are paramount (Bishop, 2003).

Mechanisms to Ensure Integrity

Several mechanisms and practices are employed to maintain integrity within information systems:

- **Cryptographic Hash Functions**: These functions generate a unique hash value for data, which can be used to verify its integrity. Any alteration to the data results in a different hash value, signaling potential tampering. Hash functions are widely used in securing data transmissions and verifying the integrity of files and software (Stallings, 2005).
- **Digital Signatures**: Digital signatures provide a means to ensure the integrity and authenticity of digital documents. By encrypting the hash of a document with a private key, the sender can create a signature that the recipient can verify using the sender's public key. This process ensures that the document has not been altered since it was signed (Pfleeger & Pfleeger, 2012).

- **Version Control Systems**: In software development and document management, version control systems track changes to files, enabling the restoration of earlier versions and the verification of modifications. This aids in maintaining the integrity of the development process and ensuring that changes are authorized and documented (Collins-Sussman, Fitzpatrick, & Pilato, 2004).
- **Access Controls and Audit Trails**: Implementing strict access controls prevents unauthorized modifications to data, while audit trails record who accessed or modified data and when. These records are crucial for detecting breaches of integrity and tracing the source of unauthorized changes (Sandhu & Samarati, 1994).

Challenges in Maintaining Integrity

Maintaining integrity in the digital age faces several challenges, including sophisticated cyber threats like malware designed to alter or corrupt data and insider threats where individuals with legitimate access intentionally or accidentally compromise data integrity. Moreover, the increasing complexity of IT systems and the proliferation of interconnected devices expand the attack surface, necessitating comprehensive security measures to safeguard data integrity across multiple platforms and networks.

The Impact of Integrity on Trust and Compliance

The integrity of data directly impacts trust in information systems and their compliance with regulatory standards. In sectors like finance, healthcare, and government, where decisions are based on digital information, the integrity of data is essential for maintaining operational trust and legal compliance. Regulations such as the Sarbanes-Oxley Act and the Health Insurance Portability and Accountability Act (HIPAA) underscore the importance of data integrity by setting stringent requirements for information management and protection (United States Congress, 2002; United States Department of Health and Human Services, n.d.).

Integrity is a cornerstone of information security, ensuring that data remains accurate, complete, and unaltered. Through mechanisms like cryptographic hash functions, digital signatures, version control systems, and comprehensive access controls, organizations can safeguard the integrity of their data. As technology evolves and the threat landscape expands, maintaining data integrity remains a critical challenge, underpinning trust, compliance, and the overall security of information systems.

Availability:

Ensures that information and resources are accessible to authorized users when needed. This aspect of information security involves protecting against disruptions to systems and networks, employing redundancy, failover systems, and robust disaster recovery plans (Easttom, 2016).

Availability, as a critical component of the Confidentiality, Integrity, and Availability (CIA) Triad, is essential in the realm of information security. It ensures that information systems, data, and services are accessible to authorized users when needed, thus supporting the continuous functionality of business operations and services. The concept of availability extends beyond mere access to data; it encompasses the resilience of systems against disruptions, the timely recovery from incidents, and the assurance that critical business processes remain operational despite cyber threats or technical failures.

The Importance of Availability

In today's interconnected world, the availability of digital resources is crucial for the day-to-day operations of organizations across all sectors. Disruptions to the availability of information systems can lead to significant financial losses, damage to reputation, and in some cases, impact public safety and welfare. For instance, in healthcare, the availability of patient records and medical systems is vital for patient care. Similarly, in finance, the availability of online banking systems is critical for customer transactions (Dhillon & Backhouse, 2000).

Ensuring Availability

Ensuring the availability of information systems involves several key practices and technologies:

- **Redundancy and Failover Systems**: Implementing redundancy in hardware, software, and connectivity can prevent single points of failure, ensuring that backup components take over in case of a malfunction. Failover systems automatically switch to a redundant system upon the failure of the primary system, minimizing downtime (Patterson, Gibson, & Katz, 1988).
- **Disaster Recovery and Business Continuity Planning**: Disaster recovery plans outline procedures for data backup and system restoration in the event of a disaster. Business continuity planning goes further to ensure that essential business functions can continue during and after a disaster. Both are critical for maintaining availability during unexpected events (Wallace & Webber, 2017).
- **Regular Maintenance and Updates**: Conducting regular maintenance and updates of hardware and software helps in preventing failures due to outdated or malfunctioning components. Patch management is particularly important for addressing vulnerabilities that could be exploited to disrupt services (Stallings, 2005).
- **Distributed Denial of Service (DDoS) Mitigation**: DDoS attacks, which flood servers with excessive traffic to overwhelm resources and disrupt services, are a significant threat to availability. DDoS mitigation techniques include traffic analysis to identify and filter out malicious traffic, along with the use of cloud-based DDoS protection services that can absorb and disperse the excessive traffic (Mirkovic & Reiher, 2004).

Challenges to Availability

Maintaining the availability of information systems faces challenges from both cyber threats and natural disasters. Cyber attacks such as ransomware can encrypt data and systems, rendering them inaccessible. Physical threats such as fires, floods, or power outages can also disrupt the availability of critical systems. Moreover, the increasing complexity of IT infrastructures and the reliance on third-party services and cloud computing introduce additional vulnerabilities and potential points of failure that can impact availability (Jansen & Grance, 2011).

The Evolution of Availability Measures

As technology evolves and the landscape of threats changes, the measures to ensure availability also advance. Cloud computing, for example, offers opportunities for enhanced availability through distributed resources and scalability. However, it also requires new approaches to security and risk management to protect against service disruptions. The concept of availability is thus continually evolving, reflecting the changing nature of technology, threats, and organizational dependencies on digital systems.

Availability is a fundamental aspect of information security, ensuring that data and systems are accessible to authorized users when needed. Through a combination of technological solutions, planning, and proactive management, organizations can enhance the resilience of their information systems against disruptions. As the digital landscape continues to evolve, so too will the strategies and technologies employed to maintain the availability of critical digital resources.

Expanding the Triad: Additional Considerations

While the CIA Triad forms the core of information security, the evolving digital landscape has introduced additional considerations, expanding the model to include aspects such as:

Authentication and Non-Repudiation:

Ensuring that users are who they claim to be and cannot deny their actions. This expansion reflects the need for robust identity management and access control systems (Vacca, 2013).

While the Confidentiality, Integrity, and Availability (CIA) Triad forms the core foundation of information security principles, the evolving digital landscape necessitates additional considerations to address complex cybersecurity challenges. Among these are the concepts of Authentication and Non-Repudiation, which have become increasingly critical in ensuring secure and trustworthy digital interactions.

Authentication

Authentication is the process of verifying the identity of a user, system, or entity. In the context of information security, authentication ensures that individuals or systems are who they claim to be before granting access to sensitive information or critical functionalities. This process is fundamental to maintaining the confidentiality and integrity of data, as it helps to prevent unauthorized access and potential security breaches (Stallings & Brown, 2012).

Authentication mechanisms typically involve one or more of the following factors:

- **Something you know**: A password, PIN, or another piece of knowledge unique to the user.
- **Something you have**: A physical token, smart card, or a mobile device used to generate one-time passcodes.
- **Something you are**: Biometric identifiers such as fingerprints, facial recognition, or retina scans.

The use of multiple factors, known as Multi-Factor Authentication (MFA), significantly enhances security by adding layers of defense against unauthorized access (Jain, Ross, & Nandakumar, 2016).

Non-Repudiation

Non-Repudiation refers to the ability to ensure that a party in a communication or transaction cannot deny the authenticity of their signature on a document or the sending of a message that they origi-nated. This concept is particularly important in digital communications and transactions, where proving the origin and integrity of data can be crucial in legal disputes, financial transactions, and secure messaging (Zhou, Gollmann, & Mitchell, 2013).

Digital signatures and cryptographic techniques are commonly used to provide non-repudiation. A digital signature, created using the sender's private key, can be verified by anyone who has the sender's public key, thereby authenticating the origin and confirming that the message or document has not been altered after signing. This mechanism not only ensures the integrity of the data but also provides a cryptographic proof of origin (Pfleeger & Pfleeger, 2012).

The Importance of Authentication and Non-Repudiation

As digital interactions continue to proliferate, the importance of authentication and non-repudiation in information security cannot be overstated. These principles address critical security challenges in online banking, e-commerce, electronic voting, and any application where trust, privacy, and security are paramount. By verifying identities and securing the origins of digital communications, authentication and non-repudiation help to build trust in digital systems and ensure the reliability of electronic transactions.

Challenges and Future Directions

Implementing robust authentication and non-repudiation measures poses challenges, particularly in balancing security with user convenience and privacy concerns. As technology evolves, so too do the methods employed by cybercriminals to bypass security measures. This ongoing arms race necessitates continuous innovation in authentication and non-repudiation techniques, including advancements in biometric authentication, decentralized identity systems, and quantum-resistant cryptographic algorithms.

Expanding the CIA Triad to include Authentication and Non-Repudiation reflects the complexity of modern cybersecurity challenges. These additional considerations are essential in ensuring secure, trustworthy digital interactions and transactions. As the digital landscape continues to evolve, the development and implementation of advanced authentication and non-repudiation mechanisms will be crucial in safeguarding information security in an increasingly interconnected world.

Privacy:

Addressing concerns related to the collection, storage, and use of personal information. The rise of regulations like the General Data Protection Regulation (GDPR) underscores the importance of privacy as an integral component of information security (European Parliament and Council, 2016).

In the realm of information security, the traditional focus on the CIA (Confidentiality, Integrity, and Availability) Triad has been instrumental in guiding security practices. However, the evolving digital landscape, characterized by vast data exchanges and the ubiquity of personal information online, has necessitated a broader perspective that includes Privacy as a critical component of information security. The expansion of the CIA Triad to incorporate Privacy reflects a growing recognition of the importance of protecting personal information from unauthorized access and misuse.

The Importance of Privacy in Information Security

Privacy, in the context of information security, pertains to the right of individuals to control the collection, use, and disclosure of their personal information. It encompasses the protection of personal data from unauthorized access, ensuring that individuals' preferences regarding data sharing are respected, and safeguarding the confidentiality of personal communications (Solove & Schwartz, 2015).

As digital technologies become increasingly integrated into daily life, the volume of personal data generated and collected by organizations has surged, elevating privacy concerns. Data breaches, unauthorized surveillance, and the misuse of personal information have underscored the need for robust privacy protections as a fundamental aspect of information security.

Mechanisms to Ensure Privacy

Ensuring privacy within information systems involves implementing a combination of technical, legal, and procedural measures:

- **Data Minimization and Purpose Limitation**: Collecting only the data necessary for the specified purpose and limiting the use of data to those purposes for which it was collected. These principles are critical for reducing the risk of harm from data breaches and misuse (European Parliament and Council, 2016).
- **Encryption**: Protecting the confidentiality of personal data through encryption, both at rest and in transit, to prevent unauthorized access. Encryption serves as a foundational technology for securing personal communications and sensitive information (Stallings & Brown, 2012).
- **Access Controls and Authentication**: Implementing stringent access controls and authentication mechanisms to ensure that only authorized individuals can access personal data, thereby protecting against unauthorized disclosure and modification.
- **Anonymization and Pseudonymization**: Techniques such as anonymization and pseudonymization reduce the risks associated with personal data processing by making it difficult to attribute data to specific individuals without additional information (Voigt & Von dem Bussche, 2017).

Privacy Legislation and Regulations

The importance of privacy has led to the development of comprehensive privacy laws and regulations around the world. The General Data Protection Regulation (GDPR) in the European Union represents a landmark in privacy legislation, setting stringent standards for data protection and granting individuals significant rights over their personal data. Similar regulations, such as the California Consumer Privacy Act (CCPA) in the United States, reflect a global trend toward strengthening privacy protections and accountability for organizations handling personal data (European Parliament and Council, 2016; State of California Department of Justice, n.d.).

Challenges and Future Directions

Ensuring privacy in the digital age presents numerous challenges, including the complexity of managing personal data across different jurisdictions, the potential for conflict between privacy and other objectives such as national security, and the rapid pace of technological change that can outstrip existing regulatory frameworks. Future directions in privacy protection may involve the development of privacy-enhancing technologies (PETs), the adoption of privacy-by-design principles in the development of new technologies, and ongoing efforts to harmonize privacy regulations across jurisdictions.

The inclusion of Privacy as an expansion of the traditional CIA Triad underscores the critical importance of safeguarding personal information in the digital ecosystem. Protecting privacy requires a comprehensive approach that integrates technical measures, robust legal frameworks, and ethical considerations. As technology and data practices continue to evolve, privacy will remain a central concern in information security, demanding continuous attention and adaptation to ensure the protection of individuals' rights in the digital age.

Challenges in Information Security

Information security faces numerous challenges, from the technical complexities of protecting against sophisticated cyber threats to the organizational challenges of implementing comprehensive security policies. The dynamic nature of cyber threats, including malware, phishing, and advanced persistent threats (APTs), requires continuous vigilance and adaptation of security measures.

Additionally, the human factor remains one of the most significant vulnerabilities in information security. Social engineering attacks exploit human psychology rather than technical vulnerabilities, highlighting the need for ongoing security awareness and training (Hadnagy, 2018).

Understanding the challenges in information security is crucial for developing effective strategies to protect digital assets in an increasingly complex and evolving cyber threat landscape. The Confidentiality, Integrity, and Availability (CIA) Triad serves as the foundational framework for information security practices. However, ensuring the confidentiality, integrity, and availability of information systems in the face of sophisticated and rapidly evolving threats presents a myriad of challenges.

Emerging Cyber Threats

One of the primary challenges in information security is the constant evolution of cyber threats. Cybercriminals are continually developing new methods and technologies to breach security measures, exploit vulnerabilities, and gain unauthorized access to sensitive data. Advanced Persistent Threats (APTs), ransomware, phishing attacks, and zero-day exploits represent just a fraction of the tactics employed by adversaries to compromise the CIA triad (Manky, 2013). The dynamic nature of these threats necessitates continuous vigilance, threat intelligence, and adaptive security measures to protect against potential breaches.

Complexity of IT Systems and Infrastructure

The growing complexity of IT systems and infrastructure poses significant challenges to information security. The widespread adoption of cloud computing, Internet of Things (IoT) devices, and mobile technologies has expanded the attack surface, introducing new vulnerabilities and making it more difficult to manage and secure information systems (Jansen & Grance, 2011). Additionally, the integration of third-party services and the reliance on complex supply chains further complicate the security landscape, as vulnerabilities in any component can potentially compromise the entire system.

Insider Threats and Human Error

Insider threats, whether intentional or accidental, represent a significant challenge to maintaining the CIA triad. Malicious insiders with access to sensitive information can cause substantial damage, while unintentional actions by employees, such as falling for phishing scams or mishandling data, can also lead to security breaches (Hadnagy, 2018). Addressing insider threats requires a combination of technical controls, such as access management and data monitoring, and organizational measures, including security awareness training and a strong culture of security.

Legal and Regulatory Compliance

Navigating the complex landscape of legal and regulatory requirements adds another layer of challenge to information security. Regulations such as the General Data Protection Regulation (GDPR) in the European Union and various sector-specific regulations worldwide impose strict data protection and privacy requirements on organizations. Compliance with these regulations necessitates comprehensive data governance and security practices, but the diverse and sometimes conflicting nature of international regulations can complicate compliance efforts (Voigt & Von dem Bussche, 2017).

Balancing Security with Usability

Achieving a balance between security and usability is an ongoing challenge in information security. Overly restrictive security measures can hinder productivity and frustrate users, potentially leading to non-compliance or the adoption of workarounds that compromise security. Conversely, insufficient security controls can leave systems vulnerable to attack. Finding the right balance requires a user-centric approach to security, designing measures that are both effective and user-friendly (Zurko & Simon, 1996).

The challenges in information security are diverse and multifaceted, reflecting the complexity of the digital environment and the ingenuity of cyber adversaries. Addressing these challenges requires a comprehensive and adaptive approach that encompasses technological solutions, organizational policies, and a culture of security awareness. As the digital landscape continues to evolve, so too will the challenges and strategies for protecting the confidentiality, integrity, and availability of information.

Future Directions

As technology continues to advance, information security will increasingly rely on artificial intelligence (AI) and machine learning (ML) to predict, detect, and respond to threats more efficiently. However, the ethical implications and potential biases within AI-driven security tools will necessitate careful consideration and governance.

Moreover, the concept of Zero Trust architecture, which assumes that threats could be present both outside and inside the network, is gaining traction. This approach requires strict identity verification, least privilege access, and microsegmentation to secure the organization's resources (Rose, Borchert, Mitchell, & Connelly, 2020).

The realm of information security, underpinned by the foundational principles of the Confidentiality, Integrity, and Availability (CIA) Triad, is on the cusp of transformative changes. As digital technologies evolve at an unprecedented pace, the future directions of information security are poised to address emerging challenges with innovative solutions. This evolution is driven by advancements in technology, the changing nature of cyber threats, and the growing complexity of the global information landscape.

Integration of Artificial Intelligence and Machine Learning

The integration of Artificial Intelligence (AI) and Machine Learning (ML) into information security represents a significant future direction. AI and ML offer the potential to revolutionize threat detection and response by analyzing vast datasets to identify patterns indicative of cyber threats. These technologies can automate the process of threat intelligence, providing real-time, adaptive responses to emerging threats (April Tanner & Cam, 2018). As AI and ML capabilities continue to advance, their application in predictive analytics, anomaly detection, and automated incident response is expected to become more sophisticated, enhancing the ability to protect against advanced persistent threats (APTs) and zero-day exploits.

Embracing Zero Trust Security Models

The concept of Zero Trust security models is gaining traction as a future direction in information security. Zero Trust operates on the principle that no entity, whether inside or outside the network perimeter, should be automatically trusted. This approach requires strict identity verification, least privilege access controls, and micro-segmentation to secure resources. As organizations continue to embrace cloud computing and remote work, the implementation of Zero Trust architectures is expected to become more prevalent, offering a more dynamic and flexible approach to securing digital assets (Rose, Borchert, Mitchell, & Connelly, 2020).

Advancements in Quantum Computing and Cryptography

The advent of quantum computing poses both challenges and opportunities for information security. Quantum computers have the potential to break current cryptographic algorithms, threatening the confidentiality and integrity of digital communications. In response, the development of quantum-resistant cryptography is a critical future direction. Post-quantum cryptographic algorithms are being designed to secure information against the capabilities of quantum computing, ensuring the long-term viability of encryption as a cornerstone of information security (Chen et al., 2016).

Increasing Importance of Privacy and Data Protection

The future of information security will also see an increased emphasis on privacy and data protection. As data breaches and privacy concerns continue to rise, there is a growing demand for more robust privacy-preserving technologies and practices. This includes the adoption of Privacy by Design principles, which integrate privacy considerations into the development of IT systems and business practices. Furthermore, global data protection regulations, such as the GDPR, are likely to evolve and possibly converge, setting higher standards for privacy and compelling organizations worldwide to enhance their data protection measures (European Parliament and Council, 2016).

Collaborative Cybersecurity and Information Sharing

The complexity and sophistication of cyber threats necessitate a collaborative approach to cybersecurity. Future directions in information security will likely emphasize greater information sharing and cooperation among organizations, industries, and governments. Initiatives such as the Cyber Threat Alliance and Information Sharing and Analysis Centers (ISACs) exemplify this trend, facilitating the exchange of threat intelligence and best practices. Collaborative cybersecurity efforts are essential for building collective resilience against cyber threats and addressing the shared challenges of securing the digital landscape.

The future directions of information security are characterized by the adoption of advanced technologies, new security models, and an increased focus on privacy and collaboration. As the digital world continues to evolve, so too will the strategies and tools employed to protect information assets. Navigating this future will require continuous innovation, adaptability, and a proactive stance toward emerging threats and opportunities.

Security Policies, Standards, and Frameworks:

Understanding Information Security within the context of Security Policies, Standards, and Frameworks is pivotal for organizations aiming to safeguard their digital assets against a vast array of cyber threats. These elements—policies, standards, and frameworks—form the backbone of an organization's information security program, providing a structured approach to managing and mitigating cybersecurity risks.

Security Policies

Security policies are formalized statements from an organization's management, outlining the company's approach to security, its objectives, and the responsibilities of its employees and users. These policies serve as a guide for the behavior of individuals and the use of resources within the organization, ensuring that activities are conducted in a secure manner. Security policies are foundational in establishing a security-conscious culture and in setting the direction for the implementation and management of security controls (Dhillon & Backhouse, 2000).

Security policies form the cornerstone of an organization's information security program, defining the framework within which the organization manages its security processes, protects its digital assets, and aligns its cybersecurity efforts with its business objectives. These policies are essential documents that dictate how information security is implemented, managed, and maintained across the organization.

Definition and Purpose of Security Policies

Security policies are formal statements issued by an organization's management, laying out the rules, guidelines, and practices for securing its information technology and data assets. They serve multiple purposes, including:

- **Establishing a Security Culture**: Security policies communicate the importance of information security to all members of the organization, fostering a culture of security awareness and compliance.
- **Guiding Behavior**: They provide clear guidelines on expected behaviors and practices regarding the use of IT resources, data handling, and response to security incidents.
- **Defining Roles and Responsibilities**: Security policies outline the responsibilities of various roles within the organization concerning information security, ensuring accountability and clarity in security operations (Dhillon & Backhouse, 2000).

Components of Security Policies

Effective security policies typically include the following components:

- **Scope and Objectives**: A description of the policy's scope and the security objectives it aims to achieve.
- **Compliance Requirements**: Information on relevant legal, regulatory, and contractual compliance requirements the policy addresses.
- **Roles and Responsibilities**: Detailed descriptions of the security responsibilities of different roles within the organization.
- **Specific Security Requirements**: Guidelines and rules for specific areas of security, such as access control, data encryption, incident response, and physical security.

- **Review and Enforcement Mechanisms**: Procedures for the ongoing review, update, and enforcement of the policy, including disciplinary measures for non-compliance (von Solms & van Niekerk, 2013).

Developing and Implementing Security Policies

The development and implementation of security policies involve several key steps:

- **Assessment of Risk and Compliance Needs**: Identifying the organization's security risks and compliance requirements to ensure the policies address these areas effectively.
- **Stakeholder Engagement**: Involving stakeholders from various departments to ensure the policies are comprehensive and align with business processes.
- **Drafting and Review**: Writing the policy documents and reviewing them with legal, compliance, and security experts within the organization.
- **Approval and Communication**: Obtaining approval from senior management and communicating the policies across the organization.
- **Training and Awareness**: Conducting training sessions and awareness programs to ensure employees understand the policies and their roles in upholding them.
- **Monitoring and Review**: Regularly monitoring compliance with the policies and reviewing them periodically to adapt to changes in the threat landscape, technology, and business operations (Whitman & Mattord, 2013).

Challenges in Security Policy Management

Managing security policies presents several challenges, including keeping the policies up to date with the rapidly evolving cyber threat landscape and technological advancements. Additionally, ensuring that the policies are effectively communicated and adhered to throughout the organization requires continuous effort and resources. Balancing security needs with business functionality and user convenience is also crucial to avoid overly restrictive policies that can hinder productivity.

Security policies are vital for establishing a robust information security framework within an organization. They set the foundation for a secure organizational culture, guide the behavior of employees, and define the mechanisms for managing and protecting information assets. Developing, implementing, and maintaining effective security policies require a strategic approach, stakeholder engagement, and ongoing management to ensure they remain relevant and effective in securing the organization against cyber threats.

Security Standards

Security standards are specific requirements or rules that must be followed to achieve policy objectives and maintain the security posture of an organization. Standards can be internal, developed by the organization to address specific security needs, or external, adopted from established industry or international standards. Examples of widely recognized security standards include the ISO/IEC 27000 series for information security management systems (ISMS) and the Payment Card Industry Data Security Standard (PCI DSS) for payment card data protection. Standards provide a measurable and consistent approach to implementing security controls and achieving compliance with regulatory requirements (von Solms & van Niekerk, 2013).

Security standards are critical components within the domain of information security, acting as the bridge between high-level policies and the specific controls and procedures implemented by organizations. These standards provide a set of established criteria, best practices, and guidelines designed to help organizations enhance their security posture, ensure compliance, and protect their information assets from cyber threats.

The Role of Security Standards

Security standards serve several key functions in the realm of information security:

- **Benchmarking and Best Practices**: They offer a consensus-driven set of benchmarks and best practices developed through the expertise and experience of industry professionals and organizations.
- **Consistency and Interoperability**: Standards promote consistency in implementing security measures across different systems and organizations, facilitating interoperability and the seamless exchange of information.
- **Compliance and Assurance**: Many standards have regulatory or industry-specific requirements, providing a framework for compliance that organizations can use to demonstrate their commitment to security to stakeholders, customers, and regulatory bodies (ISO/IEC, 2013).

Notable Security Standards

Several security standards are widely recognized and adopted across industries and sectors, each serving specific aspects of information security:

- **ISO/IEC 27000 Series**: This series, particularly ISO/IEC 27001, provides a framework for an information security management system (ISMS), offering guidelines for implementing, maintaining, and continually improving information security (ISO/IEC, 2013).
- **NIST Special Publication 800 Series**: Developed by the National Institute of Standards and Technology (NIST) in the United States, this series offers comprehensive guidelines, best practices, and recommendations on various aspects of information security, including risk management, cybersecurity, and privacy controls (NIST, 2018).

- **Payment Card Industry Data Security Standard (PCI DSS)**: This standard is mandatory for all entities that store, process, or transmit cardholder data, outlining measures to secure transactions and protect cardholder information against theft and fraud (PCI Security Standards Council, 2018).

Developing and Implementing Security Standards

The development and implementation of security standards within an organization involve several critical steps:

- **Assessment and Gap Analysis**: Assessing the current security posture and conducting a gap analysis to identify areas where the organization does not meet the desired standards.
- **Customization and Integration**: While standards provide a general framework, they often need to be customized to fit the specific needs, context, and risk profile of the organization.
- **Training and Awareness**: Educating employees about the standards and their role in the organization's security posture is essential for effective implementation.
- **Continuous Monitoring and Improvement**: Standards are not static; they require continuous monitoring, review, and updates to adapt to new threats, technologies, and business practices.

Challenges and Considerations

Implementing security standards poses challenges, including the complexity of integrating standards into existing processes, the costs associated with compliance, and the need for ongoing updates to keep pace with evolving threats. Moreover, the effectiveness of standards depends on their acceptance and adoption by the organization's personnel and the continuous improvement of security practices.

Security standards are indispensable in guiding organizations toward robust and effective information security practices. By providing a comprehensive set of guidelines and best practices, standards help organizations protect against cyber threats, ensure compliance, and maintain the trust of stakeholders. The successful implementation of security standards requires a commitment to continuous improvement, customization to fit organizational needs, and engagement across all levels of the organization.

Security Frameworks

Security frameworks offer a comprehensive approach to managing and mitigating cybersecurity risks. Unlike standards, which can be prescriptive, frameworks typically provide a flexible structure that organizations can adapt to their specific needs. Frameworks often encompass best practices, methodologies, and guidelines to assist organizations in developing and refining their information security programs.

Security frameworks in information security provide comprehensive structures for managing and mitigating cybersecurity risks. Unlike specific security policies and standards, which might focus on particular aspects of security or compliance requirements, security frameworks offer a more holistic approach. They integrate policies, standards, and best practices into a cohesive system that organizations can tailor to their unique needs and objectives. The adoption of security frameworks is crucial for establishing a resilient information security posture that addresses a broad spectrum of threats and compliance demands.

Role of Security Frameworks

Security frameworks serve multiple roles within an organization's information security program:

- **Strategic Planning**: They provide a strategic outline for managing cybersecurity risk aligned with business objectives, enabling organizations to prioritize resources effectively.
- **Risk Management**: Frameworks facilitate a systematic approach to identifying, assessing, and managing cybersecurity risks, ensuring that protective measures are proportional to the risks identified.

- **Compliance and Governance**: By encompassing various compliance requirements, frameworks help organizations meet legal and regulatory obligations while promoting good governance practices.
- **Continuous Improvement**: Offering a structured approach to security, these frameworks support continuous monitoring and improvement of cybersecurity practices (National Institute of Standards and Technology, 2018).

Prominent Security Frameworks

Several security frameworks have gained prominence, each with its unique focus and application domain. Among these, a few stand out for their widespread adoption and impact:

- **NIST Cybersecurity Framework (NIST CSF)**: Developed by the National Institute of Standards and Technology, the NIST CSF offers a flexible and voluntary framework primarily intended for critical infrastructure organizations but applicable across sectors. It outlines five core functions—Identify, Protect, Detect, Respond, and Recover—that provide a high-level taxonomy of cybersecurity outcomes and a systematic approach to managing cybersecurity risk (National Institute of Standards and Technology, 2018).
- **ISO/IEC 27001**: Part of the ISO/IEC 27000 family, ISO/IEC 27001 specifies the requirements for establishing, implementing, maintaining, and continually improving an information security management system (ISMS). It is designed to help organizations secure their information assets in a systematic and cost-effective manner (International Organization for Standardization, 2013).
- **Control Objectives for Information and Related Technologies (COBIT)**: COBIT is a framework for IT management and governance, developed by ISACA. It provides a comprehensive set of best practices for IT governance and control, aiming to

align IT processes with business objectives while managing risks and resources effectively (ISACA, 2018).

Implementing Security Frameworks

Implementing a security framework involves several key steps:

- **Gap Analysis**: Assessing the current cybersecurity practices against the framework to identify gaps.
- **Adaptation and Customization**: Tailoring the framework to the organization's specific context, risk appetite, and business objectives.
- **Integration**: Integrating the framework into existing processes and systems, ensuring it complements other standards and policies in place.
- **Training and Awareness**: Educating staff about the framework and their roles in supporting it.
- **Continuous Assessment and Improvement**: Regularly reviewing and updating the implementation to reflect changing threats, technologies, and business requirements.

Challenges and Future Directions

While security frameworks provide a valuable structure for managing cybersecurity, their implementation can present challenges. These include the potential complexity of adapting frameworks to an organization's specific needs, the resources required for implementation and ongoing management, and the need to keep the framework aligned with evolving cybersecurity threats and business objectives.

As cybersecurity threats continue to evolve, so too will security frameworks. Future directions may include greater emphasis on cloud security, privacy protection, and the integration of artificial intelligence and machine learning technologies for dynamic risk management.

Security frameworks play a pivotal role in shaping an organization's approach to managing cybersecurity risks. By providing a comprehensive and flexible structure that encompasses best practices, standards, and governance models, these frameworks are instrumental in building resilient cybersecurity postures. Organizations that effectively implement and maintain security frameworks are better positioned to protect their assets, comply with regulatory requirements, and adapt to the rapidly changing cyber threat landscape.

One of the most influential security frameworks is the National Institute of Standards and Technology (NIST) Cybersecurity Framework, which is designed to help organizations manage cybersecurity risks in a prioritized, flexible, and cost-effective manner. The Framework is organized into five core functions—Identify, Protect, Detect, Respond, and Recover—that provide a high-level strategic view of an organization's approach to managing cybersecurity risk (National Institute of Standards and Technology, 2018).

The Importance of Policies, Standards, and Frameworks

The development and implementation of security policies, standards, and frameworks are crucial for several reasons:

- **Risk Management**: They provide a structured approach to identifying, assessing, and mitigating cybersecurity risks.
- **Regulatory Compliance**: They ensure that organizations meet legal and regulatory requirements related to information security.
- **Consistency and Efficiency**: They standardize security practices across the organization, improving consistency and operational efficiency.
- **Continuous Improvement**: They facilitate the ongoing assessment and improvement of security practices in response to evolving threats and business needs.

Challenges and Considerations

Implementing security policies, standards, and frameworks presents challenges, including keeping up with rapidly evolving cyber threats, ensuring alignment with business objectives, and managing the complexity of compliance with multiple regulatory requirements. Organizations must remain adaptable, continually assessing and updating their security practices to address new risks and technologies.

Security Policies, Standards, and Frameworks are integral components of an effective information security program. They provide the necessary structure, guidance, and benchmarks for organizations to protect their information assets and manage cybersecurity risks effectively. As the digital landscape continues to evolve, the role of these elements in fostering a secure and resilient digital environment will remain paramount.

Conclusion

Understanding information security is critical in the digital age, requiring a comprehensive approach that encompasses technical, organizational, and human factors. The foundational principles of the CIA Triad, expanded to address modern challenges, guide the development of effective security measures. As the digital landscape evolves, so too will the strategies and technologies employed to protect information, necessitating ongoing adaptation and innovation in information security practices.

Chapter 4: Cryptography: The Art of Secrecy

Cryptography, often described as the art and science of secrecy, has been an integral part of human communication and information security for centuries. From ancient ciphers to modern encryption algorithms, cryptography enables the confidential communication of information, protecting data from unauthorized access and ensuring its integrity and authenticity. In the digital age, cryptography has become a cornerstone of information security, underpinning the secure transmission of data across the internet and safeguarding sensitive information stored on digital devices.

The Evolution of Cryptography

The evolution of cryptography is a fascinating journey through history, reflecting the continuous cat-and-mouse game between code makers and code breakers. From ancient methods of secret communication to the complex algorithms that secure modern digital transactions, the art and science of cryptography have been fundamental to the development of societies and technologies. This evolution is not just a technical narrative but also a reflection of the changing needs, threats, and capabilities of civilizations over time.

Ancient Cryptography

The earliest forms of cryptography can be traced back to ancient civilizations. The Egyptians used non-standard hieroglyphs on monuments, while the Spartans used the scytale, a tool for performing a transposition cipher, to send secret military messages. One of the most famous ancient ciphers is the Caesar cipher, named after Julius Caesar, who used it to encode his military communications. These early methods were primarily based on simple substitution or transposition techniques, where the letters in a message were replaced or reordered (Kahn, 1967).

The Middle Ages to the Renaissance

During the Middle Ages and the Renaissance, cryptography became more sophisticated, reflecting the increased complexity of political and military communication. The development of polyalphabetic ciphers, such as the Vigenère cipher, introduced a new level of security by using multiple alphabets to encrypt a message. Despite these advancements, the fundamental principles of cryptography remained relatively unchanged until the advent of mechanical encryption devices (Singh, 1999).

The Mechanical Era

The mechanical era of cryptography began in the 15th century with the invention of cryptographic devices that could automate the encryption and decryption processes. The most famous of these is the Enigma machine, developed by the Germans in the 1920s and used extensively during World War II. The Enigma machine's complexity and the secrecy surrounding its operation made it one of the most secure cryptographic devices of its time. However, the successful efforts of Allied cryptanalysts to break the Enigma code highlighted the ongoing challenge of maintaining the security of cryptographic systems (Sebag-Montefiore, 2000).

The Digital Era

The advent of digital computing in the mid-20th century revolutionized cryptography, leading to the development of modern cryptographic algorithms. The introduction of the Data Encryption Standard (DES) in the 1970s marked the beginning of the digital era of cryptography, providing a standardized method for secure electronic communication. The subsequent development of asymmetric (public key) cryptography by Diffie and Hellman in 1976 solved the key distribution problem that had plagued cryptography for centuries, enabling secure communication between parties without the need to share a secret key (Diffie & Hellman, 1976).

The Modern Landscape

Today, cryptography is an indispensable part of digital security, protecting everything from personal communications to global financial transactions. The development of advanced cryptographic algorithms, such as RSA and AES, and secure protocols, such as SSL/TLS for internet security, exemplify the ongoing innovation in the field. However, the potential development of quantum computing poses a significant threat to current cryptographic methods, prompting researchers to explore post-quantum cryptography as the next frontier in the evolution of cryptography (Bernstein & Lange, 2017).

The evolution of cryptography is a testament to human ingenuity in the quest for secure communication. From ancient ciphers to quantum-resistant algorithms, the history of cryptography is a narrative of constant adaptation and innovation. As the digital world continues to evolve, so too will cryptography, playing a crucial role in safeguarding the future of information security.

Principles of Cryptography

Cryptography is based on several fundamental principles:

Encryption and Decryption: Encryption is the process of converting plaintext into ciphertext, a scrambled message unreadable without the key to decrypt it. Decryption is the reverse process, converting ciphertext back into plaintext using the appropriate key.

Keys: Cryptographic keys are used to encrypt and decrypt messages. The security of cryptographic systems often depends on the secrecy of the keys.

Algorithms: Cryptographic algorithms define the mathematical operations used for encryption and decryption. These algorithms can be symmetric, where the same key is used for both encryption and decryption, or asymmetric, involving a pair of keys (public and private keys) for secure communication (Stallings, 2017).

Modern Cryptographic Techniques

Modern cryptography encompasses a wide range of techniques, including:

Symmetric Key Cryptography: Also known as secret key cryptography, this involves a single key shared between the sender and receiver. Algorithms like AES (Advanced Encryption Standard) are widely used for encrypting data at rest and in transit.

Asymmetric Key Cryptography: Also known as public key cryptography, this involves two keys: a public key for encryption and a private key for decryption. RSA (Rivest-Shamir-Adleman) is one of the most well-known asymmetric algorithms, enabling secure data transmission and digital signatures.

Hash Functions: Hash functions convert input data into a fixed-size string of characters, which represents the data uniquely. Hash functions are used for data integrity checks and are a fundamental component of digital signatures and various security protocols (Menezes, van Oorschot, & Vanstone, 1996).

Applications of Cryptography

Cryptography underpins numerous applications in the digital world, including:

Secure Communications:

Encrypting emails, instant messages, and other forms of digital communication to protect against eavesdropping.

The applications of cryptography in secure communications represent a significant aspect of its evolution, reflecting the growing need to protect information as it traverses increasingly complex and potentially insecure digital landscapes. Secure communications, encompassing everything from military communications to everyday internet transactions, have been fundamentally transformed by cryptographic techniques, ensuring confidentiality, integrity, and authenticity of the data exchanged.

Historical Context

The use of cryptography for secure communications dates back to ancient civilizations, where simple substitution ciphers were used for military secrecy. However, the real transformation began with the advent of the telegraph and later the telephone, which introduced new challenges for secure communication over long distances. World War I and II saw extensive use of cryptography, with machines like the Enigma and the Lorenz cipher machine being used to protect military communications. The breaking of these ciphers by Allied cryptanalysts not only had significant wartime implications but also pushed the development of cryptography further into the modern era (Kahn, 1967).

Digital Era and Public Key Cryptography

The digital revolution marked a pivotal shift in the applications of cryptography for secure communications. The invention of public key cryptography by Whitfield Diffie and Martin Hellman in 1976 addressed one of the most significant challenges in digital communications: secure key exchange over an insecure channel. This breakthrough made it possible to encrypt and decrypt messages without the need for the sender and receiver to have shared a secret key in advance, paving the way for secure email, secure web browsing, and the secure transmission of data over the internet (Diffie & Hellman, 1976).

Internet and Digital Communications

The proliferation of the internet and digital communications in the late 20th and early 21st centuries has made cryptography an indispensable tool. Protocols such as the Secure Sockets Layer (SSL) and its successor, Transport Layer Security (TLS), utilize cryptographic techniques to secure web browsing and online transactions. Similarly, encrypted messaging apps use end-to-end encryption to ensure that only the communicating users can read the messages, protecting against eavesdropping and interception (Stallings, 2017).

Cryptography in Mobile Communications

The advent of mobile communications has further expanded the applications of cryptography in secure communications. The encryption of voice and text messages, secure mobile payment systems, and encrypted virtual private networks (VPNs) are just a few examples of how cryptography is used to protect information in the mobile domain. The widespread use of smartphones has made cryptographic security an everyday necessity for individuals and businesses alike (Zimmermann, 1995).

<u>*Challenges and Future Directions*</u>

Despite its advancements, the application of cryptography in secure communications faces ongoing challenges. The rise of quantum computing poses a potential threat to current cryptographic algorithms, prompting research into quantum-resistant cryptography. Additionally, the increasing sophistication of cyber threats and the evolving regulatory landscape regarding encryption and privacy necessitate continuous innovation in cryptographic techniques and their applications in secure communications (Bernstein & Lange, 2017).

The application of cryptography in secure communications has evolved from simple ciphers used in ancient times to sophisticated algorithms that secure modern digital transactions and communications. This evolution reflects the critical role of cryptography in protecting the confidentiality, integrity, and authenticity of information in an increasingly interconnected world. As technology advances, the importance of cryptography in secure communications will continue to grow, underscoring the need for ongoing research, development, and innovation in cryptographic techniques.

Data Security:

Encrypting data stored on devices or in the cloud to protect against unauthorized access.

The evolution of cryptography has been pivotal in advancing data security, an area that has grown in complexity and importance with the digital transformation of society. As data has become one of the most valuable assets in the modern world, the application of cryptographic techniques to ensure its security is a testament to cryptography's adaptability and enduring relevance. Data security, encompassing the protection of data from unauthorized access, disclosure, alteration, and destruction, leverages cryptographic principles to safeguard information across various states: at rest, in transit, and during processing.

Cryptography in Data Security

Cryptography's role in data security is multifaceted, involving encryption, hashing, and digital signatures to protect data's confidentiality, integrity, and authenticity:

- **Encryption** is used to secure data at rest (e.g., stored on hard drives, cloud storage) and data in transit (e.g., transmitted over networks). By converting plain text into unreadable ciphertext, encryption ensures that data can only be accessed by authorized parties possessing the decryption key. Advanced Encryption Standard (AES) and Rivest-Shamir-Adleman (RSA) are among the most widely used encryption algorithms for securing digital data (Daemen & Rijmen, 2002; Rivest, Shamir, & Adleman, 1978).

- **Hashing** functions generate a fixed-size string (hash) from data of any size, providing a unique fingerprint of the data. Hashing is crucial for verifying data integrity, as even a minor change in the original data results in a different hash. This property is instrumental in detecting unauthorized alterations to data (Menezes, van Oorschot, & Vanstone, 1996).

- **Digital Signatures** combine hashing and encryption to authenticate the origin of data and confirm its integrity. A digital signature is created by encrypting the hash of the data with a private key, which can then be verified by others using the corresponding public key. Digital signatures are fundamental to establishing trust in digital transactions and communications (Diffie & Hellman, 1976).

Applications in Data Security

Cryptographic techniques are employed in a wide range of data security applications:

- **Secure File Storage**: Encryption algorithms protect sensitive files stored on computers, servers, or cloud platforms, ensuring that data is inaccessible to unauthorized users.
- **Secure Communications**: Cryptography secures email, messaging apps, and other forms of digital communication, protecting the confidentiality and integrity of the information exchanged.
- **Data Integrity Checks**: Hash functions are used to verify the integrity of data transferred or stored, ensuring that it has not been tampered with or corrupted.
- **Digital Transactions**: Cryptography secures online transactions, including e-commerce and banking, through SSL/TLS protocols and digital signatures, safeguarding financial and personal information.

Challenges and Evolution

The application of cryptography in data security faces challenges, notably from the advancement of computing capabilities such as quantum computing, which could potentially break current cryptographic algorithms. This threat has spurred research into quantum-resistant cryptographic methods, ensuring the future security of data against emerging computational advancements (Bernstein & Lange, 2017).

Additionally, the increasing volume of data and its importance across sectors drive the continuous evolution of cryptographic techniques to address scalability, performance, and privacy concerns. Innovations such as homomorphic encryption, which allows computations on encrypted data without decrypting it, illustrate the ongoing advancement in cryptography to meet the changing needs of data security (Gentry, 2009).

Cryptography's role in data security is indispensable, providing the tools and techniques to protect the confidentiality, integrity, and authenticity of data in an increasingly digital world. From securing personal communications to protecting global financial systems, the applications of cryptography in data security are vast and varied. As technology evolves and new challenges emerge, the field of cryptography will continue to advance, ensuring that data security can keep pace with the growing reliance on digital information.

E-commerce and Online Transactions:

Securing online transactions, including the exchange of financial information, through encryption and digital signatures.

The advent and proliferation of e-commerce and online transactions have been significantly underpinned by the advancements in cryptography, showcasing its pivotal role in the digital economy. As consumers and businesses increasingly engage in online financial activities, the need for secure and trustworthy mechanisms to protect these transactions has become paramount. Cryptography, through its ability to ensure confidentiality, integrity, and authenticity, has emerged as the cornerstone of secure e-commerce and online transactions.

Cryptography in E-commerce and Online Transactions

The integration of cryptographic techniques in e-commerce platforms and online transaction systems addresses several key security concerns:

- **Confidentiality**: Ensuring that sensitive information, such as credit card numbers and personal details, is encrypted and kept confidential from unauthorized parties. SSL/TLS (Secure Sockets Layer/Transport Layer Security) protocols establish an encrypted link between a web server and a browser, safeguarding all data passed between them (Dierks & Rescorla, 2008).
- **Integrity**: Protecting data from being altered in transit. Cryptographic hash functions can verify the integrity of the transaction data, ensuring that what was sent is exactly what is received.
- **Authentication**: Verifying the identity of parties involved in a transaction. Digital certificates and public key infrastructure

(PKI) provide a means to authenticate the identities of websites and users, ensuring that transactions are conducted between legitimate parties (Stallings, 2017).

- **Non-repudiation**: Preventing either party from denying a transaction. Digital signatures, generated using public key cryptography, ensure that once a party has committed to a transaction, they cannot deny their participation (Zimmermann, 1995).

Secure Electronic Transaction (SET) Protocol

One notable application of cryptography in e-commerce is the Secure Electronic Transaction (SET) protocol, developed to secure credit card transactions over the internet. Although not widely adopted, SET laid the groundwork for many of the secure payment methods used today by employing encryption and digital signatures to ensure privacy and authentication (MasterCard & Visa, 1997).

Impact on E-commerce Growth

The application of cryptography has had a profound impact on the growth and development of e-commerce. By addressing security concerns, cryptographic techniques have increased consumer confidence in online transactions, facilitating the expansion of the digital marketplace. Cryptography enables not only the secure exchange of financial information but also the protection of consumer data, compliance with privacy regulations, and the establishment of trust in digital interactions.

Challenges and Future Directions

Despite the advancements in cryptographic applications for e-commerce and online transactions, challenges remain. The increasing sophistication of cyber threats, the emergence of quantum computing, and the need for seamless yet secure user experiences present ongoing challenges to cryptographic implementations. Future directions may include the development of quantum-resistant algorithms, enhanced authentication mechanisms, and innovative payment systems that balance security with user convenience.

Moreover, the advent of blockchain technology and cryptocurrencies offers a new paradigm for secure and decentralized transactions, illustrating the evolving nature of cryptography's role in e-commerce and digital finance (Narayanan et al., 2016).

The application of cryptography in securing e-commerce and online transactions is a testament to its critical role in the digital age. By ensuring the confidentiality, integrity, authentication, and non-repudiation of digital transactions, cryptography has become the backbone of the digital economy, enabling the secure and trusted exchange of financial information online. As e-commerce continues to evolve, so too will the cryptographic techniques that protect it, ensuring that the digital marketplace remains a safe and secure environment for consumers and businesses alike.

Authentication and Access Control:

Using cryptographic techniques for user authentication and to control access to resources.

The evolution of cryptography has played a critical role in enhancing authentication and access control mechanisms, pivotal components in safeguarding information systems and ensuring that sensitive data and resources are accessible only to authorized users. As digital technologies have become integral to personal, corporate, and governmental operations, the need for robust authentication and access control systems has grown exponentially. Cryptography provides the foundational elements for these systems, leveraging encrypted keys, digital signatures, and secure protocols to verify identities and enforce access policies.

Cryptography in Authentication

Authentication processes involve verifying the identity of a user or device, often as a prerequisite to granting access to systems and data. Cryptographic techniques are central to various authentication methods:

- **Password-Based Authentication**: While the concept of passwords predates modern cryptography, cryptographic hashing functions play a crucial role in securing password storage. Instead of storing passwords directly, systems store cryptographic hashes of passwords. When a user logs in, the system compares the hash of the entered password with the stored hash, enhancing security by protecting the actual password (Pfleeger & Pfleeger, 2012).

- **Digital Certificates and Public Key Infrastructure (PKI)**: PKI systems use a combination of public and private keys for user authentication. A digital certificate, issued by a trusted Certificate Authority (CA), binds a public key to an individual or entity. The certificate's authenticity, ensured through digital signatures, enables secure, encrypted communications and authenticates the identity of the certificate holder (Stallings, 2017).

- **Two-Factor and Multi-Factor Authentication (2FA/MFA)**: Cryptography enhances the security of 2FA/MFA by incorporating something the user has (like a token or mobile device) in addition to something the user knows (like a password). Tokens or apps generate time-limited, cryptographic codes that users must provide alongside their passwords, significantly increasing authentication security (Jain, Ross, & Nandakumar, 2016).

Cryptography in Access Control

Access control mechanisms determine the resources that users are permitted to access and the operations they are allowed to perform. Cryptography is instrumental in enforcing access control policies:

- **Encrypted Access Tokens**: Systems can use encrypted tokens to manage user sessions and resource access. These tokens, which include user identity and permission claims, are encrypted and/or signed using cryptographic algorithms to prevent tampering and eavesdropping.

- **Role-Based Access Control (RBAC) with Cryptography**: In RBAC systems, access decisions are based on the roles assigned to users within an organization. Cryptographic techniques ensure that role assignments and the permissions associated with those roles are securely managed and communicated within the system.

- **Attribute-Based Encryption (ABE):** ABE is an advanced cryptographic scheme that enables access control at the encryption level. Data is encrypted with policies that specify the attributes required for decryption. Only users with the matching attributes (e.g., specific roles, credentials, or properties) can decrypt and access the data, providing a highly granular level of access control (Sahai & Waters, 2005).

Challenges and Future Directions

As digital systems become more complex and pervasive, the challenges surrounding authentication and access control also evolve. Issues such as managing cryptographic keys, ensuring user privacy, and protecting against sophisticated cyber attacks require ongoing attention. The future of cryptographic applications in authentication and access control may involve advancements in biometric encryption, decentralized identity systems, and quantum-resistant cryptographic algorithms to address these challenges.

The evolution of cryptography has been shaped by an ongoing battle between the development of cryptographic methods and the efforts to break them. This dynamic interplay has driven the field forward, but it also highlights the challenges and future directions that cryptography faces in a rapidly changing digital landscape. As we look toward the future, several key challenges stand out, each pointing to new directions for research and development in cryptography.

Quantum Computing

One of the most significant challenges to modern cryptography is the potential advent of quantum computing. Quantum computers, leveraging the principles of quantum mechanics, are expected to perform certain calculations much faster than the best current classical computers. This capability poses a threat to widely used cryptographic algorithms, such as RSA and ECC (Elliptic Curve Cryptography), which rely on the difficulty of factoring large prime numbers or solving discrete logarithm problems—tasks that quantum computers could solve efficiently (Bernstein & Lange, 2017).

Future Direction: The threat of quantum computing has spurred interest in post-quantum cryptography, which aims to develop cryptographic systems that are secure against both quantum and classical computers. Research in lattice-based cryptography, hash-based cryptography, and other quantum-resistant algorithms is active, with the goal of creating secure systems for the quantum era.

Scalability and Performance

As digital systems become more integrated into every aspect of life, the scalability and performance of cryptographic solutions become increasingly critical. The need to secure vast amounts of data in real-time, often in resource-constrained environments such as IoT devices, presents a challenge for traditional cryptographic methods, which can be computationally intensive.

Future Direction: Efforts are underway to develop lightweight cryptographic algorithms that maintain strong security while requiring less computational power. Additionally, new cryptographic protocols and architectures, such as edge computing models, are being explored to distribute the computational load more efficiently.

Privacy-Preserving Cryptography

The tension between the need for security and the desire for privacy is a longstanding issue in cryptography. With increasing surveillance and data collection, there is a growing demand for cryptographic techniques that can protect user privacy without compromising security.

Future Direction: Privacy-preserving cryptographic techniques, such as homomorphic encryption and zero-knowledge proofs, offer promising solutions. Homomorphic encryption allows computations on encrypted data without needing to decrypt it first, enabling data analysis while preserving privacy. Zero-knowledge proofs enable one party to prove to another that a statement is true without revealing any additional information. These and other advancements in cryptographic privacy are critical for future secure and private digital interactions.

Integration with Emerging Technologies

The integration of cryptography with emerging technologies, such as blockchain and distributed ledger technologies, presents both challenges and opportunities. Ensuring the security of these new technologies, particularly in areas such as cryptocurrency and smart contracts, is crucial for their widespread adoption and trust.

Future Direction: Cryptography is fundamental to the security and functionality of blockchain technologies. Research into cryptographic protocols for secure multi-party computation, consensus mechanisms, and secure smart contracts is essential for addressing the security challenges of these emerging technologies.

The evolution of cryptography is characterized by a continuous cycle of challenge and innovation. The impending arrival of quantum computing, the need for scalable and efficient cryptographic solutions, the demand for privacy-preserving techniques, and the integration with new technologies represent significant challenges but also directions for future research and development. As the digital landscape evolves, so too will cryptography, adapting to meet the security needs of tomorrow's digital world.

Cryptography's applications in authentication and access control are fundamental to securing digital identities and resources. By ensuring that only authorized users can access sensitive data and systems, cryptographic techniques are essential in maintaining the integrity, confidentiality, and availability of information in the digital age. As technology and threats evolve, so too will the cryptographic strategies employed to protect against unauthorized access and ensure the secure authentication of users in an interconnected world.

Challenges and Future Directions

Despite its advances, cryptography faces challenges, including the threat posed by quantum computing to current encryption algorithms and the ongoing arms race between cryptographic developments and techniques designed to break them. Future directions in cryptography are focused on developing quantum-resistant algorithms, enhancing the security of cryptographic protocols, and exploring new applications in blockchain technology and secure multiparty computation.

Introduction To Encryption and Decryption

Encryption and decryption form the core mechanisms of cryptography, providing the means to secure communications and protect information in the digital age. Encryption is the process of converting plaintext, the original message, into ciphertext, a scrambled and unreadable version, using a cryptographic algorithm and a key. Decryption reverses this process, converting the ciphertext back into plaintext, making the information accessible to the intended recipient. These processes are foundational to maintaining the confidentiality, integrity, and authenticity of data.

The Principles of Encryption

Encryption relies on two primary components: the algorithm and the key. The algorithm is a set of mathematical rules that determines how the plaintext is transformed into ciphertext. The key is a piece of information known only to the sender and the intended recipient, which dictates the specific output of the algorithm. The security of encrypted data is thus dependent on both the strength of the algorithm and the secrecy of the key.

There are two main types of encryptions:

Symmetric Encryption:

Uses the same key for both encryption and decryption. This method is efficient and suitable for encrypting large amounts of data but requires secure key exchange between the communicating parties. Examples of symmetric algorithms include AES (Advanced Encryption Standard) and DES (Data Encryption Standard) (Daemen & Rijmen, 2002; National Institute of Standards and Technology, 2001).

Asymmetric Encryption:

Also known as public-key cryptography, uses a pair of keys: a public key for encryption and a private key for decryption. The public key can be shared openly, while the private key is kept secret by the owner. Asymmetric encryption facilitates secure key exchange and digital signatures but is generally slower than symmetric encryption. RSA (Rivest-Shamir-Adleman) is a well-known asymmetric algorithm (Rivest, Shamir, & Adleman, 1978).

The Process of Decryption

Decryption is the process of converting ciphertext back into its original plaintext form, using the same algorithm as the encryption process but typically applying the inverse operation. In symmetric encryption, the same key used for encryption is used for decryption. In asymmetric encryption, the private key, which corresponds to the public key used for encryption, is used for decryption. The effectiveness of decryption relies on the exclusivity of the decryption key; only the intended recipient, who possesses the correct key, should be able to decrypt and access the information.

Applications of Encryption and Decryption

Encryption and decryption are utilized in various applications to ensure the security of digital information:

Secure Communications:

Protecting the confidentiality and integrity of messages exchanged over the internet, such as emails and instant messaging.

Secure communications are a principal application of cryptography, ensuring that information can be shared over potentially insecure channels without being intercepted, understood, or altered by unauthorized parties. This aspect of cryptography is foundational to the digital era, facilitating everything from private conversations to international financial transactions. The drive to secure communications has led to the development and implementation of a range of cryptographic techniques and protocols designed to protect the confidentiality, integrity, and authenticity of messages.

Cryptographic Techniques for Secure Communications

Secure communications rely on several cryptographic techniques:

- **Symmetric Encryption**: This method uses a single key for both encryption and decryption. It's efficient for encrypting large volumes of data and is commonly used for securing the content of messages once a secure channel has been established. Algorithms like AES (Advanced Encryption Standard) are widely used in symmetric encryption (Daemen & Rijmen, 2002).

- **Asymmetric Encryption (Public Key Cryptography)**: Utilizing a pair of keys (a public key for encryption and a private key for decryption) allows secure communication between parties without the need for a shared secret key. This method is foundational for establishing secure channels over public networks and is exemplified by algorithms such as RSA (Rivest, Shamir, & Adleman, 1978).

- **Digital Signatures**: Digital signatures provide a means for verifying the authenticity and integrity of messages. By using the sender's private key to sign a message, recipients can verify the message's origin and integrity using the sender's public key, ensuring the message has not been tampered with in transit.

- **Hash Functions**: Cryptographic hash functions generate a fixed-size hash value from messages of any length, which helps ensure data integrity. Any alteration to the message would result in a different hash value, signaling potential tampering.

Secure Communication Protocols

The application of cryptographic techniques has led to the development of secure communication protocols:

- **SSL/TLS (Secure Sockets Layer/Transport Layer Security)**: These protocols provide a secure channel between two devices over the internet, used extensively in web browsing, email, and other forms of online communication. SSL/TLS uses a combination of symmetric and asymmetric encryption to protect the confidentiality and integrity of data in transit (Dierks & Rescorla, 2008).

- **HTTPS (Hypertext Transfer Protocol Secure)**: Building on SSL/TLS, HTTPS adds an additional layer of security to the HTTP protocol, ensuring that data transferred between web browsers and websites is encrypted and secure from interception.
- **VPN (Virtual Private Network)**: VPNs create a secure, encrypted tunnel for data to travel across the internet, protecting the data from eavesdropping and allowing for secure communication over public networks.

Challenges in Secure Communications

Despite advancements, securing communications faces several challenges:

- **Quantum Computing**: The potential advent of quantum computing poses a threat to current cryptographic algorithms, potentially rendering them ineffective and compromising the security of communications (Bernstein & Lange, 2017).
- **Key Management and Distribution**: The secure generation, distribution, and management of cryptographic keys are critical to maintaining secure communications but pose logistical and security challenges.
- **Interception and Surveillance**: The increasing capabilities of surveillance and interception by various actors necessitate continual advancements in cryptographic techniques to stay ahead of potential threats.

Future Directions

Future directions in securing communications involve developing quantum-resistant cryptographic algorithms, enhancing the security and usability of cryptographic protocols, and exploring innovative technologies such as blockchain for decentralized secure communications. Moreover, ongoing research in homomorphic encryption and zero-knowledge proofs aims to enable secure computations on encrypted data, expanding the possibilities for secure communication and data sharing.

Secure communications represent a critical application of cryptography, enabling the confidential, integral, and authentic exchange of information in an increasingly digital and interconnected world. Through the application of symmetric and asymmetric encryption, digital signatures, and secure communication protocols like SSL/TLS and HTTPS, cryptography provides the foundation for private and secure digital interactions. As challenges evolve, so too will cryptographic solutions, ensuring the ongoing protection of communications in the digital age.

Data Security:

Encrypting data stored on devices or in the cloud to protect against unauthorized access.

Data security, a pivotal aspect of information security, ensures the protection of data from unauthorized access, use, disclosure, disruption, modification, or destruction. In the realm of digital communications and computing, cryptography serves as a fundamental tool in achieving data security, providing mechanisms for safeguarding the confidentiality, integrity, and availability of data. The application of cryptographic techniques to data security encompasses a broad spectrum of practices, from encrypting data to secure it against unauthorized access, to hashing and digital signatures for maintaining data integrity and authenticity.

Cryptographic Techniques in Data Security

Encryption is at the heart of protecting data confidentiality. It transforms readable data (plaintext) into an unreadable format (ciphertext) unless one has the key to decrypt it. This process ensures that sensitive information remains confidential, whether stored on a device (data at rest) or transmitted over a network (data in transit). Symmetric key encryption, where the same key is used for both encryption and decryption, is efficient for bulk data processing, while asymmetric key encryption, which uses a pair of public and private keys, is crucial for secure key exchange and digital signatures (Stallings, 2017).

Digital Signatures and **Hashing** are essential for maintaining the integrity and authenticity of data. Hash functions create a unique digital fingerprint of data, which is used to detect alterations. Digital signatures, combining hashing with asymmetric encryption, allow for verification of data origin and integrity, ensuring that the data received is exactly what was sent and that it came from the specified sender (Pfleeger & Pfleeger, 2012).

Applications of Cryptography in Data Security

Secure File Storage: Encrypting files and databases on hard drives, servers, or cloud storage protects sensitive data against unauthorized access, a practice made increasingly relevant with the rise of data breaches and cyber theft.

Secure Communications: Cryptography secures email, instant messaging, and other forms of digital communication, safeguarding the confidentiality and integrity of the information exchanged against eavesdropping or tampering.

E-Commerce and Online Banking: Cryptographic protocols such as SSL/TLS are employed to secure online transactions, protecting financial data and personal information as it moves across the internet.

Digital Identities and Authentication: Cryptography underpins digital identities, using certificates and public key infrastructure (PKI) for authentication processes, ensuring that access to data and resources is restricted to authorized users (Jain, Ross, & Nandakumar, 2016).

Challenges in Cryptographic Data Security

Despite its strengths, cryptographic data security faces several challenges. **Key management** — the secure creation, storage, distribution, and destruction of cryptographic keys — is a complex issue, particularly as systems and their cryptographic needs scale. Additionally, **quantum computing** presents a future threat to current cryptographic algorithms, necessitating the development of quantum-resistant cryptography (Bernstein & Lange, 2017).

Future Directions in Cryptographic Data Security

Homomorphic Encryption allows computations on encrypted data, providing new ways to process sensitive information securely without exposing it. **Blockchain Technology**, with its cryptographic underpinnings, offers a decentralized model for secure, tamper-evident transactions and data storage. Moreover, the ongoing development of **post-quantum cryptographic algorithms** aims to secure data against the potential capabilities of quantum computers, ensuring the longevity of cryptographic protection (Gentry, 2009).

Cryptography is a cornerstone of modern data security, enabling the secure storage and transmission of data across a myriad of digital environments. Through encryption, hashing, digital signatures, and secure protocols, cryptography provides the mechanisms necessary to protect the confidentiality, integrity, and authenticity of data. As the digital landscape evolves, so too will cryptographic methods, continuously adapting to address emerging threats and challenges in data security.

E-commerce:

Securing financial transactions online, including credit card information and personal identification numbers (PINs).

The integration of cryptography into e-commerce has been transformative, enabling the secure online exchange of goods, services, and information. As e-commerce platforms have proliferated, ensuring transaction security, data confidentiality, and user authenticity has become paramount. Cryptography, through its mechanisms for encryption, digital signatures, and secure protocols, underpins the trust and security framework essential for the functioning of the global digital marketplace.

Cryptography's Role in E-commerce

Secure Transactions: The primary application of cryptography in e-commerce is to secure transactions. This involves protecting the confidentiality of payment information, such as credit card numbers and bank account details, as they are transmitted over the internet. The Secure Sockets Layer (SSL) and its successor, Transport Layer Security (TLS), create an encrypted channel between the customer's browser and the e-commerce website, safeguarding transaction data from interception or tampering (Dierks & Rescorla, 2008).

Authentication: Cryptographic techniques facilitate the authentication of users and websites in e-commerce interactions. Digital certificates, issued by trusted Certificate Authorities (CAs), authenticate the identities of websites to users. Similarly, digital signatures and password-based authentication mechanisms, underpinned by cryptographic hashing, verify the identity of users to the service providers, ensuring that transactions are initiated by genuine parties (Stallings, 2017).

Data Integrity: Cryptography ensures the integrity of transaction data, confirming that the information has not been altered in transit. Digital signatures and cryptographic hashing functions are employed to detect any unauthorized changes to transaction data, thus maintaining the accuracy and reliability of transaction records.

Non-repudiation: In e-commerce transactions, it is crucial to ensure that neither party can deny their participation in the transaction. Digital signatures provide non-repudiation by creating a unique signature for each transaction, which can be definitively linked to the transaction initiator, providing a legal audit trail (Zimmermann, 1995).

Impact on E-commerce Development

The integration of cryptographic security measures has had a profound impact on the development and growth of e-commerce. By addressing key security concerns, cryptography has enhanced consumer confidence in online transactions, facilitating the expansion of the digital economy. Furthermore, cryptographic technologies have enabled new business models and services, such as digital wallets and blockchain-based transactions, which offer increased security and efficiency.

Challenges and Future Directions

Despite its successes, the application of cryptography in e-commerce faces ongoing challenges. The evolving landscape of cyber threats necessitates continual updates and improvements to cryptographic protocols and algorithms. Additionally, the emergence of quantum computing presents a potential future challenge to current cryptographic systems, which may be vulnerable to quantum attacks (Bernstein & Lange, 2017).

Future Directions in cryptographic applications for e-commerce may include the development of quantum-resistant algorithms, the use of blockchain technology for decentralized and transparent transactions, and the implementation of more user-friendly authentication mechanisms that do not compromise security.

Cryptography is integral to the security and trust that underpin e-commerce. By securing transactions, authenticating users and websites, ensuring data integrity, and providing non-repudiation, cryptographic techniques have enabled the safe and efficient exchange of goods, services, and information online. As e-commerce continues to evolve, so too will the cryptographic technologies that protect it, ensuring that the digital marketplace remains a secure environment for consumers and businesses alike.

Digital Identities and Authentication:

Using encryption to verify the identity of users and devices in digital networks.

Digital identities and authentication form a crucial nexus in the realm of cryptography, addressing the fundamental question of verifying the identity of users or devices in digital environments. As our lives and transactions increasingly migrate online, establishing trust through secure authentication has become paramount. Cryptography offers robust mechanisms for creating, managing, and validating digital identities, ensuring that digital interactions and transactions are both secure and reliable.

Foundations of Digital Identities and Authentication

Digital Identities represent the digital counterpart of individual identities, encompassing the credentials and attributes associated with a user or device in the digital realm. These identities are crucial for accessing services, performing transactions, and interacting within digital ecosystems.

Authentication is the process of verifying the claimed identity of a user or device, typically through one or more of the following factors:

- **Something you know**: a password or PIN.
- **Something you have**: a smart card, a mobile device, or a security token.
- **Something you are**: biometric characteristics, such as fingerprints, facial recognition, or iris scans (Jain, Ross, & Nandakumar, 2016).

Cryptographic Techniques in Authentication

Public Key Infrastructure (PKI): PKI uses asymmetric cryptography to secure communications and validate digital identities. It involves the use of digital certificates issued by trusted Certificate Authorities (CAs). These certificates link public keys with the identities of their owners, allowing users to verify the authenticity of public keys and the identity of their holders (Stallings, 2017).

Digital Signatures: Digital signatures employ asymmetric cryptography to provide proof of the integrity and origin of digital messages. A digital signature is created by encrypting the hash of a message with the sender's private key. Receivers can verify the signature with the sender's public key, confirming both the message's integrity and the sender's identity (Diffie & Hellman, 1976).

Multi-factor Authentication (MFA): MFA enhances security by requiring two or more authentication factors, combining something the user knows, has, or is. Cryptographic techniques are used to secure the transmission and verification of these factors, protecting against unauthorized access (Schneier, 2015).

Applications and Implications

Secure Online Transactions: Digital identities and cryptographic authentication are fundamental to secure e-commerce, online banking, and any transaction requiring identity verification, protecting against fraud and unauthorized access.

Access Control: In corporate and cloud environments, digital identities and cryptographic authentication ensure that only authorized users can access sensitive data and systems, based on predefined roles and permissions.

Internet of Things (IoT): As IoT devices proliferate, cryptographic authentication becomes critical for verifying device identities and securing communications between devices and networks, addressing concerns about IoT security and privacy.

Challenges and Future Directions

Despite their effectiveness, cryptographic approaches to digital identities and authentication face challenges, including:

Usability: Balancing security with user convenience remains a challenge, particularly for complex or multi-factor authentication systems.

Management: The secure management of digital identities, including the issuance, revocation, and renewal of digital certificates, presents logistical and security challenges.

Quantum Computing: The potential ability of quantum computers to break current cryptographic algorithms poses a long-term threat to digital identity and authentication systems (Bernstein & Lange, 2017).

Future Directions involve the development of quantum-resistant cryptographic algorithms, decentralized identity solutions leveraging blockchain technology, and advances in biometric authentication that offer both enhanced security and greater user convenience.

Digital identities and authentication represent a critical application of cryptography, securing the foundation of trust in the digital world. By verifying identities and ensuring the integrity and origin of digital communications, cryptographic techniques provide the essential mechanisms for secure digital interactions. As technology evolves, so too will the cryptographic solutions that underpin digital identities and authentication, adapting to new challenges and opportunities in the digital age.

Challenges and Considerations

As the digital landscape continues to evolve, cryptography remains a cornerstone of information security, providing essential mechanisms for protecting data confidentiality, integrity, and authentication. However, the field of cryptography faces numerous challenges and considerations, shaped by technological advancements, emerging threats, and the complex requirements of modern digital systems. Addressing these challenges is crucial for maintaining the efficacy of cryptographic protections and ensuring the security of digital information.

Quantum Computing Threat

One of the most significant challenges to current cryptographic standards is the potential development of quantum computing. Quantum computers, leveraging the principles of quantum mechanics, promise to perform certain computations much faster than conventional computers, potentially breaking widely used encryption algorithms such as RSA and ECC (Elliptic Curve Cryptography) that underpin much of today's digital security. This threat necessitates the development and adoption of quantum-resistant cryptographic algorithms to secure data against future quantum attacks (Bernstein & Lange, 2017).

Scalability and Performance

As digital systems become more integrated into every aspect of life, the scalability and performance of cryptographic solutions are increasingly under scrutiny. Cryptographic operations, particularly those involving complex algorithms like those used in public-key cryptography, can be resource-intensive. This poses challenges for large-scale systems and resource-constrained environments, such as IoT devices, where efficient cryptography is necessary to maintain operational performance without compromising security (Menezes, van Oorschot, & Vanstone, 1996).

Key Management

Effective key management is essential for the security of cryptographic systems. Generating, storing, distributing, and revoking cryptographic keys in a secure and efficient manner remains a complex challenge, especially for large organizations and systems employing public key infrastructure (PKI). The loss or compromise of cryptographic keys can lead to significant security breaches, underscoring the need for robust key management practices and systems (Stallings, 2017).

Regulatory and Ethical Considerations

The use of cryptography intersects with various regulatory and ethical considerations, particularly concerning privacy and surveillance. Governments and regulatory bodies around the world have different stances on the use of encryption, with some advocating for backdoors to assist law enforcement. These positions raise concerns about privacy rights, the security of digital systems, and the potential for abuse. Balancing the need for security with ethical considerations and legal requirements is a continuing challenge for the field of cryptography (Schneier, 2015).

Accessibility and Usability

Ensuring that cryptographic systems are accessible and usable by non-experts is crucial for widespread adoption and effective security. Complex cryptographic interfaces or processes can lead to user errors, potentially compromising security. Developing user-friendly cryptographic solutions that do not sacrifice security for convenience is an ongoing challenge, requiring innovation in design and user education (Whitfield Diffie, 2018).

Future Directions

Addressing these challenges involves both technological innovations and policy considerations. Research into post-quantum cryptography, lightweight cryptographic algorithms, advanced key management solutions, and user-centric design is critical for the future of cryptography. Moreover, engaging with regulatory and ethical debates is essential for ensuring that cryptographic technologies serve the broader interests of security, privacy, and societal values.

Cryptography faces a complex array of challenges and considerations, from the technical to the regulatory. Addressing these issues is vital for ensuring the continued security of digital information in an ever-evolving technological landscape. Through ongoing research, innovation, and dialogue, the field of cryptography can continue to provide the foundational security mechanisms necessary for the digital age.

Types Of Cryptographic Algorithms and Their Uses

Cryptography, the science of secret writing, is fundamental to securing digital information. Its algorithms, which are mathematical procedures for encrypting and decrypting data, underpin various aspects of information security. These cryptographic algorithms are broadly categorized into three main types: symmetric-key, asymmetric-key, and hash functions. Each type serves distinct purposes in the realm of digital security, from protecting data confidentiality and integrity to authenticating users and devices.

Symmetric-Key Algorithms

Symmetric-key algorithms, also known as secret-key cryptography, use a single key for both encryption and decryption. The key must be shared between the sender and receiver in a secure manner, as anyone with access to the key can decrypt the encrypted data. Symmetric-key algorithms are highly efficient, making them suitable for encrypting large volumes of data or for applications where speed is critical.

Uses:

- **Data Encryption**: Symmetric-key algorithms are commonly used for encrypting data at rest, such as files on a hard drive or data stored in a database, to protect against unauthorized access.

- **Secure Communication**: In secure communication protocols, such as those used for secure web browsing, symmetric-key encryption secures the bulk of data transmission due to its efficiency.

Examples: Advanced Encryption Standard (AES), Data Encryption Standard (DES), and Triple DES (3DES) are well-known symmetric-key algorithms (Daemen & Rijmen, 2002; National Institute of Standards and Technology, 2001).

Asymmetric-Key Algorithms

Asymmetric-key algorithms, or public-key cryptography, utilize a pair of keys: a public key, which can be shared openly, for encryption, and a private key, kept secret by the owner, for decryption. This separation addresses the key distribution problem of symmetric-key algorithms, allowing secure communication between parties without the need to share a secret key beforehand.

Uses:

- **Secure Key Exchange**: Asymmetric cryptography facilitates the secure exchange of symmetric encryption keys over public channels, as used in SSL/TLS protocols for secure internet communications.
- **Digital Signatures**: Asymmetric algorithms enable digital signatures, which provide integrity, authenticity, and non-repudiation for digital documents and transactions.

Examples: Rivest-Shamir-Adleman (RSA), Elliptic Curve Cryptography (ECC), and Digital Signature Algorithm (DSA) are prominent examples of asymmetric-key algorithms (Rivest, Shamir, & Adleman, 1978).

Hash Functions

Hash functions are algorithms that take an input (or 'message') and return a fixed-size string of bytes, typically a digest that is unique to the input data. Hash functions are designed to be one-way operations, meaning it is infeasible to invert or "reverse" the process to retrieve the original input from its hash value.

Uses:

- **Data Integrity**: Hash functions are used to verify the integrity of data by generating a digest of the original data and comparing it with the digest of the received data. Any alteration in the data results in a different hash, indicating tampering.
- **Password Storage**: Hashing is used to securely store passwords. Instead of storing the actual passwords, systems store hashed values of passwords. During authentication, the password provided by the user is hashed and compared with the stored hash.

Examples: Secure Hash Algorithm (SHA) series, including SHA-1, SHA-256, and SHA-3, and the Message Digest algorithm series, such as MD5 (though MD5 and SHA-1 are now considered vulnerable and are not recommended for secure applications) (National Institute of Standards and Technology, 2015).

Cryptographic algorithms are the backbone of digital security, providing the tools necessary for secure communication, data protection, and integrity verification. The choice of algorithm depends on the specific security requirements, including the need for speed, the sensitivity of the data, and the context of its use. As the digital landscape evolves, so too do cryptographic algorithms and their applications, continuously adapting to meet new security challenges and technological advancements.

Conclusion

Cryptography is a fundamental aspect of information security, enabling the confidential and secure exchange of information in an increasingly interconnected world. As technology evolves, so too will cryptographic techniques, continuing to play a crucial role in protecting information and ensuring the privacy and security of digital communications.

Chapter 5: Securing Networks

Securing networks in the modern digital landscape is a complex and multifaceted challenge, involving a combination of technologies, policies, and practices designed to protect the integrity, confidentiality, and availability of data and network resources. As networks become increasingly central to organizational operations and personal communications, the importance of implementing robust network security measures cannot be overstated. The goal of network security is to safeguard the network and its components against unauthorized access, misuse, malfunction, modification, destruction, or improper disclosure, thereby providing a secure platform for computers, users, and programs to perform their permitted critical functions within a secure environment.

Core Components of Network Security

Firewalls:

Firewalls act as a barrier between trusted internal networks and untrusted external networks, such as the internet. They use a set of defined rules to allow or block traffic into and out of the network. Firewalls can be hardware-based, software-based, or a combination of both, and are essential for controlling access to network resources (Stallings, 2017).

Firewalls stand as one of the foundational elements in the architecture of network security, acting as the first line of defense in protecting information systems from external threats. A firewall is a network security device that monitors and filters incoming and outgoing network traffic based on an organization's previously established security policies. At its most basic, a firewall is a barrier between a private internal network and the public Internet, designed to prevent unauthorized access while allowing legitimate communication to pass.

Types of Firewalls

Packet Filtering Firewalls: The most basic form of firewalls, packet filtering firewalls, inspect packets transferred between computers. They make decisions to allow or block data packets based on source and destination IP addresses, ports, and protocols, without opening the packet to inspect its contents (Cheswick, Bellovin, & Rubin, 2003).

Stateful Inspection Firewalls: Also known as dynamic packet filtering firewalls, these offer more security by keeping track of the state of active connections and making decisions based on the context of the traffic and state of the connection, in addition to the attributes inspected by packet filtering firewalls (Stallings, 2017).

Proxy Firewalls (Application-Level Gateways): Proxy firewalls operate at the application layer to filter incoming traffic between your network and the traffic source, thereby providing increased security. They act as an intermediary between end-users and the web, inspecting incoming traffic content, such as URLs and web page data, for malicious content before it reaches the internal network (Zwicky, Cooper, & Chapman, 2000).

Next-Generation Firewalls (NGFW): NGFWs combine the capabilities of traditional firewalls with additional functionalities like encrypted traffic inspection, intrusion prevention systems, and the ability to identify and block sophisticated attacks. They are designed to address the evolving challenges of securing modern enterprise networks which require deeper inspection capabilities and intelligence to protect against advanced threats (Palo Alto Networks, 2014).

Firewall Configuration and Policy

The effectiveness of a firewall heavily relies on its configuration and the underlying security policies it enforces. These policies are rules defined by network administrators that specify which traffic should be allowed or blocked based on factors such as IP addresses, domain names, protocols, applications, and content types. Proper firewall configuration involves specifying default deny rules (blocking all access by default and only allowing specific, necessary communications), ensuring minimal exposure to threats.

Challenges and Considerations

Despite their critical role in network security, firewalls face challenges and limitations. Advanced threats, such as zero-day exploits and sophisticated malware, can sometimes bypass traditional firewall protections. Additionally, the increasing use of encryption in network communications poses challenges for firewalls to inspect and filter malicious content without significant decryption capabilities.

Moreover, the complexity of firewall rules and the dynamic nature of network environments require continuous management and updates to ensure that security policies remain effective and do not inadvertently block legitimate traffic or create network bottlenecks.

Firewalls are an indispensable component of network security, providing a critical barrier between secure internal networks and potentially hostile external environments. As cyber threats continue to evolve, the development and deployment of more advanced firewall technologies, along with diligent management and configuration, will remain central to effective network security strategies.

Intrusion Detection and Prevention Systems (IDPS):

These systems monitor network and system activities for malicious activities or policy violations. An intrusion detection system (IDS) produces reports of suspicious activities, while an intrusion prevention system (IPS) actively blocks or prevents those activities. IDPS technologies are crucial for identifying and responding to threats in real-time (Scarfone & Mell, 2007).

Intrusion Detection and Prevention Systems (IDPS) are critical components of comprehensive network security, providing the means to detect, analyze, and respond to malicious activities and policy violations in real-time. As networks become increasingly complex and the landscape of cyber threats evolves, IDPS play an essential role in identifying potential security breaches and mitigating their impact. These systems monitor network traffic, system activities, or both, for suspicious actions that could indicate an attack on the network's security infrastructure.

Types of IDPS

Network-based Intrusion Detection and Prevention Systems (NIDPS): NIDPS are deployed at strategic points within the network to monitor traffic to and from all devices on the network. They are particularly effective at detecting network-based attacks, such as denial-of-service (DoS) attacks, network scanning, and certain types of malware and worms (Scarfone & Mell, 2007).

Host-based Intrusion Detection and Prevention Systems (HIDPS): Unlike NIDPS, HIDPS are installed on individual hosts or devices. They monitor the inbound and outbound packets from the device only and can offer more detailed insight into the activities of specific hosts, including the detection of unauthorized access attempts, changes in system configurations, and access to protected files.

Signature-based Detection: This method relies on predefined signatures or patterns of known threats. When a piece of data or an action matches a signature, an alert is triggered. While effective against known threats, it may not detect new, unknown attacks.

Anomaly-based Detection: Anomaly-based IDPS analyze the behavior of network traffic and host activities to identify deviations from established norms, which may indicate a security incident. This method can potentially detect previously unknown threats but may generate higher false positives.

Hybrid Approaches: Many modern IDPS combine signature-based and anomaly-based detection methods to leverage the strengths of both approaches, aiming to minimize the weaknesses inherent in each.

Functions of IDPS

Monitoring and Analysis: IDPS continuously monitor network or system activities for malicious actions or policy violations, analyzing data packets and system calls to identify potential threats.

Detection of Policy Violations: Beyond identifying attacks, IDPS can detect violations of organizational policies, such as the misuse of network resources or unauthorized data access.

Automated Response: Upon detection of a threat, IDPS can execute predefined actions to mitigate the impact. This might include blocking traffic from a suspicious source, terminating a malicious process, or alerting administrators.

Reporting and Alerting: IDPS provide detailed reports on security incidents, including the nature of the attack, the targeted resources, and the outcome of automated response actions. This information is critical for incident response and forensic analysis.

Challenges and Considerations

Implementing and managing IDPS pose several challenges. The configuration of detection rules requires a deep understanding of network architectures, normal traffic patterns, and potential threat vectors to minimize false positives and false negatives. The effectiveness of IDPS also depends on the continuous updating of threat signatures and anomaly detection algorithms to keep pace with evolving cyber threats.

Furthermore, the integration of IDPS into broader security operations and incident response protocols is essential to ensure that detections lead to effective mitigation and that security insights contribute to ongoing security improvements.

Intrusion Detection and Prevention Systems are indispensable tools in the network security arsenal, providing critical capabilities for detecting and responding to cyber threats. As part of a layered security strategy, IDPS enhance the resilience of networks against attacks, contributing to the overall security posture of organizations. Continuous advancements in IDPS technologies, along with strategic planning and skilled management, are crucial for addressing the dynamic nature of cyber threats.

Virtual Private Networks (VPNs):

VPNs create a secure, encrypted connection over a public network, such as the internet, enabling remote users to access the network as if they were directly connected to the network's main infrastructure. VPNs use cryptographic tunneling protocols to provide confidentiality, sender authentication, and message integrity (Rosenberg, 2012).

Virtual Private Networks (VPNs) are a pivotal component in the architecture of network security, providing a secure means of transmitting data over public networks, such as the internet. By creating an encrypted tunnel for data packets to travel between a user's device and a VPN server, VPNs ensure that data remains confidential and immune to interception or eavesdropping. This technology is indispensable for remote access to secure network resources, safeguarding sensitive communications, and maintaining the privacy of internet activities.

Fundamentals of VPN Technology

Encryption: At the core of VPN technology is encryption, which ensures that data transmitted over the VPN is unreadable to anyone who intercepts it. VPNs utilize strong encryption protocols such as IPsec (Internet Protocol Security) or SSL/TLS (Secure Sockets Layer/ Transport Layer Security) to encrypt data at the sending end and decrypt it at the receiving end (Stallings, 2017).

Tunneling Protocols: VPNs use tunneling protocols to encapsulate encrypted data packets within standard IP packets, enabling them to traverse public networks securely. Protocols like PPTP (Point-to-Point Tunneling Protocol), L2TP (Layer 2 Tunneling Protocol), and OpenVPN support the creation of the encrypted tunnel through which the encrypted data travels (Farley, 2001).

Authentication: VPNs require authentication to verify the identity of users and devices accessing the network. This can be achieved through traditional username and password combinations, digital certificates, or more sophisticated multi-factor authentication methods, ensuring that only authorized users can establish a VPN connection (Rosenberg, 2012).

Applications of VPNs

Remote Access: VPNs enable remote workers to securely access organizational resources as if they were directly connected to the private network, crucial for businesses with a distributed workforce or those adopting telecommuting practices.

Secure Data Transmission: For individuals and organizations alike, VPNs secure the transmission of data over public Wi-Fi networks, protecting against data theft and cyberattacks.

Privacy and Anonymity: VPNs mask the user's IP address and encrypt internet traffic, enhancing privacy and providing anonymity online. This is particularly valuable in regions with strict internet censorship or surveillance practices.

Inter-organizational Connectivity: VPNs facilitate secure communication and data sharing between different organizations, creating a virtual network that spans across multiple physical locations while ensuring data security and privacy.

Challenges and Considerations

While VPNs offer robust security benefits, they are not without challenges:

VPN Blocking and Filtering:

Some networks and countries actively block or filter VPN traffic, complicating the use of VPNs for bypassing geo-restrictions or accessing restricted content.

VPN (Virtual Private Network) blocking and filtering represent significant challenges in the realm of network security and digital freedom. This phenomenon involves the deliberate restriction of VPN traffic by organizations, ISPs (Internet Service Providers), and even governments. The motivations behind VPN blocking and filtering vary, including enforcing corporate security policies, complying with national regulations, or restricting access to content based on geographic locations. Despite the legitimate uses of VPNs for privacy, security, and bypassing censorship, the ability of entities to block or filter VPN traffic poses questions about user privacy, security, and the open internet.

Mechanisms of VPN Blocking and Filtering

Port Blocking: One common method of VPN blocking involves identifying and blocking the ports used by VPN protocols. For instance, PPTP VPNs commonly use port 1723, and blocking this port can disrupt PPTP VPN traffic (Farley, 2001).

Deep Packet Inspection (DPI): DPI is a more sophisticated method that examines the data part (and possibly also the header) of a packet as it passes an inspection point. DPI can identify, classify, and block VPN traffic based on specific signatures or patterns characteristic of VPN protocols (Rosenberg, 2012).

IP Blocking: VPN services typically use a range of known IP addresses for their servers. By identifying and blocking these IP addresses, organizations and governments can effectively prevent users from connecting to VPN servers.

Protocol Fingerprinting: Some blocking mechanisms analyze the characteristics of specific VPN protocols, such as OpenVPN or L2TP/IPSec, to detect and block VPN traffic. This method requires a detailed understanding of the protocol's operational specifics.

Challenges and Implications

Privacy and Security: VPN blocking challenges the fundamental premise of VPNs to provide secure and private access to the internet. It can expose users to surveillance and data interception, especially in environments with strict internet censorship and monitoring.

Access to Information: VPN blocking can restrict access to information by preventing users from bypassing geo-restrictions or censorship, impacting freedom of information and expression.

Corporate and Personal Use: While organizations may block VPNs to enforce security policies and prevent data leakage, such measures can also affect legitimate uses of VPNs for secure remote access to corporate networks.

Countermeasures and Future Directions

VPN Obfuscation: Some VPNs offer obfuscation techniques that disguise VPN traffic as regular HTTPS traffic, making it more challenging to detect and block using conventional methods.

Alternative Protocols: The development and use of alternative VPN protocols that are less detectable and easier to disguise can help bypass VPN blocks. Examples include WireGuard, which is designed to be simpler and more efficient than older protocols.

Decentralized VPNs (dVPNs): Emerging technologies like decentralized VPNs leverage blockchain technology to create a distributed network of peers. dVPNs aim to offer more resilient and harder-to-block VPN services by eliminating centralized points of failure.

Legal and Policy Advocacy: Engaging in legal and policy advocacy to promote the rights to privacy and freedom of expression can help address the root causes of VPN blocking and filtering, advocating for the legitimate use of VPNs as tools for securing digital communications.

VPN blocking and filtering present significant challenges to securing networks, maintaining privacy, and accessing information freely on the internet. As entities continue to deploy sophisticated methods to restrict VPN usage, the development of advanced countermeasures and advocacy for digital rights are crucial for preserving the integrity and accessibility of the internet. The ongoing cat-and-mouse game between VPN providers and blockers underscores the dynamic nature of internet freedom and network security.

Security Vulnerabilities:

VPNs can be susceptible to vulnerabilities in their implementation, such as flaws in the encryption protocols or software vulnerabilities. Regular updates and security audits are necessary to mitigate these risks.

Security vulnerabilities within networks represent critical points of weakness that can be exploited by cyber attackers to gain unauthorized access, steal sensitive data, or disrupt network operations. These vulnerabilities can arise from a variety of sources, including software bugs, system misconfigurations, inadequate security policies, and human error. Addressing these vulnerabilities is a foundational aspect of network security, involving the identification, assessment, and remediation of potential weaknesses before they can be exploited.

Types of Security Vulnerabilities

Software Flaws and Bugs: Vulnerabilities can exist in operating systems, applications, and network devices due to programming errors or software flaws. These vulnerabilities may allow attackers to execute arbitrary code, escalate privileges, or access restricted data (Howard & Lipner, 2006).

Misconfigurations: Incorrectly configured network devices, servers, or applications can introduce vulnerabilities into a network. Common misconfigurations include open ports, unnecessary services running on devices, and default credentials not being changed.

Unpatched Systems: Failing to apply security patches in a timely manner leaves systems exposed to known vulnerabilities. Cyber attackers often exploit these vulnerabilities, as the means to mitigate them (patches) are publicly known but not applied (Scarfone, Souppaya, & Cody, 2008).

Insecure Network Protocols: Some network protocols do not provide adequate security features, such as encryption for data in transit, leaving transmitted data vulnerable to interception and eavesdropping.

Physical Vulnerabilities: Physical access to network devices can lead to security breaches. This includes unauthorized access to data centers, unsecured network interfaces, and theft of devices containing sensitive information.

Addressing Security Vulnerabilities

Vulnerability Assessment and Penetration Testing (VAPT): Regular vulnerability assessments and penetration testing are crucial for identifying existing weaknesses in network systems and applications.

These activities simulate cyber attacks to evaluate the effectiveness of current security measures and identify vulnerabilities (Reddy, 2017).

Patch Management: Implementing a robust patch management process ensures that software and firmware updates are applied promptly, mitigating known vulnerabilities. This process involves regularly checking for updates, prioritizing patches based on the severity of vulnerabilities, and testing patches before deployment to avoid unintended consequences.

Configuration Management: Proper configuration management practices help prevent misconfigurations that could lead to vulnerabilities. This includes the use of configuration standards, regular audits of device and software configurations, and automated tools to enforce configuration policies.

Security Awareness Training: Human error is a significant factor in many security breaches. Training employees on security best practices, phishing awareness, and safe handling of sensitive information can reduce the risk of vulnerabilities being exploited due to user actions.

Use of Security Tools and Technologies: Deploying a range of security tools and technologies, such as intrusion detection and prevention systems, firewalls, and encryption, can help mitigate the impact of vulnerabilities. Additionally, employing security information and event management (SIEM) systems can provide real-time monitoring and alerting for potential security incidents.

Challenges and Future Directions

The complexity of modern networks, the increasing sophistication of cyber threats, and the rapid pace of technological change present ongoing challenges in identifying and mitigating security vulnerabilities. Future directions in addressing these challenges may involve the use of artificial intelligence and machine learning to predict and identify vulnerabilities, automated patching systems, and the development of more secure software and network protocols through secure coding practices and protocol design.

Security vulnerabilities are a critical concern in network security, requiring vigilant identification, assessment, and remediation efforts to protect against potential cyber threats. Through comprehensive vulnerability management strategies, regular security assessments, and a culture of security awareness, organizations can significantly reduce their risk exposure and enhance their overall security posture.

Performance and Latency:

The encryption and decryption processes, along with the routing of traffic through VPN servers, can introduce latency and reduce performance, impacting user experience.

Performance and latency are critical considerations in the context of network security. As organizations deploy various security measures to protect their networks from cyber threats, the impact on network performance and latency becomes a significant concern. Security mechanisms, while essential for protecting data and systems, can introduce delays and reduce the efficiency of network operations if not properly optimized. Balancing security with performance is a key challenge for network administrators, requiring a careful selection and configuration of security technologies to minimize latency without compromising security.

Impact of Security Measures on Performance and Latency

Encryption Overhead: Encryption is a fundamental security practice for protecting data in transit and at rest. However, the process of encrypting and decrypting data introduces computational overhead, which can impact network throughput and increase latency. The performance impact varies depending on the encryption algorithm, key length, and the hardware capabilities of the network devices (Stallings, 2017).

Intrusion Detection and Prevention Systems (IDPS): IDPS are deployed to monitor network traffic and identify potential threats. While essential for security, the deep packet inspection and analysis performed by these systems can significantly increase latency, especially in high-traffic environments. Optimizing the placement of IDPS and tuning their rulesets are crucial for minimizing their impact on network performance (Scarfone & Mell, 2007).

Firewalls: Firewalls act as a barrier between secured and unsecured networks, inspecting incoming and outgoing traffic based on predefined rules. Complex rule sets and deep packet inspection by advanced firewalls can introduce latency, affecting the speed of data transmission across the network (Cheswick, Bellovin, & Rubin, 2003).

VPN Tunnels: Virtual Private Networks (VPNs) secure remote connections by encrypting data traffic. The encryption and tunneling processes, however, can increase latency and reduce bandwidth, impacting the performance of applications, especially those sensitive to delays, such as VoIP and real-time video conferencing (Farley, 2001).

Strategies for Balancing Security and Performance

Selective Encryption: Applying encryption selectively based on data sensitivity and regulatory requirements can help reduce the performance impact. For example, encrypting only specific fields within a database rather than the entire database can minimize overhead while maintaining security for sensitive information.

Load Balancing and Traffic Shaping: Implementing load balancers and traffic shaping techniques can help distribute traffic evenly across network resources, preventing bottlenecks and reducing latency introduced by security devices.

Hardware Acceleration: Utilizing hardware acceleration for encryption and other security processes can significantly improve performance. Many modern network devices include dedicated cryptographic processors that handle encryption tasks more efficiently than software alone.

Segmentation and Zoning: Dividing the network into segments or zones, each with its security policies, can help localize traffic inspection and reduce unnecessary processing. This approach not only improves performance but also enhances security by limiting the potential impact of a breach.

Regular Performance Testing: Conducting regular performance testing of security devices and configurations helps identify bottlenecks and optimize settings for an ideal balance between security and network speed.

The relationship between network security and performance, particularly in terms of latency, is a critical consideration in the design and operation of secure networks. Effective network security practices must not only protect against threats but also preserve the functionality and performance of the network. By employing strategic approaches to security deployment, such as selective encryption, load balancing, and hardware acceleration, organizations can achieve a balanced security posture that protects their assets without unduly compromising network performance.

Policy and Compliance Issues:

Organizations employing VPNs must ensure that their use complies with legal and regulatory requirements, particularly those concerning data protection and privacy.

Policy and compliance issues play a critical role in securing networks, acting as the framework within which technical and operational security measures are implemented and maintained. Network security policies provide the foundation for establishing what assets need protection, who has access to those assets, and how that access is managed and audited. Compliance with relevant laws, regulations, and standards ensures that organizations not only protect their networks and data but also adhere to legal and ethical obligations, reducing the risk of financial penalties, legal action, and reputational damage.

Network Security Policies

Development and Implementation: Effective network security policies are comprehensive, clear, and tailored to the specific needs and structure of the organization. They cover aspects such as user access controls, data classification and handling, incident response procedures, and the use of security technologies. The development of these policies involves stakeholders from across the organization, including IT, legal, human resources, and executive leadership, to ensure that policies are enforceable and aligned with business objectives (Peltier, 2005).

Regular Review and Updates: The dynamic nature of cyber threats and technology means that network security policies must be regularly reviewed and updated to remain effective. This includes adjustments based on new regulatory requirements, emerging threats, technological advancements, and changes within the organization.

Compliance with Regulations and Standards

Regulatory Requirements: Organizations may be subject to various regulatory requirements depending on their industry, the type of data they handle, and their geographic location. Regulations such as the General Data Protection Regulation (GDPR) in the European Union, the Health Insurance Portability and Accountability Act (HIPAA) in the United States, and others impose specific requirements for data protection and privacy, including aspects related to network security (Voigt & Von dem Bussche, 2017).

Standards and Frameworks: In addition to regulatory requirements, organizations often adhere to industry standards and best practice frameworks to guide their network security efforts. Standards such as the ISO/IEC 27000 series for information security management, the Payment Card Industry Data Security Standard (PCI DSS) for payment card data, and the National Institute of Standards and Technology (NIST) frameworks provide guidelines and requirements for securing networks and managing cybersecurity risks (Stallings, 2017).

Challenges and Considerations

Balancing Security and Business Objectives: One of the primary challenges in addressing policy and compliance issues is balancing security measures with business objectives. Overly restrictive policies may hinder productivity or innovation, while too lenient policies can expose the organization to increased risk.

Complexity of Compliance: For organizations operating across multiple jurisdictions or in highly regulated industries, navigating the complexity of compliance with various regulations and standards can be daunting. This often requires dedicated resources and expertise to ensure ongoing compliance and to adapt to changes in the regulatory landscape.

Cost of Compliance: Implementing and maintaining compliance with including investments in technology, personnel training, and on-going audits and assessments. Organizations must weigh these costs against the potential risks of non-compliance, including legal penalties and reputational damage.

Future Directions

The increasing emphasis on data protection and privacy, along with the evolving cyber threat landscape, is likely to result in more stringent regulatory requirements and a greater focus on compliance across all sectors. Organizations will need to adopt more integrated and auto-mated approaches to compliance management, leveraging technology to streamline compliance processes and improve the effectiveness of network security measures.

Policy and compliance issues are integral to the broader strategy of securing networks, providing the guidelines and legal framework within which technical security measures operate. Effective network security policies, combined with adherence to regulatory requirements and industry standards, form the backbone of an organization's security posture. As the regulatory environment becomes more complex, orga-nizations must remain vigilant and adaptable to ensure their network security practices meet both current and future compliance obligations.

Future Directions

The increasing demand for privacy and secure remote access, coupled with the expansion of the remote workforce, points to a future where VPNs will play an even more critical role in network security. Innovations in VPN technologies, such as the development of more efficient encryption algorithms and the adoption of wireguard protocol, promise enhanced security and performance. Moreover, the integration of VPNs with other network security components, like next-generation firewalls and cloud security services, will offer more comprehensive security solutions.

VPNs are an essential tool in the network security toolkit, offering encrypted communication over public networks and enabling secure remote access to network resources. As cyber threats evolve and the need for secure, private internet access continues to grow, VPNs will remain vital for protecting data integrity, confidentiality, and user privacy in the digital realm.

Antivirus and Anti-malware Software:

This software is designed to detect, prevent, and remove malicious software, including viruses, worms, and ransomware. Antivirus and anti-malware solutions are continually updated to respond to new and evolving malware threats.

Security Information and Event Management (SIEM):

SIEM solutions provide real-time analysis of security alerts generated by applications and network hardware. They aggregate and correlate data from different sources to identify patterns of activity that may indicate a security threat, facilitating rapid detection and response to incidents (Kent & Souppaya, 2006).

Network Security Practices

Regular Updates and Patch Management:

Keeping software and systems updated is vital for protecting against vulnerabilities. Regularly applying patches and updates closes security holes that attackers could exploit.

Strong Authentication and Access Controls:

Implementing strong password policies and multi-factor authentication (MFA) helps ensure that only authorized users can access network resources. Role-based access control (RBAC) limits users' access to the information and resources necessary for their roles, reducing the potential impact of a breach.

Encryption:

Encrypting data in transit and at rest protects it from interception and unauthorized access. Encryption is particularly important for sensitive information, such as financial data and personal identifiable information (PII).

Employee Training and Awareness:

Human error is a significant security risk. Training employees on best security practices, including recognizing phishing attempts and safely handling data, is crucial for maintaining network security.

Challenges and Future Directions

As technology evolves, so too do the challenges in securing networks. The rise of IoT devices introduces new vulnerabilities, while sophisticated cyber threats like advanced persistent threats (APTs) and ransomware demand increasingly advanced security measures. The future of network security will likely involve more intelligent and adaptive systems capable of predicting and mitigating threats before they can cause harm. Furthermore, the development of quantum computing poses potential risks to cryptographic security measures, necessitating the exploration of quantum-resistant algorithms.

Basics of Network Security

The basics of network security encompass a broad range of practices, technologies, and policies designed to protect network infrastructure and the data it transports from unauthorized access, misuse, or harm. Network security is a critical aspect of information security as it not only involves protecting the data but also the pathways through which this data travels. Effective network security strategies employ multiple layers of defense at the edge and within the network, each network security layer implementing policies and controls to safeguard against threats.

Fundamental Components of Network Security

Firewalls:

Acting as a barrier between secure internal networks and untrusted external networks such as the internet, firewalls control incoming and outgoing network traffic based on an organization's security policies.

They are one of the first lines of defense in network security, filtering traffic based on predetermined security rules (Cheswick, Bellovin, & Rubin, 2003).

Antivirus and Anti-malware Software:

These tools are essential for detecting, preventing, and removing malware, which can compromise network security. Continuous updates are crucial as new malware variants are constantly being developed and deployed by cyber attackers (Symantec, 2018).

Intrusion Detection Systems (IDS) and Intrusion Prevention Systems (IPS):

IDS are designed to detect unauthorized access to a network, while IPS prevent the identified threats. These systems monitor network traffic for suspicious activity and take action to block attacks (Scarfone & Mell, 2007).

Virtual Private Networks (VPNs):

VPNs create a secure and encrypted connection over a less secure network, typically the internet. They are used to safeguard data in transit, ensuring that data remains private and secure even when transmitted over public networks (Rosenberg, 2012).

Secure Sockets Layer (SSL) and Transport Layer Security (TLS):

These cryptographic protocols provide secure communication over a computer network. Websites use SSL/TLS to secure all communications between their servers and web browsers (Dierks & Rescorla, 2008).

Network Access Control (NAC):

NAC systems control who can access the network and what they can do once they're connected. By enforcing policy compliance, NAC ensures that devices meet the organization's security standards before granting them access (Finneran, 2007).

Principles of Network Security

Confidentiality: Ensuring that sensitive information is accessible only to those authorized to access it.

Integrity: Guaranteeing the accuracy and reliability of data and information, ensuring that it is not altered or tampered with during transmission or storage.

Availability: Ensuring that network resources are accessible to authorized users when needed, which involves protecting the network against attacks that can lead to downtime.

Challenges in Network Security

Network security faces numerous challenges, including the increasing sophistication of cyber threats, the rapid expansion of network-connected devices (IoT), and the complexity of managing security across diverse network architectures. Moreover, the evolving regulatory landscape imposes additional compliance burdens on organizations, requiring them to not only secure their networks but also ensure they meet various regulatory standards.

Future Directions

The future of network security is likely to be shaped by advancements in artificial intelligence and machine learning, which can provide more proactive and predictive approaches to threat detection and response. Additionally, the adoption of zero trust security models, which assume that threats can exist both outside and inside the network, is becoming more widespread. This model emphasizes strict identity verification for every person and device trying to access resources on a private network, regardless of whether they are sitting within or outside of the network perimeter.

Network security is a comprehensive and dynamic field, requiring continuous attention and adaptation to protect against evolving threats. By understanding and implementing the basic components of network security, organizations can significantly enhance their overall security posture, protect their critical assets, and ensure the trust of their users and partners.

Defensive Technologies: Firewalls, IDS/IPS, VPNs

In the realm of network security, defensive technologies such as Firewalls, Intrusion Detection Systems (IDS)/Intrusion Prevention Systems (IPS), and Virtual Private Networks (VPNs) constitute the primary arsenal for protecting network infrastructure and data. These technologies work in concert to create a multilayered defense mechanism that can identify, mitigate, and prevent various cyber threats, ensuring the confidentiality, integrity, and availability of network resources.

Firewalls

Firewalls serve as the first line of defense in network security, acting as a barrier between secured internal networks and untrusted external networks, such as the internet. They monitor and control incoming and outgoing network traffic based on predetermined security rules and policies. Firewalls can be hardware-based, software-based, or a combination of both, and are designed to prevent unauthorized access to or from private networks.

Types of Firewalls:

Packet Filtering Firewalls: These inspect each packet that passes through the network and accept or reject it based on user-defined rules.

Stateful Inspection Firewalls: These track the operating state and characteristics of network connections traversing them, making decisions based on the context of the traffic, as well as the rules defined.

Proxy Firewalls (Application-Level Gateways): Acting as an intermediary between end-users and the internet, these firewalls evaluate requests from the perspective of the application layer (Cheswick, Bellovin, & Rubin, 2003).

IDS/IPS

Intrusion Detection Systems (IDS) and Intrusion Prevention Systems (IPS) are critical components of network security, providing continuous surveillance and protection against malicious activities and policy violations. While IDS is focused on monitoring and detecting potential threats, providing alerts when suspicious activities are identified, IPS goes a step further by taking automated actions to block or prevent those threats based on specific criteria.

Functions:

Signature-Based Detection: Matches observed events to a database of known threat signatures, effective against known threats.

Anomaly-Based Detection: Identifies deviations from a baseline of normal network activity, potentially uncovering unknown threats (Scarfone & Mell, 2007).

VPNs

Virtual Private Networks (VPNs) create a secure, encrypted tunnel for data to travel across the internet, protecting the data from interception and eavesdropping. This technology is essential for remote access to a network, securing data transmission across public networks, and ensuring privacy and confidentiality.

Key Features:

Encryption: VPNs utilize strong encryption protocols to secure all data in transit between the VPN client and the VPN server.

Remote Access: Enable users to securely connect to a private network from remote locations, extending the network's security to remote connections (Rosenberg, 2012).

Challenges and Considerations

Integration and Management: The effectiveness of these defensive technologies depends on their proper integration and management within the network's security architecture. Configurations must be regularly reviewed and updated to adapt to evolving threats.

Performance Impact: The deployment of these technologies can impact network performance. Encryption and deep packet inspection, for example, can introduce latency. Balancing security and performance is a crucial consideration for network administrators.

Emerging Threats: Cyber threats are constantly evolving, requiring defensive technologies to be adaptable and updated regularly. The development of advanced persistent threats (APTs) and the use of encryption by malicious actors pose particular challenges for traditional defense mechanisms.

Firewalls, IDS/IPS, and VPNs are fundamental to securing networks against a myriad of cyber threats. By effectively deploying and managing these defensive technologies, organizations can significantly enhance their security posture. Continuous monitoring, regular updates, and the integration of these technologies into a broader security strategy are essential for maintaining robust network security in the face of ever-evolving cyber threats.

Conclusion

Securing networks is an ongoing process that requires a comprehensive approach, combining technical solutions with effective policies and user education. As cyber threats continue to evolve, so too must network security strategies, ensuring that networks remain robust against both current and future threats.

Chapter 6: The Anatomy of Cyber Attacks

Part III: Threats and Defenses

Understanding the anatomy of cyber attacks is crucial for developing effective cybersecurity strategies and defenses. Cyber attacks can vary widely in their objectives, methods, and impacts, but they typically follow a structured process or lifecycle, including reconnaissance, weaponization, delivery, exploitation, installation, command and control (C&C), and actions on objectives. By dissecting these stages, organizations can better anticipate potential vulnerabilities, detect ongoing attacks, and respond more effectively to breaches.

Stages of a Cyber Attack

Reconnaissance:

This initial phase involves gathering information about the target. Attackers use various techniques to collect data on potential vulnerabilities, including social engineering, public databases, network scans, and phishing attempts. The goal is to identify the weakest links in the target's security posture (Graves, 2007).

Reconnaissance, often considered the first phase in the anatomy of a cyber attack, involves the careful gathering of information about the target system, network, or organization. This preliminary phase is crucial for attackers as it helps them identify vulnerabilities, understand the target's defenses, and plan subsequent stages of the attack with greater precision. Reconnaissance can be either passive, involving the collection of publicly available information without directly interacting with the target, or active, where the attacker engages with the target's systems to glean information.

Techniques Used in Reconnaissance

Open Source Intelligence (OSINT): Attackers use publicly available sources to collect information about the target. This includes data from websites, social media platforms, professional networks, forums, and other online sources where companies and individuals might share sensitive information unwittingly (Hassan, 2020).

Social Engineering: A more interactive form of reconnaissance, social engineering involves manipulating individuals into disclosing confidential information. Phishing emails, pretexting, baiting, and quid pro quo are common tactics used to trick employees into revealing details about internal systems, processes, or credentials (Hadnagy, 2010).

Network Scanning and Enumeration: Attackers may use various tools to scan the target's network for open ports, running services, and the types of devices connected to the network. Enumeration further involves extracting specific details such as usernames, group information, and service settings, which can aid in planning the attack (Bejtlich, 2004).

DNS Digging: The Domain Name System (DNS) can provide valuable information about the target, including subdomains, IP addresses associated with the domain, and sometimes the email addresses of system administrators. Tools like nslookup and dig are commonly used for DNS reconnaissance.

Defensive Strategies Against Reconnaissance

Limiting Information Disclosure: Organizations can minimize exposure by controlling the amount of information shared publicly. This includes reviewing social media policies, training employees on the risks of oversharing, and regularly auditing publicly accessible information.

Network Segmentation: Segmenting the network can obscure the internal structure from an external viewpoint, making it more difficult for attackers to gather useful information from any reconnaissance activities.

Implementing Intrusion Detection Systems (IDS): IDS can detect and alert on active reconnaissance efforts such as port scans and enumeration attempts, allowing security teams to respond to potential threats in real-time (Scarfone & Mell, 2007).

Regular Penetration Testing and Vulnerability Assessments: By regularly testing their own networks for vulnerabilities and simulating reconnaissance activities, organizations can identify and address weaknesses before attackers can exploit them.

Reconnaissance plays a critical role in the success of cyber attacks, providing attackers with the insights needed to breach defenses effectively. Understanding the tactics used in this phase allows organizations to implement targeted defensive measures, reducing their attack surface and strengthening their overall security posture. By prioritizing data privacy, monitoring network traffic, and educating employees about the risks of information disclosure, organizations can significantly mitigate the threat posed by reconnaissance activities.

Weaponization:

Once sufficient information is collected, attackers create malware or a cyber weapon tailored to exploit the identified vulnerabilities. This stage may involve developing custom malware or modifying existing tools and exploits to avoid detection.

Following the reconnaissance phase, where attackers gather necessary information about their target, the next critical stage in the anatomy of a cyber attack is weaponization. This phase involves creating or repurposing a cyber weapon, such as malware, a virus, or a worm, tailored to exploit the vulnerabilities identified during reconnaissance. The weaponization stage is where the theoretical knowledge gained about the target is transformed into a practical tool for attack, marking a shift from preparation to active aggression.

The Process of Weaponization

Malware Creation: Based on the vulnerabilities identified, attackers either develop new malware or modify existing malicious code to suit their specific objectives. This could involve crafting a payload to exploit a software vulnerability, creating a backdoor, or developing ransomware to encrypt and hold data hostage (Perkins, 2017).

Exploit Development: Sometimes, the weaponization phase involves developing an exploit, which is code that takes advantage of a software vulnerability. Exploits can be packaged with malware to create an exploit kit, making it easier to deploy the attack against the target.

Packaging: The crafted malware or exploit is then packaged in a manner that facilitates delivery and execution. This could involve embedding the malware in a seemingly benign document or application, known as a Trojan horse, or using a loader or dropper to install the malware without detection.

Testing Against Security Measures: Before deploying the weaponized code, attackers often test it against common antivirus software and security measures to ensure it can bypass detection. Tools and services exist in the cybercrime ecosystem that allow attackers to test their malware against up-to-date antivirus engines (Symantec, 2018).

Defensive Strategies Against Weaponization

Patch Management: Regularly updating software and systems with the latest patches is crucial for fixing vulnerabilities that could be exploited. A robust patch management policy can significantly reduce the attack surface available to adversaries.

Endpoint Protection: Utilizing comprehensive endpoint security solutions that include antivirus, anti-malware, and intrusion prevention capabilities can help detect and neutralize weaponized attacks before they execute.

Application Whitelisting: Allowing only pre-approved applications to run on systems can prevent unauthorized or malicious software, including weaponized malware, from executing.

Security Awareness Training: Educating employees about the dangers of malicious attachments and links can reduce the risk of weaponized attacks succeeding via social engineering methods.

The weaponization phase is a critical juncture in the anatomy of a cyber-attack, transitioning from planning to action. By understanding the tactics and techniques used by attackers to weaponize information against them, organizations can implement targeted defenses to protect against these threats. Maintaining rigorous patch management, deploying advanced endpoint protection, and fostering a culture of security awareness are essential strategies for mitigating the risk posed by weaponized cyber-attacks.

Delivery:

The weaponized threat is then delivered to the target. This could be through email attachments, malicious links, compromised websites, USB drives, or other methods designed to ensure that the malware reaches the intended system or network.

The delivery stage in the anatomy of a cyber-attack is when the attacker deploys the weaponized payload to the target. This phase is crucial as it determines how the malicious code reaches the victim, setting the stage for exploitation. The delivery mechanisms are diverse, leveraging various vectors to ensure the payload reaches the intended target without detection. This phase's success largely depends on the attacker's ability to disguise the attack and exploit the target's vulnerabilities or human errors.

Delivery Methods

Phishing Emails: One of the most common delivery methods involves sending emails that entice or trick the recipient into opening an attachment or clicking on a link that contains the malicious payload. Spear-phishing, a targeted form of phishing, involves crafting messages that are personalized to the recipient, increasing the likelihood of success (Hadnagy, 2010).

Drive-by Downloads: Attackers can compromise legitimate websites to serve malicious code. When a user visits the infected site, the code automatically downloads and executes on their system, often exploiting vulnerabilities in web browsers or plugins (Provos et al., 2007).

Removable Media: USB drives and other removable media can be used to deliver malware. Once connected to a system, the malicious code can execute automatically, exploiting the autorun feature in many operating systems.

Social Media and Instant Messaging: These platforms can be used to spread malicious links or files. The use of social engineering techniques can persuade users to click on links or download files that appear to come from trusted contacts.

Watering Hole Attacks: Attackers compromise a website frequently visited by the target group (the "watering hole") and use it to distribute malware. This method targets specific organizations or groups and relies on the victims visiting the compromised site (Cova et al., 2010).

Defensive Measures Against Delivery Attacks

Email Filtering and Anti-Phishing Solutions: Implementing advanced email filtering solutions that can detect phishing attempts, malicious attachments, and links is crucial. Employee training on recognizing phishing emails complements these technical solutions.

Web Security Gateways: Deploying web security gateways can block access to malicious websites, prevent drive-by downloads, and filter unwanted software from internet traffic.

Endpoint Security: Comprehensive endpoint security solutions can detect and prevent the execution of malware delivered through various means. Regularly updating these solutions ensures they can protect against the latest threats.

Disable Autorun: Disabling the autorun feature for removable media can prevent the automatic execution of malware when a USB drive or other media is inserted into a system.

Security Awareness Training: Educating users about the risks associated with clicking on links, downloading files from unknown sources, and the importance of reporting suspicious activities can significantly reduce the risk of successful deliveries.

The delivery stage is a critical step in the execution of a cyber attack, determining how the weaponized payload reaches the victim. By understanding the common delivery methods used by attackers, organizations can implement targeted defensive strategies to protect against these attacks. Combining technical controls with ongoing security awareness training for users creates a robust defense against the delivery of malicious payloads.

Exploitation:

Upon successful delivery, the malware exploits the identified vulnerabilities to gain unauthorized access to the system or network. This stage can involve executing code, escalating privileges, or bypassing security controls.

The exploitation stage is a pivotal phase in the anatomy of a cyber-attack, where the attacker leverages the delivered payload to exploit vulnerabilities within the target system or network. This stage follows the successful delivery of the weaponized payload, using various techniques to execute malicious activities that breach the target's defenses. Exploitation is the point at which the potential damage of a cyber-attack becomes actual, leading to unauthorized access, data theft, or other forms of compromise.

Mechanisms of Exploitation

Exploiting Software Vulnerabilities: Attackers often target known vulnerabilities in software applications, operating systems, or network infrastructure components that have not been patched or for which patches are not yet available. Common vulnerabilities include buffer overflows, SQL injections, and cross-site scripting (XSS) flaws (Howard & LeBlanc, 2003).

Zero-Day Exploits: These are attacks against previously unknown vulnerabilities, for which no patch exists at the time of the attack. Zero-day exploits are particularly dangerous because they give system administrators no time to react and secure the systems against the exploit (Bilge & Dumitras, 2012).

Configuration Weaknesses: Beyond software vulnerabilities, attackers exploit misconfigurations in systems and networks, such as default passwords, unnecessary services running on servers, or improperly configured access controls.

Social Engineering and Phishing: In some cases, exploitation involves manipulating users into performing actions that compromise security, such as disclosing passwords or downloading and executing malicious code.

Countermeasures and Defenses

Patching and Vulnerability Management: Regularly updating software and systems with the latest patches is critical for mitigating known vulnerabilities. A robust vulnerability management program helps identify, prioritize, and remediate vulnerabilities before attackers can exploit them.

Security Configuration and Hardening: Ensuring that systems and applications are securely configured and regularly audited can prevent exploitation. This includes disabling unnecessary services, changing default credentials, and applying the principle of least privilege.

Intrusion Prevention Systems (IPS): IPS solutions can detect and block attempts to exploit known vulnerabilities in real time, providing an additional layer of defense against exploitation (Scarfone & Mell, 2007).

User Education and Awareness: Training users to recognize and respond to social engineering tactics can reduce the likelihood of successful exploitation. This includes awareness of phishing, suspicious email attachments, and unsolicited requests for sensitive information.

Application Whitelisting: Limiting the software that can execute on a system to a known list of secure applications can prevent the execution of unauthorized or malicious programs.

Challenges in Preventing Exploitation

Despite the best efforts of security teams, preventing exploitation remains challenging due to the constantly evolving nature of vulnerabilities and attack techniques. The use of sophisticated, targeted zero-day exploits and the ability of attackers to rapidly adapt to defensive measures necessitate a proactive and adaptive security posture. Furthermore, the human factor often remains the weakest link in security, underscoring the importance of ongoing user education and behavioral change.

The exploitation stage is critical within the anatomy of a cyber-attack, marking the attacker's transition from potential threat to active adversary. By understanding the mechanisms of exploitation and implementing comprehensive countermeasures, organizations can significantly enhance their resilience against cyber-attacks. Continuous vigilance, rapid response to emerging threats, and a culture of security awareness are essential components of effective cyber defense strategies.

Installation:

After gaining access, the attacker installs additional tools or malware to maintain persistence within the target's environment. This allows the attacker to continue operating even if the initial entry point is discovered and closed.

Following the exploitation stage in the anatomy of a cyber-attack, where vulnerabilities are exploited to gain unauthorized access, comes the installation phase. This stage is characterized by the attacker's efforts to establish a persistent presence within the target's system or network. Installation allows attackers to maintain access to the compromised system, even if the initial exploit vector is discovered and remediated. This persistence is crucial for conducting further malicious activities, such as data exfiltration, lateral movement within the network, and the deployment of additional payloads.

Techniques Used in the Installation Phase

Malware Installation: Once a vulnerability has been exploited, attackers often install malware on the compromised system. This malware can take various forms, including backdoors, which allow remote access to the system; Trojans, which appear as legitimate software; or rootkits, which conceal the existence of other malware or themselves from detection mechanisms (Szor, 2005).

Credential Theft and Privilege Escalation: Attackers may use the initial access gained during exploitation to steal credentials and escalate their privileges within the system. This can involve installing software designed to capture keystrokes, extract password hashes, or exploit system vulnerabilities to gain higher-level access.

Creating Persistent Mechanisms: To ensure continued access, attackers often create mechanisms that allow the malware to survive system reboots and user logouts. This can include adding registry entries, creating scheduled tasks, or modifying startup scripts (Skoudis & Zeltser, 2019).

Establishing Command and Control Channels: Installation often involves setting up command and control (C&C) channels, which enable attackers to communicate with and control the compromised system remotely. These channels are used to exfiltrate data, receive further instructions, and download additional malicious payloads.

Countermeasures and Defenses

Advanced Endpoint Protection: Utilizing endpoint protection platforms (EPP) that include antivirus, anti-malware, and behavior-based detection can identify and block the installation of malicious software.

Privilege Management: Implementing strict privilege management and access controls can limit what attackers can do if they gain access to a system. The principle of least privilege (PoLP) ensures that users and applications have only the minimum level of access required to perform their functions.

Application Control and Whitelisting: Controlling which applications can execute on a system and employing application whitelisting can prevent unauthorized software, including malware, from running.

Regular System and Network Monitoring: Continuous monitoring of systems and networks for unusual activity can help detect the presence of unauthorized software or access. This includes monitoring for changes to files, configurations, and behavior indicative of malware or an attacker establishing persistence.

Security Awareness Training: Educating users about the dangers of installing unverified software and the importance of using secure, unique passwords can reduce the risk of credential theft and unauthorized software installation.

The installation stage is a critical phase in a cyber attack, enabling attackers to solidify their foothold within a target's system or network. By understanding the techniques used by attackers to maintain persistence, organizations can develop targeted defenses to detect and mitigate these threats. Implementing advanced endpoint protection, strict access controls, and regular monitoring, combined with fostering a culture of security awareness, are key strategies for preventing attackers from establishing a persistent presence within networks.

Command and Control (C&C):

The attacker establishes a command and control channel to communicate with and control the compromised systems remotely. This phase is crucial for exfiltrating data, issuing commands, and expanding the attacker's foothold within the network (Tankard, 2011).

The Command and Control (C&C) stage, also known as "Command and Control," marks a critical juncture in the anatomy of a cyber attack. Following successful exploitation and installation, attackers establish a C&C channel to maintain communication with the compromised system or network. This phase allows attackers to remotely commandeer the infected systems, directing them to execute specific actions that align with their malicious objectives. The versatility of C&C infrastructure enables continuous control over compromised assets, facilitating data exfiltration, spreading of malware, and further network penetration.

Nature and Functionality of C&C Channels

C&C channels are the means through which attackers communicate with compromised systems. These channels can be direct or indirect, leveraging various protocols and methods to evade detection:

Direct Connections: Some C&C infrastructures involve direct communication between the attacker's server and the compromised system. While straightforward, these connections can be easier to detect and block.

Domain Generation Algorithms (DGAs): DGAs dynamically generate a large number of domain names as potential C&C servers. This technique complicates efforts to block C&C communications by requiring defenders to predict or block a vast array of domains.

Peer-to-Peer (P2P) Networks: Utilizing P2P networks for C&C communications distributes control among numerous infected systems. This decentralization makes disrupting the C&C infrastructure more challenging.

Social Media and Cloud Services: Some attackers leverage legitimate social media platforms and cloud services to relay commands, exploiting these services' widespread use and trustworthiness to camouflage their activities (Myers, 2007; Stuttard & Pinto, 2011).

Impact of C&C Channels

The establishment of C&C channels signifies that attackers have secured a foothold within the target environment. Through these channels, attackers can:

Exfiltrate Sensitive Data: Steal intellectual property, personal information, financial data, or any valuable data accessible through the compromised system.

Expand Compromise: Use the initial foothold to explore and compromise other systems within the network, increasing their control and the potential impact of the attack.

Deploy Additional Malware: Introduce additional malicious tools or software, such as ransomware, to further their attack objectives.

Disrupt Operations: Execute commands that disrupt or degrade the performance of the target network or system, potentially leading to denial of service.

Defenses Against C&C Activity

Mitigating the threat posed by C&C channels requires a multi-faceted approach, focusing on both detection and disruption:

Network Segmentation: Dividing the network into segments can limit the spread of malware and restrict the communication capabilities of compromised systems.

Traffic Analysis and Monitoring: Continuous monitoring of network traffic for unusual patterns can help identify C&C communications. Deep packet inspection and behavioral analysis are key tools in this effort.

Domain Filtering and Blacklisting: Blocking known malicious domains and IP addresses can disrupt C&C communications, although attackers frequently change or obfuscate these addresses to evade blacklisting.

Endpoint Detection and Response (EDR): EDR solutions can detect and respond to signs of C&C activity on individual endpoints, providing granular control over the threat.

Education and Awareness: Training users to recognize signs of compromise can aid in early detection. Encouraging prompt reporting of suspicious behavior can significantly reduce the window of opportunity for attackers.

The Command and Control stage is a pivotal phase in cyber attacks, enabling attackers to exert ongoing influence over compromised systems. By understanding the mechanisms and implications of C&C channels, organizations can better prepare to detect and disrupt these communications, thereby mitigating the impact of cyber attacks. Employing comprehensive monitoring, domain filtering, and adopting proactive defense strategies are essential in countering the threat posed by C&C activities.

Actions on Objectives:

With control over the compromised systems, the attacker can now take actions to achieve their ultimate objectives. This can include data theft, data encryption for ransom, destruction of data, creating backdoors for future access, or using the compromised systems as part of a botnet for further attacks.

The "Actions on Objectives" stage represents the culmination of a cyber attack, where attackers execute their intended actions using the access and control established through earlier stages. This phase is the ultimate realization of the attackers' goals, which can vary widely depending on their motivations, ranging from financial gain, espionage, and sabotage to reputational damage. By this point, attackers have navigated past initial defenses, secured persistent access, and possibly established command and control (C&C) mechanisms, positioning them to carry out specific, targeted actions against the compromised entity.

Types of Actions on Objectives

Data Exfiltration: One of the most common objectives is the theft of sensitive data, including personal information, intellectual property, financial records, or strategic plans. Exfiltrated data can be used for financial fraud, competitive advantage, or public release to damage the victim's reputation (Mandiant, 2013).

Deployment of Ransomware: Attackers may encrypt critical data or systems and demand a ransom for the decryption key. This type of attack directly monetizes access to the compromised systems and can significantly disrupt operations (Symantec, 2019).

Sabotage and Disruption: Actions may include deleting critical data, disabling hardware or software, or otherwise disrupting operations. In state-sponsored or ideologically motivated attacks, the goal might be to damage infrastructure, undermine trust, or cause financial loss to the target.

Establishment of Backdoors: Installing backdoors ensures continued access to the compromised system for future attacks or to maintain a stealthy presence within the network, often for ongoing espionage activities.

Manipulation of Data or Systems: Rather than stealing or encrypting data, some attackers may alter data or system configurations to achieve their goals, such as manipulating financial systems, altering records, or changing operational parameters in industrial control systems.

Defensive Measures Against Actions on Objectives

Data Loss Prevention (DLP): DLP technologies can detect and prevent unauthorized attempts to copy or transmit sensitive data, mitigating the risk of data exfiltration.

Endpoint Detection and Response (EDR) and **Security Information and Event Management (SIEM)**: These systems provide real-time monitoring and analysis of security alerts generated by network hardware and applications, enabling the rapid detection and response to malicious activities indicative of an attacker moving towards their objectives (Caltagirone, Pendergast, & Betz, 2013).

Segmentation and Access Control: Limiting the ability of an attacker to move laterally within a network and access sensitive systems or data can significantly reduce the impact of actions on objectives. Implementing strict access controls and network segmentation are key strategies.

Incident Response Planning: A well-developed incident response plan ensures that an organization can quickly and effectively respond to signs of a compromise, potentially stopping attackers before they achieve their objectives.

Regular Backups and System Redundancy: Maintaining regular backups and system redundancy can mitigate the impact of ransomware or sabotage, enabling the rapid restoration of affected systems and data.

The "Actions on Objectives" stage is where the attacker's plans come to fruition, directly impacting the target through theft, disruption, or manipulation. Understanding the variety of actions attackers might undertake enables organizations to tailor their defensive strategies to detect and mitigate these actions more effectively. By implementing robust security measures, such as DLP, EDR, SIEM, strict access controls, and incident response plans, organizations can significantly reduce the likelihood and impact of attackers successfully achieving their objectives.

Mitigation Strategies

Comprehensive Security Training:

Educating employees on the risks of phishing emails, social engineering tactics, and safe internet practices is vital for preventing the initial compromise.

Comprehensive security training is a pivotal mitigation strategy in the broader context of defending against cyber attacks. In an era where technical defenses can be bypassed by exploiting human vulnerabilities, investing in human capital through security awareness and training programs becomes indispensable. This strategy not only aims to inform and educate employees about the various cyber threats but also fosters a culture of security within the organization, making each member a proactive participant in the organization's defense mechanisms.

Importance of Comprehensive Security Training

Human Factor as a Primary Vector: Numerous cyber attacks exploit human errors—such as falling for phishing scams, using weak passwords, or mishandling sensitive information. Comprehensive security training addresses these vulnerabilities by equipping employees with the knowledge to recognize and respond appropriately to security threats (Hadnagy, 2010).

Evolving Threat Landscape: The dynamic nature of cyber threats requires that employees stay informed about the latest tactics used by attackers. Regular training updates can help keep the workforce abreast of new threats and the latest best practices for defense.

Regulatory Compliance: Many industries are subject to regulations that mandate security awareness training. Regular, documented training sessions can help organizations comply with these requirements, avoiding potential legal and financial penalties.

Components of Effective Security Training Programs

Risk-Based Approach: Training programs should be tailored to the specific risks and needs of the organization. This involves identifying the most relevant threats and designing training content that addresses these risks directly.

Engaging and Accessible Content: To be effective, security training should be engaging, understandable, and accessible to all employees, regardless of their technical expertise. The use of interactive elements, real-life scenarios, and gamification can enhance engagement and retention of knowledge (SANS Institute, 2019).

Continuous Learning: Cybersecurity training should not be a one-time event but a continuous process. Regular updates, reminders, and follow-up training sessions help reinforce key concepts and keep security at the forefront of employees' minds.

Testing and Phishing Simulations: Simulated phishing exercises can be an effective tool for reinforcing training and assessing the readiness of employees to identify and respond to attempts at social engineering.

Reporting Mechanisms: Employees should be encouraged and empowered to report suspicious activities. Training programs should include clear instructions on how to report potential security threats, underscoring the role of each employee in the organization's security posture.

Challenges in Implementing Security Training

Engagement and Participation: One of the main challenges is ensuring high levels of engagement and participation from all employees. Overcoming this challenge requires making the training relevant, interesting, and interactive.

Measuring Effectiveness: Assessing the effectiveness of security training programs can be difficult. Organizations must develop metrics and evaluation methods to measure changes in behavior and reductions in vulnerability to attacks.

Resource Allocation: Comprehensive security training requires an investment of time and resources. Organizations must balance these costs against the benefits of a more informed and vigilant workforce.

Comprehensive security training is a crucial element of a holistic cybersecurity strategy, addressing the human element of cyber defense. By educating employees on the risks and equipping them with the skills to act as the first line of defense, organizations can significantly enhance their overall security posture. Effective security training requires careful planning, engaging content, and continuous reinforcement, but the benefits—reduced vulnerability to attacks and enhanced regulatory compliance—far outweigh the challenges.

Regular Software Updates and Patch Management:

Keeping software and systems up to date with the latest patches significantly reduces the vulnerabilities available for exploitation.

Regular software updates and patch management form a critical pillar in the mitigation strategies against cyber-attacks. Vulnerabilities in software are among the most common entry points for attackers. When software developers discover vulnerabilities, they issue updates or patches to fix them. Without these updates, organizations leave themselves exposed to attackers who exploit known vulnerabilities to gain unauthorized access, steal data, or deploy malware. Effective patch management is not merely about applying updates; it's about systematically ensuring that all software across the organization is current and secure.

The Significance of Regular Software Updates and Patch Management

Closing Security Gaps: Regular updates close security gaps that attackers could exploit. The 2017 WannaCry ransomware attack, for example, exploited a vulnerability in Microsoft Windows for which a patch was available but not universally applied (Mohurle & Patil, 2017).

Compliance Requirements: Many regulatory frameworks require up-to-date security measures, including patch management, as part of their compliance criteria. Regular patching can thus also be a matter of legal and regulatory compliance.

Maintaining System Integrity and Availability: Beyond security, updates often contain improvements to the functionality and efficiency of software, helping ensure systems operate optimally and remain available for business needs.

Challenges in Patch Management

Inventory Management: A prerequisite for effective patch management is a comprehensive inventory of all assets within the organization. Without a clear understanding of what software is running and where vulnerabilities might exist, patch management becomes a hit-or-miss affair.

Prioritization of Patches: Not all vulnerabilities pose the same level of risk. Organizations must assess and prioritize patches based on the severity of the vulnerability, the importance of the affected system, and the potential impact of exploitation (Krsul, Spafford, & Tripunitara, 1998).

Testing for Compatibility: Before deployment, patches should be tested in a non-production environment to ensure they do not interfere with existing systems or applications, potentially causing more harm than the vulnerabilities they intend to fix.

Best Practices in Patch Management

Automated Patch Management Tools: Automation can significantly streamline the patch management process, from identifying available updates to deploying patches across the organization. Automated tools can also help in maintaining an inventory of assets and in prioritizing patches.

Establish a Patch Management Policy: A formal policy should outline the process for regular updates, define roles and responsibilities, and set timelines for patch deployment following the release of an update.

Continuous Monitoring and Reporting: Continuous monitoring for new vulnerabilities and patches is essential. Reporting mechanisms should be in place to ensure accountability and to document compliance with internal and external audit requirements.

User Education: Educating users about the importance of updates, especially for personal devices that may access corporate resources, can help maintain security across the organization.

Regular software updates and patch management are indispensable strategies in mitigating the risk of cyber attacks. By systematically addressing vulnerabilities through timely updates, organizations can protect against a wide range of threats. While challenges exist, including the need for comprehensive asset inventories and the potential for compatibility issues, the benefits of maintaining up-to-date software far outweigh the risks of neglect. Through a combination of automated tools, well-defined policies, and ongoing education, organizations can establish a robust patch management process that supports their overall cybersecurity posture.

Network Segmentation and Access Controls:

Limiting access to sensitive information and segmenting networks can help contain the spread of an attack, minimizing its impact.

Network segmentation and access controls stand as fundamental components in the arsenal of strategies to mitigate cyber attacks. These strategies are instrumental in not only preventing unauthorized access but also in minimizing the potential damage should an attacker gain entry into the network. By dividing larger networks into smaller, manageable segments and enforcing strict access controls, organizations can significantly reduce the attack surface and limit the lateral movement of attackers within the network. This approach enhances the overall security posture by applying the principle of least privilege across network resources and users.

Network Segmentation: Principles and Implementation

Definition and Purpose: Network segmentation involves dividing a network into multiple segments or subnets, each acting as a separate security domain. This division is typically based on factors like departmental functions, user roles, or types of data processed. The primary purpose is to reduce the network's complexity, improve performance, and enhance security by isolating critical assets and limiting the spread of potential attacks (Stouffer, Pillitteri, Lightman, Abrams, & Hahn, 2015).

Techniques: Segmentation can be achieved through various means, including physical separation, virtual local area networks (VLANs), and firewalls. Advanced technologies like software-defined networking (SDN) offer dynamic and flexible segmentation capabilities, adapting to changing security requirements.

Benefits: Segmentation helps in containing security breaches within a single segment, thereby protecting the rest of the network. It also simplifies security monitoring and management by reducing the number of systems within each segment that need to be monitored.

Access Controls: Principles and Implementation

Definition and Purpose: Access controls are security measures that regulate who or what can view or use resources in a computing environment. These controls are essential for ensuring that only authorized users, systems, or applications have access to certain data or resources, based on their roles and responsibilities.

Types of Access Controls: Access controls can be categorized into discretionary access control (DAC), mandatory access control (MAC), and role-based access control (RBAC). RBAC, in particular, is widely used in enterprise environments, where access permissions are assigned to roles rather than individuals, simplifying the administration of access rights (Ferraiolo, Sandhu, Gavrila, Kuhn, & Chandramouli, 2001).

Implementation: Effective access control implementation requires a comprehensive understanding of the organization's assets, data classification, and user roles. Policies should be regularly reviewed and updated to reflect changes in the organization's structure, roles, or security posture.

Challenges and Best Practices

Complexity and Management Overhead: Both network segmentation and access control can introduce complexity and require significant management overhead. Best practices include using automated tools for managing access rights and continuously monitoring network traffic patterns to adjust segmentation rules as needed.

Continuous Monitoring and Auditing: Implementing segmentation and access controls is not a set-and-forget solution. Continuous monitoring for unauthorized access attempts and regular auditing of access control policies are critical for maintaining their effectiveness.

Integration with Other Security Measures: For optimal results, network segmentation and access controls should be integrated with other security measures, such as intrusion detection systems, firewalls, and endpoint protection solutions, creating a layered defense strategy.

Network segmentation and access controls are vital strategies for mitigating the risk of cyber attacks. By effectively implementing these measures, organizations can enhance their security posture, limit the potential impact of breaches, and ensure that only authorized users have access to sensitive information and critical systems. While these strategies require careful planning, management, and regular review, the security benefits they provide are indispensable in the current threat landscape.

Intrusion Detection and Response:

Implementing advanced intrusion detection systems (IDS) and having a proactive incident response plan can help in early detection of attack activities and reduce the time to respond to incidents.

Intrusion Detection and Response (IDR) systems play a crucial role in the mitigation strategies against cyber attacks, providing the means to detect, analyze, and respond to malicious activities within a network or system. As cyber threats evolve in complexity and stealth, relying solely on preventive measures is insufficient. IDR systems bridge this gap by offering real-time monitoring and analysis of network traffic and system behavior, identifying potential security breaches that slip past initial defenses, and facilitating rapid response to mitigate their impact.

Intrusion Detection Systems (IDS)

Types of IDS:

Network-based Intrusion Detection Systems (NIDS) monitor network traffic for suspicious activity and alert administrators to potential threats. NIDS are well-suited to detecting attacks that target network infrastructure, such as denial-of-service (DoS) attacks or certain types of malware propagation.

Host-based Intrusion Detection Systems (HIDS) are installed on individual hosts or devices to monitor inbound and outbound traffic from the device, as well as system logs and file integrity. HIDS can detect attacks aimed directly at host systems, including malware infections and unauthorized access attempts.

Detection Methodologies:

Signature-based Detection relies on a database of known threat patterns or signatures to identify malicious activities. While effective against known threats, it may not detect new, unknown attacks.

Anomaly-based Detection compares current network or system activities against a baseline of "normal" behavior to identify deviations that may indicate a security incident. This method can potentially detect previously unknown threats but may generate higher false positives (Scarfone & Mell, 2007).

Intrusion Response Systems (IRS)

Intrusion Response Systems automate the process of responding to detected threats, often integrating with IDS to provide a seamless detection and response solution. Response actions can range from simple alerts to system administrators, to automatically isolating affected systems, blocking malicious traffic, or executing scripts to remove malware.

Challenges in Intrusion Detection and Response

Volume of Alerts: One of the significant challenges with IDS is the volume of alerts generated, which can overwhelm security teams.

Prioritizing alerts based on severity and potential impact is crucial for effective response.

False Positives and Negatives: Balancing the sensitivity of detection algorithms to minimize false positives (benign activities flagged as malicious) and false negatives (missed attacks) requires continuous tuning and optimization of the system.

Skilled Personnel: Effective intrusion detection and response require skilled security personnel who can analyze alerts, distinguish between false alarms and genuine threats, and take appropriate action.

Best Practices for Intrusion Detection and Response

Comprehensive Security Policy: A well-defined security policy should outline the procedures for monitoring, detecting, and responding to intrusions, including roles and responsibilities.

Regular Updates and Maintenance: Keeping the IDS/IRS updated with the latest signatures and software versions ensures the system can detect and respond to the latest threats.

Integration with Other Security Tools: Integrating IDS/IRS with other security tools, such as Security Information and Event Management (SIEM) systems, firewalls, and endpoint protection platforms, can provide a more comprehensive security posture.

Continuous Training and Awareness: Ongoing training for security teams on the latest threat landscapes, detection techniques, and response strategies is essential for maintaining an effective IDR capability.

Intrusion Detection and Response systems are critical components of a robust cybersecurity strategy, enabling organizations to detect and mitigate threats that bypass other defenses. By implementing a comprehensive IDR solution, continuously tuning detection mechanisms, and fostering a skilled security team, organizations can significantly enhance their resilience against cyber attacks.

Endpoint Protection:

Utilizing comprehensive endpoint protection platforms (EPP) that include antivirus, anti-malware, and personal firewalls can prevent the installation of malware and block command and control communications.

Endpoint Protection plays a pivotal role in the landscape of cybersecurity mitigation strategies, aiming to secure endpoints, or entry points of end-user devices such as desktops, laptops, and mobile devices, from being exploited by malicious actors or campaigns. As endpoints often serve as gateways for cyber attacks, safeguarding them is critical for the overall security of network infrastructure and data.

Overview of Endpoint Protection

Endpoint protection platforms (EPP) provide comprehensive security solutions designed to detect, investigate, and neutralize threats at the device level. Unlike traditional antivirus software that primarily focuses on removing malware after it has been identified, modern EPPs offer a broader range of defense mechanisms, including prevention, detection, and response capabilities.

Core Features of Endpoint Protection:

Antivirus and Anti-malware: These are foundational elements that protect against known viruses and malware through signature-based detection.

Behavioral Analysis: This feature monitors the behavior of applications and processes to identify suspicious activities that may indicate a zero-day exploit or previously unknown malware.

Sandboxing: Suspicious programs are executed in a virtual environment separate from the system to observe their behavior without risking the endpoint's security.

Endpoint Detection and Response (EDR): EDR capabilities enable the detailed tracking and investigation of security incidents, providing tools for alert triage, forensic investigation, and remediation (Gartner, 2019).

The Importance of Endpoint Protection

Diverse Threat Landscape: Endpoints face a variety of threats, from phishing attacks and ransomware to sophisticated state-sponsored espionage. Effective endpoint protection must therefore employ a multi-layered defense strategy to address these threats.

The Rise of Remote Work: The increase in remote working arrangements has expanded the perimeter that organizations must defend, making endpoint protection more critical as employees access corporate resources from various, often unsecured, networks.

Compliance and Data Protection: Many regulatory frameworks require the protection of sensitive data. Endpoint protection helps ensure compliance by safeguarding data stored on or accessed by endpoints.

Challenges in Implementing Endpoint Protection

Managing Complexity: The diversity of endpoint devices and operating systems can complicate the deployment and management of endpoint protection solutions.

Balancing Performance and Security: Endpoint protection tools must be optimized to minimize their impact on system performance while still providing robust security.

Evolving Threats: The constant evolution of cyber threats necessitates continuous updates and adjustments to endpoint protection strategies.

Best Practices for Endpoint Protection

Regular Updates and Patch Management: Keeping endpoint protection software and operating systems up to date is crucial for defending against known vulnerabilities and threats.

Comprehensive Configuration Policies: Configuring endpoint protection tools according to best practices and organizational security policies ensures maximum effectiveness.

Integration with Security Infrastructure: Endpoint protection should be integrated with the broader security infrastructure, including network security tools and SIEM systems, for coordinated detection and response efforts.

User Education and Awareness: Training users on best practices for cybersecurity, including how to recognize phishing attempts and the importance of using strong passwords, enhances the overall effectiveness of endpoint protection.

Endpoint protection is a cornerstone of contemporary cybersecurity strategies, addressing the myriad threats that target individual user devices. By employing a blend of traditional and advanced security features, organizations can significantly enhance their defensive posture. As the landscape of threats continues to evolve, so too must the strategies and technologies deployed to protect endpoints, necessitating a commitment to continuous improvement and adaptation.

Understanding Malware:

Understanding malware is crucial in the realm of cybersecurity, as it encompasses various forms of malicious software designed to infiltrate, damage, or take control of a computer system without the user's consent. Malware is a broad term that includes viruses, worms, trojans, and ransomware, each with unique characteristics and methods of propagation. By comprehending the nuances of these malware types, individuals and organizations can better prepare and implement effective defense mechanisms against such cyber threats.

Viruses

A virus is a type of malware that attaches itself to a legitimate program or document and executes malicious code when the host program is run. Viruses are designed to spread from host to host and have the potential to corrupt or modify files, steal data, or impair system functionality. They require user interaction, such as opening an infected email attachment or downloading and executing a malicious file, to activate and propagate (Szor, 2005).

Viruses constitute a significant category within the spectrum of malware, characterized by their ability to replicate and spread across systems and networks. A computer virus is essentially a piece of code that attaches itself to a host file or program, leveraging the execution of the host to activate its malicious payload. Once activated, a virus can compromise system integrity, steal data, corrupt files, or even take control of the system to execute arbitrary commands. The unique aspect of viruses is their dependency on human action such as opening an infected email attachment or downloading malicious software—for propagation and activation.

Characteristics of Computer Viruses

Replication: Viruses are designed to replicate themselves and spread to other programs or systems. This replication process is what distinguishes viruses from other types of malware.

Concealment: Many viruses use sophisticated techniques to avoid detection by antivirus software, such as polymorphism (changing their code appearance without altering their functionality) and metamorphism (rewriting themselves entirely to appear different each time they infect a new host).

Payload Delivery: The payload of a virus can vary widely, from relatively benign pranks that may display messages on the user's screen to destructive actions like deleting files or formatting hard drives. More sophisticated viruses may establish backdoors, steal information, or integrate the infected machine into a botnet for coordinated attacks.

Mechanisms of Virus Propagation

File Infection: The most common method of virus spread is through file infection, where the virus code attaches itself to executable files. When the file is executed, the virus is also run, allowing it to infect other files and systems.

Boot Sector Infection: Some viruses target the boot sector of a hard drive, which contains the code executed during the system's boot process. Infecting the boot sector ensures that the virus is executed each time the computer is started.

Macro Viruses: These viruses exploit the macro programming languages built into software applications like Microsoft Word or Excel. They are embedded in documents and are executed when the document is opened, leveraging the application's capabilities to execute malicious activities.

Mitigation and Defense Strategies

Antivirus Software: Effective antivirus software remains one of the most reliable defenses against viruses. Modern antivirus solutions use signature-based detection to identify known viruses, heuristic analysis to detect new or modified viruses, and real-time scanning to monitor system activities.

Regular Software Updates: Keeping operating systems and applications up to date is critical for closing security vulnerabilities that viruses might exploit. Patch management policies should be implemented to ensure timely updates.

User Education: Training users to recognize potential threats, such as phishing emails or suspicious downloads, can significantly reduce the risk of virus infection. Users should be cautioned against opening attachments or clicking links from unknown sources.

Backup and Recovery: Regularly backing up important data ensures that, in the event of a virus infection, the lost or corrupted data can be restored. A robust backup strategy should include off-site or cloud backups that are not directly connected to the system networks.

Computer viruses represent a persistent threat in the cybersecurity landscape, capable of causing significant damage to individuals and organizations alike. Understanding the nature of viruses, their propagation mechanisms, and potential payloads is essential for developing effective strategies to combat them. By combining technical safeguards such as antivirus software and regular updates with user education and robust backup strategies, organizations can enhance their resilience against virus attacks.

Worms

Worms are similar to viruses in their destructive capabilities but differ in their method of propagation. Worms are standalone software that do not require host programs or user interaction to spread. They exploit vulnerabilities in operating systems or applications to propagate across networks, making them particularly effective at spreading quickly and widely. Worms can carry payloads that perform specific actions, such as deleting files, installing backdoors, or launching denial-of-service attacks (Nachenberg, 1997).

Worms constitute a distinct and particularly virulent form of malware, characterized primarily by their ability to replicate and spread across networks autonomously, without the need for direct human action to propagate. Unlike viruses, which require a host program to infect and trigger their execution, worms are standalone software that exploit vulnerabilities in operating systems, applications, or network protocols to spread themselves to other computers. Once infiltrated, worms can perform a variety of malicious actions, from consuming bandwidth and overloading systems to installing backdoors and delivering harmful payloads.

Characteristics of Worms

Self-Replicating: The hallmark of a worm is its ability to replicate itself independently. After infecting one system, a worm scans for other systems with the same vulnerability and spreads itself without user interaction, leveraging network connections.

Exploitation of Vulnerabilities: Worms often exploit specific security vulnerabilities in software or protocols to spread. Notable examples include the SQL Slammer worm, which exploited a buffer overflow vulnerability in Microsoft SQL Server and Desktop Engine database products, and the WannaCry ransomware worm, which targeted the Microsoft Windows operating system by exploiting the EternalBlue vulnerability.

Payload Delivery: While some worms merely propagate and consume system resources, others carry payloads designed to perform specific malicious actions. These actions can include deleting files, encrypting data for ransom, stealing information, or creating a botnet by installing remote control software on the infected machines.

Mechanisms of Worm Propagation

Network Services: Worms frequently target vulnerabilities in network services, such as email servers, web servers, or file-sharing systems, to spread from one host to another.

Email Attachments: Some worms spread by sending copies of themselves as email attachments to contacts found on the infected host. Opening the attachment on another system results in infection and further propagation.

Instant Messaging and Social Networks: Worms can also spread through instant messaging applications or social networks by sending links or files that lead to the worm's executable.

Removable Media: Although less common, some worms spread through removable media like USB drives, exploiting the autorun feature of operating systems to execute automatically when the media is accessed.

Mitigation and Defense Strategies

Patching and Vulnerability Management: Regularly updating operating systems and applications to patch known vulnerabilities is critical to defending against worms. Organizations should prioritize vulnerability management and timely patching to reduce the attack surface.

Intrusion Detection Systems (IDS) and Firewalls: Deploying IDS and firewalls can help detect and block worm activity, especially when configured to recognize and halt unusual network traffic patterns or known worm signatures.

Network Segmentation: Dividing the network into segments can contain the spread of worms within an organization, limiting the impact of an infection to isolated parts of the network.

Security Awareness and Training: Educating users about the dangers of opening unsolicited email attachments or clicking on unknown links can reduce the risk of worm infection through social engineering tactics.

Regular Backups: Maintaining regular backups of critical data ensures that, in the event of a worm infection, lost or corrupted data can be restored, minimizing operational disruption.

Worms are a formidable threat in the cybersecurity landscape, capable of rapid and wide-reaching propagation. Understanding their characteristics, mechanisms of spread, and potential impacts is crucial for developing effective defenses against them. By implementing a combination of technical controls, regular software updates, and user education, organizations can significantly reduce their vulnerability to worm infections and mitigate the potential damage they can cause.

Trojans

Trojan malware, or Trojans, deceive users by masquerading as legitimate software. Unlike viruses and worms, Trojans do not self-replicate but rely on social engineering to trick users into executing them. Once activated, Trojans can perform a range of actions, including creating backdoors for attackers to gain access, spying on users, or stealing data. The versatility and stealth of Trojans make them a potent tool for cybercriminals (Provos et al., 2007).

Trojans, named after the infamous Trojan Horse of Greek mythology, are a type of malware designed to mislead users of its true intent. Unlike viruses and worms, trojans do not replicate themselves but disguise themselves as legitimate software or are hidden within legitimate software to trick users into installing them. Once activated, trojans can carry out their malicious functions, which range from spying on the user to stealing data, installing additional malware, or creating backdoors for attackers to exploit.

Characteristics of Trojans

Deceptive Nature: The defining characteristic of a trojan is its ability to deceive users into willingly executing them, often by masquerading as legitimate software. This deception differentiates trojans from viruses and worms, which spread through exploitation or replication.

Diverse Malicious Functions: Trojans are versatile in their malicious capabilities. Depending on their design, they can serve various purposes, such as remote access trojans (RATs) for unauthorized access, data-stealing trojans for exfiltrating sensitive information, or destructive trojans that delete files or crash systems.

Lack of Self-Replication: Trojans do not self-replicate or infect other files. Their spread relies on social engineering tactics to trick users into executing them or on being bundled with other software.

Mechanisms of Trojan Propagation

Social Engineering: The most common propagation method for trojans involves social engineering techniques to convince users to execute them, often through phishing emails, malicious advertisements, or spoofed websites.

Software Bundles: Trojans may be bundled with legitimate software, either by compromising legitimate software distribution sites or by tricking users into downloading from untrustworthy sources.

Exploit Kits: Some trojans are delivered using exploit kits that probe for vulnerabilities on a user's system to silently install the trojan without the user's knowledge.

Mitigation and Defense Strategies

Security Software: Effective antivirus and anti-malware solutions can detect and remove trojans. Modern security software uses heuristic analysis, behavior monitoring, and signature-based detection to identify and neutralize trojans.

User Education and Awareness: Since trojans often rely on deception, educating users about the risks of downloading software from unverified sources, the dangers of clicking on links in unsolicited emails, and the importance of verifying the authenticity of software can significantly reduce the risk of trojan infections.

Software and Operating System Updates: Keeping software and operating systems updated can close vulnerabilities that trojans and their delivery mechanisms might exploit.

Application Whitelisting: Implementing application whitelisting can prevent unauthorized applications, including trojans disguised as legitimate software, from executing on the system.

Regular Backups: Maintaining regular backups of important data can help mitigate the damage caused by data-stealing or destructive trojans, ensuring that critical information can be restored.

Trojans represent a significant threat in the cybersecurity landscape due to their deceptive nature and the broad range of malicious activities they can perform. Understanding the characteristics of trojans, their propagation mechanisms, and their potential impacts is essential for developing effective strategies to combat them. By combining technical security measures with robust user education programs, organizations can significantly enhance their defenses against trojan malware and mitigate the potential risks they pose.

Ransomware

Ransomware is a type of malware that encrypts the victim's files or locks users out of their systems, demanding a ransom payment in exchange for the decryption key or release of the system. Ransomware attacks can target individuals, businesses, and government agencies, causing significant data loss and financial damage. The rise of cryptocurrencies has facilitated anonymous ransom transactions, further emboldening attackers (Kharraz et al., 2015).

Ransomware represents a formidable and increasingly prevalent form of malware that restricts access to the victim's data or systems until a ransom is paid, typically in cryptocurrency. This cyber extortion can lock users out of their systems, encrypt files making them inaccessible, or threaten to release sensitive data unless the demands are met. The impact of ransomware can range from minor inconvenience to significant financial loss and disruption of critical services, highlighting the importance of understanding and preparing for such attacks.

Characteristics of Ransomware

Encryption-Based Lockout: Many ransomware variants encrypt the victim's files with strong encryption algorithms, making them inaccessible without the decryption key, which is held by the attacker until the ransom is paid.

Payment Demands: Victims are presented with a ransom note demanding payment, often in Bitcoin or another cryptocurrency, to receive the decryption key. The note may include instructions on how to pay the ransom and deadlines for payment, after which the price may increase or the decryption keys may be destroyed.

Anonymity of Transactions: The use of cryptocurrencies for the payment of ransoms provides anonymity to the attackers, making it difficult to trace and prosecute the perpetrators.

Psychological Manipulation: Ransomware often employs scare tactics, such as countdown timers or threats of data destruction, to pressure victims into paying the ransom quickly.

Mechanisms of Ransomware Propagation

Phishing Emails: Ransomware is often spread through phishing emails that trick users into downloading and opening malicious attachments or clicking links that lead to malware-laden websites.

Exploit Kits: These kits target vulnerabilities in software and systems to automatically distribute ransomware without the need for user interaction, making them a particularly stealthy and effective propagation method.

Remote Desktop Protocol (RDP) Exploits: Attackers may exploit weak or default passwords in RDP services to gain remote access to systems and manually install ransomware.

Malvertising: Malicious advertising can redirect users to ransomware-distributing sites or directly exploit browser vulnerabilities to download ransomware.

Mitigation and Defense Strategies

Regular Backups: Regular, secure, and isolated backups of critical data are the most effective defense against ransomware. Restoring data from backups can negate the need to pay the ransom.

Patch Management: Keeping systems and software updated with the latest security patches can close vulnerabilities that ransomware exploits to infiltrate systems.

Security Awareness Training: Educating users on the dangers of phishing emails, malicious attachments, and dubious links can reduce the likelihood of initial infection.

Endpoint Protection and Antivirus Software: Comprehensive antivirus and anti-ransomware solutions can detect and block ransomware before it can encrypt files.

Network Segmentation: Limiting the ransomware's ability to spread through network segmentation can contain the infection to isolated parts of the network, reducing its overall impact.

Ransomware poses a significant threat to individuals, businesses, and government entities alike, with its ability to incapacitate critical systems and data. Understanding its characteristics, propagation mechanisms, and the devastating potential impact underscores the importance of implementing robust mitigation and defense strategies. By prioritizing regular backups, maintaining up-to-date systems, fostering security awareness, and deploying effective security solutions, organizations can significantly reduce their vulnerability to ransomware attacks and their reliance on paying ransoms to recover data.

Mitigation Strategies

Regular Software Updates and Patch Management: Keeping software and operating systems up to date with the latest patches is critical for protecting against vulnerabilities that malware exploits.

Antivirus and Anti-Malware Software: Comprehensive antivirus solutions can detect and remove malware infections. Regularly updating antivirus signatures is essential for defending against new malware variants.

Backup and Disaster Recovery: Regularly backing up critical data and having a disaster recovery plan in place can mitigate the impact of ransomware and other destructive malware.

User Education and Awareness: Training users to recognize and avoid phishing attempts, suspicious downloads, and other social engineering tactics is a vital line of defense against malware.

Malware, including viruses, worms, trojans, and ransomware, represents a significant cybersecurity threat with the potential to cause extensive damage and disruption. Understanding the characteristics and behaviors of different malware types is fundamental to developing effective security strategies. Implementing a combination of technical defenses, regular updates, user education, and preparedness planning is essential for mitigating the risks posed by malware.

Phishing And Social Engineering Tactics

Phishing and social engineering represent some of the most insidious methods employed by cyber attackers to breach security defenses. Unlike direct hacking attacks that exploit technical vulnerabilities, these tactics target the human element, manipulating individuals into surrendering confidential information or performing actions that compromise security. Understanding the nature of these threats is crucial for developing effective countermeasures.

Phishing: The Art of Deception

Phishing involves sending fraudulent communications that appear to come from a reputable source, typically via email, but also through SMS (smishing) or voice calls (vishing). The goal is to trick the recipient into revealing sensitive information, clicking on malicious links, or downloading infected attachments.

Phishing stands as a principal vector for cyber attacks, leveraging deceptive communications to manipulate individuals into divulging confidential information, clicking on malicious links, or downloading compromised attachments. This form of cyber deception mimics legitimate sources, often exploiting trust to breach security perimeters. Understanding the diverse types of phishing is vital for developing effective countermeasures and enhancing organizational and individual resilience against these attacks.

Types of Phishing

Spear Phishing:

Unlike broad, indiscriminate phishing campaigns, spear phishing targets specific individuals or organizations. Attackers conduct detailed research to personalize their messages, making them appear as credible as possible. This type of phishing might use personal information, such as names, job titles, and specific interests, to create a sense of legitimacy and urgency, significantly increasing the chances of the recipient taking the bait (Jagatic et al., 2007).

Spear phishing represents a more targeted approach within the phishing spectrum, focusing on specific individuals or organizations rather than casting a wide net. This method is distinguished by its personalized nature, leveraging detailed information about the target to craft convincing messages that appear legitimate and relevant. The precision of spear phishing increases its effectiveness, making it a preferred tactic for attackers seeking to infiltrate organizations or compromise high-value targets.

Characteristics of Spear Phishing

Targeted: Spear phishing campaigns are meticulously planned, with attackers often spending considerable time gathering information about their targets. This might include employment details, personal interests, or professional connections, typically sourced from social media, corporate websites, or previous breaches.

Customized Messages: The emails sent in spear phishing attacks are highly customized to appear as though they come from a trusted sender—often a colleague, superior, or known organization. The content is tailored to resonate with the recipient, increasing the likelihood of the email's call to action being followed.

Objective: The primary goals of spear phishing vary from stealing sensitive information, such as login credentials or financial data, to installing malware on the target's device. In corporate settings, spear phishing may aim to gain access to confidential systems or data, serving as a foothold for further penetration into the network.

Mechanisms of Spear Phishing Propagation

Email Communication: The most common delivery method for spear phishing is email. Attackers leverage compromised email accounts or craft email addresses that mimic legitimate ones to avoid raising suspicion.

Social Engineering: Beyond the technical aspects, spear phishing relies heavily on social engineering principles. By creating a scenario that appears credible to the target, attackers manipulate the recipient into taking actions such as clicking on a link, downloading an attachment, or directly providing sensitive information.

Utilization of Compromised Information: Spear phishing often utilizes information obtained from previous data breaches. Attackers might include specific details known only to the target and the legitimate sender to lend credibility to their fraudulent communications.

Mitigation and Defense Strategies

Education and Awareness Training: Regular training for employees on recognizing spear phishing attempts is crucial. This includes scrutinizing email addresses for slight deviations from legitimate ones, questioning unexpected requests for sensitive information, and verifying the authenticity of requests through alternate communication channels.

Email Filtering and Anti-Phishing Solutions: Advanced email security solutions can help filter out many spear phishing attempts, especially those utilizing known malicious domains or identified phishing patterns.

Multi-Factor Authentication (MFA): MFA adds an additional layer of security, ensuring that compromised credentials alone are not enough to grant access to sensitive systems or information.

Information Sharing Controls: Organizations should limit the amount of personal and operational information publicly available, reducing the data attackers can use to craft their spear phishing campaigns.

Spear phishing is a highly effective cyber attack tactic due to its targeted and personalized nature. By understanding its characteristics and mechanisms, organizations can better prepare their employees to recognize and respond appropriately to such threats. Combining awareness training with technical defenses and information sharing controls forms a comprehensive approach to mitigating the risk of spear phishing attacks.

Whaling:

A subset of spear phishing, whaling, targets high-profile individuals within organizations, such as executives, managers, or other key decision-makers. These attacks are meticulously crafted, often involving fake legal subpoenas, executive summaries, or other documents that a high-ranking official might consider urgent and relevant. The objective can range from financial fraud to espionage or gaining access to restricted corporate resources (Hadnagy, 2018).

Whaling, a specialized form of phishing, targets high-ranking individuals within an organization, such as CEOs, CFOs, or other senior executives. Termed "whaling" due to the high value and influence of the targets, akin to catching a large whale instead of smaller fish, these attacks are meticulously crafted to deceive the "big fish" of an organization into divulging sensitive information, authorizing fraudulent transactions, or unwittingly facilitating access to corporate networks.

Characteristics of Whaling

Highly Personalized: Whaling attacks are characterized by their high degree of personalization. Attackers spend considerable time researching their targets, often using publicly available information to craft emails that are highly relevant and convincing to the executive. The messages may reference recent company announcements, ongoing business deals, or other specific activities known to the target.

Sophisticated Social Engineering: Unlike broader phishing campaigns, whaling employs sophisticated social engineering tactics, often impersonating other high-ranking individuals within the organization or trusted external partners. The use of authoritative language and urgent tones compels the target to act swiftly, bypassing usual security protocols or verification steps.

Objective: The objectives of whaling can include financial gain through the authorization of fraudulent transactions, data theft by acquiring sensitive company information, or gaining direct access to the organization's network for espionage or sabotage purposes.

Mechanisms of Whaling Propagation

Email Communication: Email is the primary vector for whaling attacks, with messages crafted to appear as though they come from a trusted source within or closely related to the organization. These emails often bypass traditional phishing filters due to their unique and specific content.

Spoofing and Domain Masquerading: Attackers may use email spoofing techniques or register domain names that closely mimic legitimate corporate domains, making the fraudulent communication appear more authentic.

Attachment and Link Manipulation: Whaling emails may include attachments or links that claim to direct the recipient to documents requiring their immediate attention. These attachments or links can lead to malware infections or phishing sites designed to capture credentials.

Mitigation and Defense Strategies

Executive Awareness and Training: Given their targeted nature, educating executives about the risks and indicators of whaling attacks is crucial. This includes scrutinizing emails for subtle signs of fraud, verifying the authenticity of requests through alternate channels, and exercising caution with emails demanding urgent action or sensitive information.

Advanced Email Security Solutions: Implementing advanced email security solutions that include anti-spoofing, domain authentication, and anomaly detection can help identify and block whaling attempts before they reach the target.

Verification Procedures: Establishing internal verification procedures for requests involving financial transactions or sensitive information can prevent successful whaling attacks. This might include multi-person approval processes or direct verbal confirmation.

Limit Public Exposure: Executives should be cautious about the amount of personal and professional information shared publicly. Reducing the availability of such information can make it more challenging for attackers to personalize whaling attacks effectively.

Whaling represents a significant threat to organizational leadership, exploiting their authority and access within the organization to achieve malicious ends. By understanding the unique aspects of whaling attacks, including their personalized and sophisticated nature, organizations can better prepare their executives to recognize and respond to these threats. Combining targeted awareness training with advanced email security measures and internal verification processes creates a robust defense against whaling, safeguarding both individuals and the organization as a whole.

Clone Phishing:

This technique involves creating a nearly identical replica of a previously sent legitimate email but with malicious alterations. The cloned email may claim that the original contained an error or omitted something and thus provide a new, harmful link or attachment. Because the email appears to come from a known and trusted sender, recipients may be more likely to overlook subtle discrepancies and comply with the request (Hong, 2012).

Clone phishing represents a sophisticated phishing technique where attackers create a nearly identical replica of a previously sent legitimate email, but with malicious alterations. This method leverages the trust established by the original, legitimate communication to deceive the recipient into believing that the cloned email is also genuine. In the context of whaling, where high-value targets within an organization are specifically targeted, clone phishing can be particularly effective due to the personalized nature of the attack, ensuring that the deceptive email aligns closely with the executive's expectations and past communications.

Characteristics of Clone Phishing

Replication of Legitimate Emails: Clone phishing attacks start by choosing a legitimate email to replicate. This could be an email previously sent by a trusted entity, such as a financial institution, service provider, or internal department within the organization.

Malicious Modifications: The cloned email is modified to include malicious elements. This could involve changing the links within the email to point to phishing websites, replacing attachments with malware-infected files, or altering the contact information to redirect responses to the attacker.

Urgency and Authenticity: To prompt immediate action, the cloned email often includes a sense of urgency or importance. The use of an email that the recipient recognizes adds to the authenticity, making the request seem more plausible.

Clone Phishing in the Context of Whaling

When clone phishing is used as part of a whaling attack, the emails are highly customized to target senior executives with the authority to make significant decisions or access sensitive information. The attackers might replicate an email chain related to financial transactions, sensitive negotiations, or strategic decisions, altering the content to direct the executive towards the malicious objective.

Mitigation and Defense Strategies

Email Verification: Encouraging the verification of suspicious emails through alternative communication channels can help confirm the authenticity of the request. Executives should be trained to verify emails by contacting the sender directly via phone or in person, especially if the email involves unusual requests or high-stakes information.

Advanced Email Security Features: Utilizing email security solutions that offer advanced features, such as link analysis, attachment sandboxing, and anti-spoofing technologies, can help detect and block clone phishing attempts.

Awareness and Training: Regular awareness programs that include examples of clone phishing attacks can prepare executives to recognize and respond appropriately to suspicious emails. Simulated phishing exercises can reinforce this training by providing practical experience in identifying phishing attempts.

Controlled Sharing of Information: Limiting the amount of publicly available information regarding organizational processes, decision-making chains, and executive communications can reduce the attackers' ability to craft convincing cloned emails.

Clone phishing, particularly when used in whaling attacks, exploits the established trust in existing communications to deceive targets into compromising security. By understanding the mechanics of clone phishing and implementing a multi-layered defense strategy that includes technological solutions, verification processes, and targeted awareness training, organizations can significantly mitigate the risk posed by these sophisticated phishing attacks.

Pharming:

Going beyond deceptive emails, pharming redirects users from legitimate websites to fraudulent ones via DNS poisoning or manipulating the victim's host file. Users believe they are visiting a trustworthy site, making them more likely to enter sensitive information such as login credentials, which are then captured by attackers.

Pharming is a sophisticated form of cyber attack that redirects a website's traffic to a fraudulent website without the user's knowledge or consent. Unlike phishing, which relies on tricking users into clicking on a malicious link, pharming manipulates the user's environment to redirect them automatically to a fake site, even if they type the legitimate URL into their browser's address bar. This technique can be particularly effective in whaling attacks targeting high-value individuals within organizations, as it can bypass some of the traditional defenses against email-based phishing.

Mechanisms of Pharming

DNS Poisoning: One common method of pharming involves poisoning the Domain Name System (DNS) cache, a key component of the internet that translates human-friendly domain names into IP addresses that computers use to access websites. By injecting false information into the DNS cache, attackers can redirect users to malicious sites without any visible discrepancy in the browser's address bar.

Malware: Another pharming technique involves installing malware on the user's device that modifies local DNS settings or the hosts file, redirecting requests for specific websites to fraudulent ones. This method can be particularly insidious, as the redirection occurs regardless of the network the device is connected to.

Pharming in the Context of Whaling

In whaling attacks, pharming can be used to compromise specific high-value targets within an organization by redirecting them to fake websites that mimic legitimate business or financial services. The attackers can then capture sensitive information, such as login credentials or financial information, directly from the executives. Given the personalized nature of whaling, the fraudulent sites might be specially crafted to deceive the targeted individuals, making the deception more convincing.

Mitigation and Defense Strategies

Secure DNS Practices: Implementing secure DNS practices, such as using DNSSEC (DNS Security Extensions), can help protect against DNS poisoning by ensuring that DNS responses are authenticated and have not been tampered with.

Regular Security Audits and Monitoring: Conducting regular audits of DNS records and monitoring network traffic for unusual redirection patterns can help identify attempts at DNS poisoning or other signs of pharming activity.

Endpoint Security Solutions: Comprehensive endpoint security solutions that include antivirus and anti-malware capabilities can detect and remove malware used for pharming. These solutions should be kept up to date to protect against the latest threats.

Education and Awareness: Training high-value targets within the organization about the risks and indicators of pharming attacks can help them recognize and avoid suspicious websites. This includes verifying website security certificates and being cautious of any discrepancies in website content or functionality.

Multi-Factor Authentication (MFA): Implementing MFA can add an additional layer of security, ensuring that access to sensitive accounts and systems is protected even if login credentials are compromised through a pharming attack.

Pharming poses a significant threat by redirecting users to fraudulent websites, making it a potent tool in the arsenal of cyber attackers, especially in targeted whaling campaigns. Understanding the mechanisms behind pharming and implementing a layered defense strategy that includes secure DNS practices, endpoint security, regular monitoring, and user education can significantly mitigate the risks associated with these attacks. For high-value targets, additional measures like MFA and personalized security awareness training are crucial for safeguarding against the sophisticated tactics employed in pharming and whaling attacks.

Smishing and Vishing:

With the increasing use of smartphones, smishing (SMS phishing) and vishing (voice phishing or phishing via phone calls) have become prevalent. Smishing involves sending text messages that lure recipients into clicking on a malicious link or divulging personal information. Similarly, vishing calls deceive the recipient into believing they are speaking with a legitimate representative from a trusted organization, urging them to reveal sensitive information or perform specific actions.

Mitigation and Defense Strategies

Education and Awareness: The first line of defense against phishing is awareness. Regular training sessions and simulated phishing exercises can help sensitize individuals to the hallmarks of phishing attempts.

Email Filtering and Verification Tools: Advanced email filtering solutions can identify and quarantine many phishing emails before they reach the recipient. Additionally, email verification technologies like DMARC (Domain-based Message Authentication, Reporting, and Conformance) help prevent email spoofing.

Multi-Factor Authentication (MFA): Implementing MFA can significantly mitigate the damage of compromised credentials, a common goal of phishing attacks.

Regular Updates and Patch Management: Keeping systems and security software up to date can protect against some of the exploits delivered via phishing, such as ransomware or trojans.

Phishing's evolving sophistication necessitates a vigilant, well-informed approach to cybersecurity. By understanding the various types of phishing and implementing comprehensive, layered defense strategies, organizations and individuals can substantially reduce their vulnerability to these deceptive attacks.

Phishing emails often create a sense of urgency, fear, or curiosity to prompt the recipient to act without due diligence. They might impersonate financial institutions, tech support, or colleagues to appear more convincing (Hadnagy, 2018).

Social Engineering: Exploiting Human Psychology

Social engineering is a broader term that encompasses a range of manipulative tactics aimed at tricking individuals into breaking normal security procedures. It relies on psychological manipulation, exploiting traits such as trust, authority, greed, or the desire to be helpful.

Common Tactics:

Pretexting: Creating a fabricated scenario or pretext to obtain information or gain access.

Baiting: Offering something enticing to the victim in exchange for information or access.

Tailgating: Following an authorized person into a restricted area under the guise of being an employee or contractor.

Social engineering attacks are meticulously planned, often involving research on the target to make the deception more effective. Attackers may gather information from social media, corporate websites, or other public sources to craft convincing narratives (Mitnick & Simon, 2002).

Mitigation Strategies

Education and Awareness Training: Regular training sessions can help employees recognize and respond appropriately to phishing and social engineering attempts. Simulated phishing exercises can be particularly effective in reinforcing these lessons.

Strong Authentication Processes: Implementing multi-factor authentication (MFA) can add an additional layer of security, making it harder for attackers to gain access even if they obtain login credentials.

Information Sharing Controls: Policies should be in place to control the sharing of sensitive corporate information, especially on social media or other public forums. Employees should be aware of the types of information that are considered confidential.

Physical Security Measures: For defending against tailgating and other physical breaches, organizations can employ security badges, entry codes, and receptionists or security personnel to verify the identity of individuals entering secure areas.

Phishing and social engineering attacks exploit human vulnerabilities, making them difficult to defend against with traditional security measures alone. A comprehensive approach that combines technical defenses with ongoing education, vigilance, and a strong organizational culture of security is essential for mitigating these threats. By understanding the tactics used by attackers and implementing robust security practices, organizations can significantly reduce the risk posed by these deceptive tactics.

Conclusion

The anatomy of cyber-attacks outlines a systematic process through which attackers compromise and exploit networks and systems. Understanding each stage of an attack enables organizations to implement layered security measures, detect breaches more effectively, and respond swiftly to mitigate impacts. As cyber threats continue to evolve, maintaining vigilance, updating security practices, and fostering a culture of security awareness are essential for defending against cyber-attacks.

Chapter 7: Defense Strategies

In the realm of cybersecurity, implementing robust defense strategies is crucial for organizations seeking to protect their digital assets from a wide array of cyber threats. These strategies encompass a multi-layered approach, combining technological solutions, organizational policies, and user education to create a comprehensive defense against potential cyber-attacks. Effective defense strategies not only aim to prevent attacks but also to detect threats promptly, respond effectively, and recover from any damage sustained.

Defense-in-Depth (DiD)

Concept: Defense-in-Depth (DiD) is a security strategy that employs multiple layers of defense across the organization's network, systems, and data. The idea is to ensure that if one defense mechanism fails, another will subsequently prevent or mitigate an attack. This approach is akin to physical security measures within a castle, including the outer wall, inner fortress, and secure keep (Scarfone & Mell, 2009).

Implementation: DiD involves the deployment of firewalls, intrusion detection systems (IDS), intrusion prevention systems (IPS), antivirus software, and other security measures. It also includes the implementation of access controls, encryption, regular patch management, and comprehensive monitoring of network traffic and user activities.

Zero Trust Model

Concept: The Zero Trust model operates on the principle that organizations should not automatically trust anything inside or outside their perimeters and must verify anything and everything trying to connect to their systems before granting access. This approach recognizes that threats can originate from both external and internal sources (Rose et al., 2020).

Implementation: Key elements of a Zero Trust architecture include microsegmentation of networks to limit lateral movement, least privilege access controls to minimize each user's access to the bare minimum required for their role, and multi-factor authentication (MFA) to enhance user verification processes.

Regular Software Updates and Patch Management

Concept: Keeping software and systems updated is essential for closing security vulnerabilities that could be exploited by attackers. Patch management is the process of distributing and applying updates to software, including operating systems and applications, to correct security vulnerabilities and improve functionality.

Implementation: Organizations should establish a routine for regularly checking for and applying software updates. Automated patch management tools can help streamline this process, ensuring that all systems are kept up to date with the latest security patches.

Security Awareness Training

Concept: Human error is a significant factor in many cybersecurity breaches. Security awareness training educates employees about the variety of cyber threats they may encounter, such as phishing, social engineering tactics, and malware, and instructs them on safe practices to minimize risks.

Implementation: Effective training programs are ongoing, incorporating regular updates on emerging threats and testing employee knowledge through simulated phishing exercises or other practical assessments.

Incident Response Planning

Concept: Despite the best preventive measures, cyber incidents can still occur. An incident response plan outlines the procedures an organization follows when a cyber attack is detected, including steps to contain the breach, eradicate the threat, recover lost data, and resume normal operations.

Implementation: The plan should designate an incident response team, define roles and responsibilities, establish communication protocols, and include procedures for documenting and analyzing the incident to prevent future occurrences.

Best Practices in Digital Hygiene

Digital hygiene encompasses the practices and habits that users and organizations should adopt to maintain the health and security of their digital assets and information systems. In the context of cybersecurity, good digital hygiene is akin to personal health hygiene; just as regular handwashing can prevent illness, consistent digital hygiene practices can help prevent cyber attacks and data breaches. Best practices in digital hygiene involve a combination of technical measures, user behavior, and policy enforcement designed to protect sensitive data and systems from a wide range of threats.

Regular Software Updates and Patching

Keeping all software up to date, including operating systems, applications, and firmware on devices, is foundational to digital hygiene. Software updates often include patches for security vulnerabilities that have been discovered since the last update. Automated patch management systems can facilitate this process, ensuring that updates are applied promptly across the organization (Spring, 2017).

Regular software updates and patching are pivotal components of digital hygiene and cybersecurity defense strategies. This practice is essential in protecting systems and networks from vulnerabilities that could be exploited by cyber attackers. As software vulnerabilities are identified, developers release updates or patches to fix these flaws.

Failing to apply these updates promptly can leave an organization exposed to attacks that exploit known vulnerabilities, leading to data breaches, system compromises, and other security incidents.

The Importance of Regular Software Updates and Patching

Closing Security Gaps: Many cyber attacks exploit known vulnerabilities in software. Regularly updating and patching software closes these gaps, making it more difficult for attackers to gain unauthorized access or execute malicious code on systems and networks (Spring, 2017).

Compliance and Risk Management: For many organizations, particularly those in regulated industries, staying current with software updates is not just best practice—it's a requirement. Compliance frameworks often mandate that systems be maintained at known security levels, which includes applying security patches within specified timeframes.

Enhancing System Performance and Stability: Beyond security, software updates often include improvements to the performance, stability, and functionality of applications and operating systems, contributing to the overall efficiency and reliability of IT environments.

Challenges in Software Updates and Patching

Identifying and Prioritizing Vulnerabilities: With the vast number of software applications used within organizations, identifying which vulnerabilities pose the most significant risk can be challenging. Prioritizing patches for critical systems and applications is essential for effective risk management.

Patch Testing and Deployment: Not all patches can be applied immediately without testing. Organizations must balance the need for prompt patching with the potential for new updates to introduce system incompatibilities or disrupt critical operations.

Resource and Time Constraints: The resources required to maintain an aggressive patching schedule can be significant, particularly for organizations with extensive IT infrastructures or those that operate continuously.

Best Practices in Regular Software Updates and Patching

Automated Patch Management Tools: Automating the process of identifying, testing, and deploying patches can significantly reduce the workload on IT staff and decrease the time it takes to secure systems against known vulnerabilities.

Vulnerability Assessment and Prioritization: Regular vulnerability assessments can help organizations identify which systems are at risk and prioritize patches based on the severity of the vulnerability and the criticality of the affected system.

Patch Testing: Before widespread deployment, patches should be tested in a controlled environment to ensure they do not introduce new issues. This step is particularly critical for updates to critical systems and applications.

Patch Deployment Schedule: Establishing a regular schedule for deploying patches during low-usage periods can minimize disruptions to operations. Emergency procedures should also be in place for deploying critical security patches outside of this schedule.

User Education and Policy: Educating users about the importance of keeping personal and mobile devices updated, particularly those used for work purposes, reinforces the organization's overall patch management strategy.

Regular software updates and patching are fundamental to maintaining digital hygiene and safeguarding organizational assets against cyber threats. By implementing structured, prioritized, and automated patch management processes, organizations can enhance their security posture, comply with regulatory requirements, and ensure the continued performance and stability of their IT systems.

Strong Password Policies and Use of Multi-Factor Authentication (MFA)

Passwords are often the first line of defense for many systems and accounts. Implementing strong password policies—requiring complexity, length, and frequent changes—can significantly enhance security. Additionally, the use of Multi-Factor Authentication (MFA) adds an extra layer of security by requiring users to provide two or more verification factors to gain access to a system or account, thereby mitigating the risk of unauthorized access (Stobert & Biddle, 2014).

Implementing strong password policies and the use of Multi-Factor Authentication (MFA) are critical components of digital hygiene and effective defense strategies against cyber attacks. These measures serve as fundamental safeguards, enhancing the security of user accounts and sensitive systems by mitigating the risk of unauthorized access.

Strong Password Policies

Importance of Strong Passwords: Passwords are often the first line of defense for securing user accounts and systems. Strong passwords—those that are complex, lengthy, and unique—are considerably more difficult for attackers to guess or crack through brute-force methods.

Characteristics of Strong Passwords: A strong password policy encourages the creation of passwords that are at least 12 characters long and include a mix of uppercase letters, lowercase letters, numbers, and special characters. Passwords should avoid predictable patterns, dictionary words, or easily accessible personal information (Stobert & Biddle, 2014).

Password Management: Encouraging the use of password managers can help users maintain unique and complex passwords for different accounts without the need to memorize them. Password managers can generate strong passwords and store them securely, reducing the risk of reuse across multiple sites.

Multi-Factor Authentication (MFA)

Layered Security: MFA adds additional layers of security by requiring two or more verification methods to gain access to an account or system—something you know (password), something you have (a security token or smartphone), or something you are (biometric verification).

Types of MFA: Common MFA methods include SMS codes sent to a mobile device, authentication apps that generate time-based one-time passwords (TOTPs), hardware tokens that produce a new code at the press of a button, and biometric factors like fingerprints or facial recognition.

Benefits of MFA: MFA significantly enhances account security by ensuring that the compromise of one factor (e.g., a password) is not sufficient for an attacker to gain unauthorized access. This is particularly important for protecting access to sensitive systems, personal data, and in fulfilling compliance requirements for data protection (O'Gorman, 2013).

Best Practices in Implementing Strong Password Policies and MFA

Enforce Password Complexity and Regular Changes: Organizations should enforce password complexity requirements through their IT policies and encourage regular password changes, though without making the intervals so frequent that users resort to creating weaker passwords.

Promote MFA Adoption: While some users may find MFA inconvenient, promoting its adoption through user education about its security benefits can help. Offering multiple MFA options can also improve user acceptance by providing flexibility in how they authenticate.

Regular Security Awareness Training: Educating users about the importance of strong passwords and MFA, along with training on how to create secure passwords and use MFA devices or apps, can significantly improve compliance and security posture.

Phased Implementation for MFA: For organizations newly implementing MFA, a phased approach can help manage the transition. Starting with the most sensitive systems and accounts before extending MFA requirements more broadly allows users and IT departments to adjust smoothly.

Strong password policies and the use of Multi-Factor Authentication are essential practices within the broader context of digital hygiene and cybersecurity. By adopting these measures, organizations and individuals can significantly reduce the risk of unauthorized access and the potential impact of cyber attacks. Continuous education and the promotion of secure authentication practices are vital for maintaining effective digital defenses in the face of evolving cyber threats.

Secure Network Practices

This includes using secure Wi-Fi connections, employing firewalls, and segmenting networks to isolate sensitive data and systems from general network traffic. Virtual Private Networks (VPN) should be used for remote access to ensure that data transmitted over public networks is encrypted and secure (Aljawarneh et al., 2020).

Secure network practices form the backbone of digital hygiene, ensuring the integrity, confidentiality, and availability of data across an organization's network. These practices encompass a range of strategies designed to protect network resources from unauthorized access, data breaches, and other cyber threats. By implementing secure network practices, organizations can safeguard their critical infrastructure and sensitive information against increasingly sophisticated cyber attacks.

Fundamental Components of Secure Network Practices

Network Segmentation and Isolation: Dividing the network into smaller, manageable segments can significantly enhance security. Segmentation helps in isolating critical systems and sensitive data, limiting the spread of cyber threats within the network. Implementing firewalls and access control lists (ACLs) between segments ensures that only authorized traffic can move between different parts of the network (Aljawarneh et al., 2020).

Use of Firewalls and Intrusion Prevention Systems (IPS): Firewalls serve as a barrier between trusted internal networks and untrusted external networks, such as the internet. IPS, on the other hand, actively monitors network and system activities for malicious actions and known threats, blocking them in real-time. Together, they form a critical line of defense against external and internal threats.

Secure Configuration of Network Devices: Ensuring that all network devices, including routers, switches, and firewalls, are securely configured is vital. Default configurations often include weak settings or credentials, making devices easy targets for attackers. Disabling unnecessary services, changing default passwords, and regularly updating device firmware can mitigate these risks.

Encryption of Data in Transit: Encrypting data as it moves across the network prevents unauthorized interception and access. Using protocols such as Secure Sockets Layer (SSL)/Transport Layer Security (TLS) for web traffic, Virtual Private Networks (VPNs) for remote access, and secure file transfer protocols can protect data integrity and confidentiality.

Regular Monitoring and Logging: Continuous monitoring of network traffic and system logs helps in the early detection of suspicious activities that could indicate a security breach. Implementing a Security Information and Event Management (SIEM) system can aggregate and analyze logs from various sources, providing real-time security alerts and enabling a swift response to potential threats.

Secure Wireless Networks: Wireless networks can be particularly vulnerable to eavesdropping and unauthorized access. Implementing strong encryption (such as WPA3), hiding network SSIDs, and controlling access through MAC address filtering are essential measures for securing wireless connections.

Employee Training and Awareness: Users are often the weakest link in network security. Regular training sessions on secure network practices, the importance of strong passwords, recognizing phishing attempts, and safe web browsing habits are crucial for maintaining network security.

Challenges in Implementing Secure Network Practices

Implementing comprehensive secure network practices presents several challenges, including the complexity of managing and configuring network devices, the need for specialized knowledge and skills, and the continuous evolution of cyber threats. However, the benefits of protecting organizational assets and data far outweigh these challenges.

Secure network practices are essential for protecting organizational assets from the myriad of cyber threats in today's digital landscape.

By implementing a layered defense strategy that includes network segmentation, the use of firewalls and IPS, secure configurations, data encryption, and regular monitoring, organizations can significantly enhance their network security posture. Coupled with ongoing employee training and awareness programs, these practices form the cornerstone of effective digital hygiene and cybersecurity defense.

Regular Data Backups

Regularly backing up critical data is a crucial aspect of digital hygiene. Backups should be stored securely, ideally in multiple locations, including off-site or cloud storage, to protect against data loss from ransomware attacks, natural disasters, or hardware failure. Backup procedures should be tested regularly to ensure data can be effectively restored (Wallace & Webber, 2017).

Regular data backups constitute a crucial aspect of digital hygiene and defense strategies, serving as a fundamental safeguard against data loss due to cyber attacks, hardware failures, natural disasters, or human error. The practice of backing up data involves creating copies of data that can be restored in the event of a primary data failure or loss. This ensures the continuity of operations and the preservation of critical information assets.

Importance of Regular Data Backups

Resilience Against Ransomware Attacks: One of the most compelling reasons for regular data backups is the protection they offer against ransomware attacks. Ransomware encrypts the victim's files, demanding a ransom for their release. Regular, secure backups allow organizations to restore encrypted data without capitulating to ransom demands (Cohen, 2016).

Mitigation of Data Loss: Beyond cyber threats, backups are essential for protecting against data loss due to hardware failures, software corruption, accidental deletions, or catastrophic events such as fires, floods, or earthquakes.

Compliance and Legal Requirements: Many industries are subject to regulatory requirements that mandate data protection measures, including regular backups. Compliance with these regulations not only ensures legal adherence but also reinforces best practices in data management and security.

Best Practices in Data Backup

3-2-1 Backup Rule: A widely recommended strategy is the 3-2-1 backup rule, which suggests having at least three total copies of your data, two of which are local but on different mediums (e.g., on a hard drive and on a network-attached storage device), and one copy off-site (e.g., cloud storage). This approach diversifies the risk and ensures data availability even in the event of a physical disaster (Koomey, 2017).

Regular Testing and Validation: Regularly testing backups to verify their integrity and the effectiveness of the restoration process is crucial. This ensures that, in the event of an actual need, the data can be reliably restored within an acceptable timeframe.

Encryption of Backup Data: Encrypting backups protects sensitive information from unauthorized access, both in transit to off-site locations and at rest. This is particularly important for off-site or cloud-stored backups, where data is potentially exposed to third-party risks.

Automated Backup Solutions: Automating the backup process can help ensure regularity and reduce the likelihood of human error. Many software solutions offer automated scheduling of backups, incremental backup options to save only changes since the last backup, and detailed logs of backup activities.

Secure Storage and Access Control: Whether stored on-site, off-site, or in the cloud, backups should be securely stored and accessible only to authorized personnel. This includes physical security measures for on-site backups and robust access controls for cloud-based or off-site storage.

In the digital age, the importance of regular data backups as a component of digital hygiene and cybersecurity defense strategies cannot be overstated. Effective backup practices provide a critical safety net against data loss, support business continuity, and are a key component of compliance with data protection regulations. By adhering to best practices such as the 3-2-1 rule, regular testing, encryption, automation, and secure storage, organizations can significantly enhance their resilience against a wide range of data loss scenarios.

Security Awareness Training

Users are often the weakest link in cybersecurity. Regular security awareness training can equip users with the knowledge to recognize and avoid potential threats, such as phishing emails, malicious downloads, and social engineering tactics. Training should be ongoing to address emerging threats and reinforce security practices (Hadnagy, 2018).

Security Awareness Training is a fundamental component of an organization's defense strategy, pivotal in bolstering the human element of cybersecurity. It encompasses educating employees about the array of cyber threats they face—phishing, social engineering tactics, malware, and safe internet practices—arming them with the knowledge to recognize and mitigate these threats. This training is not just a one-time event but an ongoing process to adapt to the evolving cyber threat landscape.

The Critical Role of Security Awareness Training

Mitigating Human Error: Human error is cited as a leading cause of security breaches. Regular training can significantly reduce incidents attributable to mistakes or lack of knowledge, such as falling for phishing scams or mishandling sensitive information (Hadnagy, 2018).

Creating a Culture of Security: Beyond imparting knowledge, effective training fosters a culture of security within the organization, where cybersecurity is viewed as a shared responsibility. This cultural shift can lead to proactive behaviors, such as reporting suspicious activities or suggesting improvements to security protocols.

Adapting to Changing Threats: The cyber threat landscape is constantly evolving, with attackers continually devising new tactics. Ongoing security awareness training ensures that employees stay informed about the latest threats and the corresponding preventive measures.

Best Practices in Security Awareness Training

Engaging and Relevant Content: Training content should be engaging and directly relevant to the employees' roles and responsibilities. Utilizing interactive modules, gamification, and real-life examples can enhance engagement and retention of information.

Regular Updates and Refreshers: Cybersecurity threats evolve rapidly, necessitating regular updates to the training content. Additionally, periodic refresher courses can help keep security top of mind for employees.

Simulated Phishing Exercises: Simulating phishing attacks can provide employees with practical experience in identifying suspicious emails. These exercises can be followed by feedback sessions to discuss the indicators of phishing and the correct responses to potential threats.

Measuring Effectiveness: Assessing the effectiveness of training programs is crucial. This can be achieved through pre- and post-training assessments, monitoring phishing simulation response rates, and tracking incident reporting rates. Feedback from employees can also guide improvements to the training program.

Executive Buy-in and Participation: Leadership participation in security training underscores its importance to the organization. When executives actively engage in training and adhere to security protocols, it sets a powerful example for the entire organization.

Incorporating Security Awareness Into Onboarding: Integrating cybersecurity training into the onboarding process ensures that new employees understand their role in maintaining organizational security from day one.

Security Awareness Training is a critical defensive measure that addresses the human aspect of cybersecurity. By equipping employees with the knowledge and skills to recognize and respond to cyber threats, organizations can significantly reduce their vulnerability to attacks. This training should be engaging, regularly updated, and embedded into the organization's culture, emphasizing security as everyone's responsibility. Through continuous education and fostering a security-conscious culture, organizations can create a robust human firewall as a first line of defense against cyber threats.

Use of Antivirus and Anti-Malware Solutions

Deploying antivirus and anti-malware solutions across all devices and keeping these solutions updated can detect and remove malicious software. Real-time scanning and heuristic analysis can provide proactive protection against known and emerging malware threats.

Least Privilege Access

Applying the principle of least privilege, where users are granted the minimum level of access necessary for their job functions, can limit the potential damage from insider threats or compromised accounts. Access rights should be regularly reviewed and adjusted based on role changes within the organization (Post & Kagan, 2015).

Effective digital hygiene practices are essential for protecting against cyber threats and ensuring the integrity and availability of information systems. By implementing a comprehensive set of practices—ranging from regular updates and strong authentication measures to secure network practices and user education—organizations can establish a robust defense against a wide spectrum of cyber risks.

Introduction To Ethical Hacking

Introduction to Ethical Hacking constitutes a pivotal component in the arsenal of defense strategies within the realm of cybersecurity. Ethical hacking, also known as penetration testing or white-hat hacking, involves the deliberate probing of a system's or network's defenses, using the same tools and techniques as a malicious hacker, but in a controlled and lawful manner. The goal is to identify and rectify vulnerabilities before they can be exploited by adversaries. This proactive approach to security provides invaluable insights into an organization's cybersecurity posture, enabling the reinforcement of defenses against actual cyber threats.

The Fundamentals of Ethical Hacking

Scope and Permission:

Central to ethical hacking is the explicit authorization to probe and test the targeted systems. This sets ethical hackers apart from malicious actors. Organizations commissioning penetration tests will typically define the scope and boundaries of the engagement, ensuring that the testing is conducted lawfully and without unintended harm to the systems (ENISA, 2018).

The fundamentals of ethical hacking hinge critically on the principles of scope and permission. These concepts delineate ethical hacking (or penetration testing) from unauthorized and potentially malicious activities. By strictly defining what areas of a network, system, or application can be tested and ensuring explicit authorization is obtained before testing begins, ethical hackers can assess the security of digital assets without overstepping legal or ethical boundaries.

Scope and Permission in Ethical Hacking

Defining the Scope: The scope of an ethical hacking engagement specifies which systems, networks, and applications can be tested, along with the methods and techniques that may be employed. A well-defined scope ensures that the testing is targeted, efficient, and within the bounds of agreed-upon limitations. This may include specifying particular IP ranges, applications, or even times of day when testing can occur to minimize potential disruptions (Weidman, 2014).

Obtaining Permission: Permission, typically granted through a formal contract or engagement letter, is a non-negotiable prerequisite for ethical hacking. This authorization comes directly from the organization's top management or the legal owner of the assets to be tested. Permission not only protects the ethical hacker legally but also reinforces the legitimacy and ethical nature of the penetration test. This formal agreement should detail the scope of the engagement, methodologies to be used, and any specific limitations or requirements stipulated by the client or asset owner.

Importance of Scope and Permission

Legal and Ethical Considerations: Operating without explicit permission or exceeding the defined scope can lead to legal consequences and ethical violations, potentially harming the ethical hacker's reputation and career. It is crucial to ensure that all activities are authorized and documented to avoid any misunderstanding or implications of malicious intent.

Protecting Client Relationships: Clear agreements regarding scope and permission help set client expectations and foster trust. By adhering to the agreed parameters, ethical hackers demonstrate professionalism and respect for the client's operational requirements and risk tolerance.

Focus and Efficiency: A clearly defined scope allows ethical hackers to concentrate their efforts on the most critical assets, making the best use of their skills and time. This targeted approach leads to more meaningful findings and actionable insights, contributing significantly to improving the organization's security posture.

Best Practices in Establishing Scope and Permission

Comprehensive Engagement Agreements: Draft detailed engagement agreements that clearly outline the scope, objectives, methodologies, and any specific exclusions or constraints. This ensures both parties have a mutual understanding of the engagement's parameters.

Regular Communication: Maintain open lines of communication with the client throughout the testing process. This allows for the adjustment of scope as necessary and ensures that any sensitive issues are promptly addressed.

Documentation and Authorization: Keep thorough documentation of all permissions granted and any communications regarding the scope of the project. This serves as a record of authorization and can be invaluable in clarifying the intent and legitimacy of the testing activities.

Ethical Considerations: Ethical hackers should always consider the potential impact of their actions on the client's operations and reputation. Testing should be conducted responsibly, with a focus on minimizing any adverse effects while still thoroughly assessing security vulnerabilities.

Scope and permission are foundational elements of ethical hacking, ensuring that security assessments are conducted legally, ethically, and effectively. By meticulously defining the scope and obtaining explicit permission, ethical hackers can perform their duties with clarity and integrity, delivering valuable insights that enhance an organization's cybersecurity defenses.

Testing Methodologies:

Ethical hackers employ a systematic approach, often aligning with established frameworks such as the Open Web Application Security Project (OWASP) for web applications or the Penetration Testing Execution Standard (PTES) for broader security assessments. These methodologies encompass reconnaissance, vulnerability assessment, exploitation, post-exploitation, and reporting phases.

Tools and Techniques:

Ethical hackers utilize a variety of tools and techniques to uncover vulnerabilities. These may include automated vulnerability scanners, manual testing tools, custom scripts, and social engineering tactics. Familiarity with the latest hacking tools and techniques is essential for effective penetration testing.

Testing methodologies in ethical hacking are systematic approaches that guide penetration testers (ethical hackers) through a series of steps to identify vulnerabilities, assess the security posture, and recommend improvements within an organization's digital infrastructure. These methodologies ensure that the testing is comprehensive, structured, and reproducible, providing valuable insights into an organization's cybersecurity strengths and weaknesses. Adhering to established methodologies allows ethical hackers to conduct assessments in a manner that is both thorough and consistent with industry best practices.

Core Phases of Testing Methodologies

Reconnaissance: The initial phase involves gathering information about the target system or network. This can include public information from websites, social media, and domain registration databases, as well as more technical data obtained through network scanning and enumeration. The goal is to map the attack surface and identify potential entry points (Kim, 2014).

Scanning and Enumeration: Using tools like port scanners, vulnerability scanners, and network mappers, ethical hackers identify open ports, running services, and specific vulnerabilities on targeted systems. This phase provides a more detailed view of the target's network and systems, allowing for the identification of exploitable weaknesses.

Gaining Access: In this phase, ethical hackers attempt to exploit identified vulnerabilities to gain unauthorized access to systems or data. This might involve bypassing authentication mechanisms, exploiting software vulnerabilities, or leveraging misconfigurations. The methods used are closely controlled and documented to minimize any potential impact on the target system.

Maintaining Access: Once access is gained, ethical hackers may attempt to maintain that access by deploying tools or methods that allow for persistent, undetected entry into the system. This simulates an attacker's efforts to maintain control over a compromised system for future exploitation or further attack stages.

Analysis and Reporting: The final phase involves analyzing the data gathered during the test, documenting the vulnerabilities discovered, the methods used to exploit them, and the potential impact on the organization. Ethical hackers then provide detailed reports and recommendations for remediation to improve the organization's security posture.

Popular Testing Methodologies

Open Web Application Security Project (OWASP): OWASP provides methodologies, documentation, tools, and forums for web application security. Its OWASP Top Ten is a widely recognized list of the most critical web application security risks (OWASP, 2021).

Penetration Testing Execution Standard (PTES): PTES offers a comprehensive penetration testing standard designed to provide detailed guidance throughout the testing process, from pre-engagement interactions to post-engagement cleanup.

Information Systems Security Assessment Framework (IS-SAF): The ISSAF seeks to integrate best practices and methodologies for performing thorough information systems security assessments, covering technical and non-technical aspects of security.

Best Practices in Applying Testing Methodologies

Tailoring Methodologies to the Target Environment: While methodologies provide a general framework, ethical hackers should adapt these guidelines to fit the specific context and requirements of the target organization, ensuring that the testing is relevant and effective.

Legal and Ethical Compliance: All testing activities should be conducted within the bounds of legal and ethical guidelines, with explicit permission from authorized parties and a clear understanding of the agreed-upon scope.

Continuous Skill Development: Ethical hackers must continuously update their skills and knowledge to keep pace with emerging threats and evolving technologies. Engaging with the cybersecurity community through forums, conferences, and training courses can provide valuable insights and new techniques.

Testing methodologies are indispensable in the practice of ethical hacking, providing structured approaches for uncovering vulnerabilities and enhancing an organization's cybersecurity measures. By meticulously following these methodologies, ethical hackers can deliver assessments that are not only comprehensive but also aligned with industry standards and best practices, ultimately contributing to a more secure digital environment.

Best Practices in Implementing Ethical Hacking

Regular and Comprehensive Testing:

Ethical hacking should not be a one-time activity but a regular part of an organization's security maintenance cycle. Regular testing ensures that newly introduced vulnerabilities, whether through system updates, new deployments, or changes in infrastructure, are identified and addressed promptly.

Diverse Skill Sets:

Effective penetration testing teams often comprise individuals with diverse backgrounds and expertise, including network security, application development, system administration, and even social engineering. This diversity ensures a comprehensive assessment of the organization's security posture from multiple angles.

Clear Reporting and Follow-Up:

The value of ethical hacking is realized through detailed reporting and actionable insights. Reports should clearly outline identified vulnerabilities, their potential impact, and recommended remediations. Equally important is the follow-up process to address these vulnerabilities and verify that they have been effectively mitigated.

Ethical Considerations:

Ethical hackers must adhere to a code of ethics, respecting the confidentiality and integrity of the client's data and systems. This includes responsibly disclosing vulnerabilities and ensuring that testing activities do not adversely affect system performance or availability.

Training and Certification:

Ongoing training and certification for ethical hackers are crucial, given the rapidly evolving nature of cybersecurity threats. Certifications such as the Certified Ethical Hacker (CEH) provide a benchmark for the skills and knowledge expected of professional penetration testers.

Ethical hacking plays a crucial role in identifying and mitigating vulnerabilities within an organization's digital infrastructure, offering a proactive approach to enhancing cybersecurity defenses. By adhering to best practices, including obtaining proper authorization, employing systematic testing methodologies, and maintaining ethical standards, ethical hacking can significantly bolster an organization's resilience against cyber threats. Regular penetration testing, conducted by skilled and diverse teams, ensures that security measures remain effective in the face of an ever-changing threat landscape, safeguarding critical assets and data

Conclusion

A robust cybersecurity posture requires a multifaceted approach, integrating various defense strategies to protect against and respond to cyber threats. By adopting a Defense-in-Depth strategy, implementing a Zero Trust model, ensuring regular software updates, conducting security awareness training, and having a solid incident response plan, organizations can significantly enhance their resilience against cyber-attacks.

Chapter 8: Incident Response and Recovery

Part IV: Real-world Applications

Incident Response and Recovery are critical components of an organization's cybersecurity strategy, designed to manage and mitigate the impact of security breaches or cyberattacks. An effective Incident Response (IR) plan enables an organization to quickly detect incidents, minimize losses, mitigate exploited vulnerabilities, restore services and processes, and reduce the risk of future incidents. Recovery processes are integral to restoring normal operations and rebuilding trust among stakeholders following a cybersecurity incident.

Incident Response: Key Phases

The Incident Response process typically follows a structured approach outlined in several key phases:

<u>Preparation</u>:

This foundational phase involves establishing an incident response team, developing IR policies and plans, setting communication protocols, and conducting regular training and simulation exercises. The goal is to ensure that the organization is ready to respond swiftly and effectively to any security incident (NIST, 2018).

The Preparation phase is the cornerstone of an effective Incident Response (IR) process, setting the groundwork for an organization's ability to respond swiftly and effectively to cybersecurity incidents. This phase involves a comprehensive set of activities aimed at ensuring that when an incident occurs, the organization is well-equipped to manage and mitigate its impact efficiently. The emphasis on preparation underscores the adage that the success of an incident response is more about the groundwork laid before an incident occurs than about the actions taken after.

Components of the Preparation Phase

Developing an Incident Response Plan: The creation of a detailed IR plan is critical. This document should outline the procedures for responding to various types of cybersecurity incidents, define roles and responsibilities within the incident response team, and specify communication protocols, both internal and external. The plan should be tailored to the organization's specific needs and operational environment (Cichonski et al., 2012).

Forming an Incident Response Team: An effective IR team is composed of members with diverse skills, including IT professionals, security analysts, legal advisors, and communication specialists. The team should have a clear understanding of their roles and responsibilities during an incident, ensuring a coordinated and efficient response.

Tools and Resources: Equipping the IR team with the necessary tools and resources is essential for effective incident management. This includes access to intrusion detection systems, forensic tools, and communication platforms. Additionally, ensuring that these tools are regularly updated and tested is crucial for maintaining their effectiveness.

Training and Awareness: Regular training exercises and simulations are vital components of preparation. These activities help familiarize the IR team and the broader organization with the IR plan, refine response procedures, and improve readiness to handle real incidents. Training should also extend to all employees, promoting cybersecurity awareness and guiding them on how to recognize and report potential security incidents.

Establishing Communication Channels: Effective communication is pivotal during incident response. Preparing communication templates, establishing protocols for internal and external communications, and identifying key contacts within and outside the organization can streamline information sharing during an incident.

Legal and Regulatory Compliance: Understanding the legal and regulatory framework relevant to incident response is a critical part of preparation. This includes knowledge of requirements for reporting incidents to authorities, data protection laws, and industry-specific regulations. Ensuring compliance can mitigate legal risks and penalties associated with cybersecurity incidents.

Importance of the Preparation Phase

The Preparation phase is foundational to the IR process, directly influencing the effectiveness and efficiency of an organization's response to cybersecurity incidents. Well-prepared organizations can minimize the impact of incidents, preserve customer trust and reputation, and ensure business continuity. Conversely, a lack of preparation can exacerbate the damage caused by incidents, leading to prolonged recovery times, increased costs, and legal consequences.

Investing time and resources in the Preparation phase of incident response is indispensable for any organization seeking to safeguard its digital assets against cyber threats. Through meticulous planning, team formation, resource allocation, training, and compliance efforts, organizations can establish a robust foundation for effective incident management and recovery, positioning themselves to navigate the challenges of cybersecurity incidents with resilience and agility.

Detection and Analysis:

Involves monitoring systems and networks for signs of a security incident, accurately identifying incidents, and assessing their scope and impact. Effective detection relies on a combination of technology solutions, such as intrusion detection systems, and human expertise to analyze and interpret the signs of potential incidents.

The Detection and Analysis phase in Incident Response (IR) is pivotal, serving as the bridge between preparation and the active management of a cybersecurity incident. This phase focuses on the initial identification of a potential security incident, its validation, and the subsequent analysis to understand its nature, scope, and potential impact. Efficient detection and analysis are critical for determining the severity of the incident and guiding the appropriate response measures.

Key Activities in Detection and Analysis

Initial Detection: The early detection of potential security incidents often relies on a combination of automated systems and human oversight. Intrusion Detection Systems (IDS), Security Information and Event Management (SIEM) solutions, antivirus software, and network monitoring tools play a crucial role in identifying unusual activities that may indicate a security threat (Kent & Souppaya, 2006).

Incident Validation: Once a potential incident is detected, it is essential to validate whether it is a false positive or a genuine security incident. This involves gathering additional information, correlating events across different systems, and using manual checks to verify the nature of the detected activity.

Incident Classification and Prioritization: After validation, incidents must be classified based on their type (e.g., malware infection, unauthorized access, data breach) and prioritized based on their impact on the organization. This prioritization helps in allocating resources effectively to address the most critical incidents first.

Impact Analysis: Conducting an impact analysis involves assessing the extent of the damage or disruption caused by the incident. This includes identifying affected systems, data, and services, as well as evaluating the potential business and operational impacts.

Forensic Analysis: In more complex incidents, forensic analysis may be necessary to understand how the breach occurred, the techniques used by the attackers, and any data that was compromised. This analysis can provide valuable insights for eradicating the threat and preventing future incidents.

Challenges in Detection and Analysis

Evolving Threat Landscape: The constant evolution of cyber threats can make detection challenging, as new types of attacks may not be immediately recognized by existing detection systems.

Volume of Alerts: Organizations often face a high volume of alerts, many of which are false positives. Sifting through these alerts to identify genuine incidents requires significant resources and can lead to alert fatigue among security personnel.

Skillset and Knowledge: Effective analysis of incidents requires a skilled workforce with knowledge of current cyber threats, forensic analysis techniques, and the organization's IT environment.

Best Practices in Detection and Analysis

Comprehensive Monitoring: Implementing comprehensive monitoring across all systems and networks can enhance the visibility of potential security incidents, making early detection more feasible.

Integration and Correlation: Integrating different security tools and systems to correlate data and alerts can improve the accuracy of incident detection and reduce false positives.

Continuous Improvement: Regularly updating detection tools and techniques to adapt to new threats and incorporating lessons learned from past incidents can improve detection capabilities over time.

Training and Development: Investing in training and professional development for IR teams can enhance their ability to detect and analyze incidents effectively, keeping pace with the evolving threat landscape.

The Detection and Analysis phase is critical for the timely and effective management of cybersecurity incidents. By employing a combination of advanced detection tools, skilled personnel, and best practices for incident analysis, organizations can improve their resilience against cyber threats, minimize the impact of incidents, and strengthen their overall security posture.

<u>Containment, Eradication, and Recovery:</u>

Once an incident is detected, the focus shifts to containing its impact, eradicating the threat, and initiating recovery efforts. Containment strategies aim to limit the spread of the incident and prevent further damage. Eradication involves removing the threat from the affected systems, while recovery focuses on restoring systems and data to normal operations, ensuring that all systems are cleared of threats before being brought back online.

The phases of Containment, Eradication, and Recovery are crucial in the Incident Response (IR) process, marking the transition from understanding the incident to taking action to mitigate its impact and restore normal operations. These stages are essential for minimizing damage, preventing the spread of the incident, and ensuring that the organization can recover swiftly and securely.

Containment

Objective: The primary goal of the Containment phase is to limit the scope and magnitude of the incident, preventing further damage to the organization. Containment strategies must be executed quickly and effectively to isolate affected systems and prevent the spread of malicious activity.

Strategies:

- **Short-Term Containment**: Involves immediate actions to limit the impact of the incident, such as disconnecting affected systems from the network or blocking malicious network traffic.
- **Long-Term Containment**: Entails more sustainable solutions to secure the environment as the organization moves towards eradication and recovery, such as implementing changes to firewall rules or enhancing system configurations.

Best Practices:

- **Rapid Execution**: Time is of the essence in the Containment phase. Organizations must act swiftly to implement containment measures and minimize damage.
- **Communication**: Effective communication within the incident response team and with other stakeholders is critical to coordinate containment efforts.

Eradication

Objective: Once an incident is contained, the focus shifts to Eradicating the root cause of the incident and any associated threats from the organization's systems. This step involves removing malware, closing vulnerabilities, and taking steps to prevent similar incidents in the future.

Strategies:

- **Removal of Malware and Artifacts**: Involves using antivirus software and other tools to remove malware and any related artifacts from affected systems.
- **System Hardening**: Enhancing the security posture of affected systems by applying patches, changing passwords, and implementing additional security controls to address vulnerabilities.

Best Practices:

- **Thoroughness**: Eradication must be thorough to prevent the recurrence of the incident. This often involves a detailed investigation to understand the full scope of the incident.
- **Documentation**: Maintaining detailed records of the eradication process is crucial for post-incident analysis and compliance purposes.

Recovery

Objective: The Recovery phase aims to restore affected systems and services to normal operations while ensuring they are no longer vulnerable to the same or similar incidents. This phase also involves monitoring for signs of resurgence of the incident.

Strategies:

- **Restoration of Systems**: Gradually restoring systems, services, and data from backups after ensuring they are not compromised.
- **Monitoring for Anomalies**: Continuous monitoring of the restored systems for any signs of malicious activity to ensure that the threat has been fully eradicated.

Best Practices:

- **Validation Before Restoration**: Before restoring data or systems, validate backups to ensure they are free of malware and that systems are fully secured.
- **Phased Restoration**: Adopt a phased approach to restoration, prioritizing critical systems and monitoring for stability and security before proceeding to less critical systems.

Post-Incident Activity

The culmination of the Containment, Eradication, and Recovery phases naturally leads to post-incident activities, where lessons are learned, and measures are implemented to strengthen the organization's defenses against future incidents.

The Containment, Eradication, and Recovery phases are vital for minimizing the impact of cybersecurity incidents and restoring normal operations. By following best practices and employing effective strategies across these phases, organizations can ensure a resilient response to incidents, safeguarding their assets and reputation.

Post-Incident Activity:

After an incident has been resolved, conducting a post-incident review is essential to document the incident's details, evaluate the effectiveness of the response, and identify lessons learned. This phase often results in updates to policies, procedures, and defenses to prevent future incidents.

The Post-Incident Activity phase is an essential component of the Incident Response (IR) process, offering an opportunity for organizations to reflect on the incident, assess the effectiveness of their response, and implement improvements to prevent future breaches. This phase ensures that lessons are learned from each incident, thereby continuously enhancing the organization's cybersecurity posture.

Key Activities in Post-Incident Activity

Incident Documentation: Comprehensive documentation of the incident and the response actions is crucial. This includes recording the nature of the incident, how it was detected, the steps taken during containment, eradication, and recovery, and the timeline of events. This documentation serves as a critical resource for post-incident analysis and for compliance and reporting requirements.

Incident Analysis and Lessons Learned: Analyzing the incident to identify what went well and what could be improved is vital. This analysis should cover the effectiveness of the detection mechanisms, the response actions, the tools used, and the coordination among the response team and other stakeholders. Lessons learned from this analysis should be documented and used to update policies, procedures, and response plans.

Updating Incident Response Plan: Based on the lessons learned and the insights gained from the incident analysis, the organization's IR plan should be reviewed and updated accordingly. This may involve adjusting roles and responsibilities, updating communication protocols, and refining response strategies to address the identified gaps.

Strengthening Defenses: The post-incident phase is also an opportunity to strengthen the organization's defenses based on the vulnerabilities exploited by the attackers. This could involve deploying new security technologies, implementing additional security controls, or enhancing existing ones.

Training and Awareness Programs: Reinforcing training and awareness programs for all employees, including the incident response team, is essential. Training programs should be updated to include new threats, tactics, and lessons learned from recent incidents to ensure that staff are aware of current risks and response procedures.

Regulatory Compliance and Reporting: Many industries and jurisdictions require organizations to report certain types of incidents to regulatory bodies or affected parties. The post-incident phase should include a review of compliance requirements to ensure that all necessary reporting has been completed and that the organization's response aligns with regulatory expectations.

Recovery and Business Continuity Planning: Reviewing and updating the organization's recovery and business continuity plans to incorporate lessons learned from the incident can help improve resilience and reduce the impact of future incidents.

Best Practices in Post-Incident Activity

Timely and Thorough Review: Conducting the post-incident review promptly after the incident ensures that details are accurately remembered and that improvements can be quickly implemented.

Inclusivity in the Review Process: Involving a broad range of stakeholders in the post-incident review, including IT staff, security personnel, management, and affected business units, can provide diverse perspectives and comprehensive insights.

Continuous Improvement: Viewing the post-incident activity as an integral part of a continuous improvement process for cybersecurity practices encourages a proactive and adaptive security posture.

The Post-Incident Activity phase is pivotal in closing the loop on the Incident Response process, ensuring that each incident serves as a learning opportunity to fortify the organization against future threats. By meticulously documenting the incident, analyzing the response, updating plans and procedures, and enhancing defenses, organizations can turn the challenge of a cybersecurity incident into a stepping stone for strengthening their overall security posture.

Recovery: Strategies and Considerations

Disaster Recovery Planning:

Part of broader business continuity planning, disaster recovery focuses on restoring IT operations following an incident. This includes restoring data from backups, repairing or replacing damaged hardware, and ensuring that critical applications are available to users.

Disaster Recovery Planning is a crucial aspect of the Recovery phase in Incident Response and Recovery, focusing on restoring IT operations and systems after a cybersecurity incident to ensure business continuity. Effective disaster recovery planning is not just about reacting to incidents but about proactively preparing for any eventuality that could disrupt operations, including cyberattacks, natural disasters, or system failures.

Strategies in Disaster Recovery Planning

Risk Assessment and Business Impact Analysis (BIA): Conducting a risk assessment and BIA is foundational to disaster recovery planning. These analyses help identify critical systems and assets, assess the potential impact of different types of disasters, and prioritize recovery efforts based on the importance to the business operations (Wallace & Webber, 2017).

Identification of Recovery Objectives: Defining Recovery Point Objectives (RPOs) and Recovery Time Objectives (RTOs) is essential for setting the goals of the disaster recovery plan. RPOs dictate the maximum acceptable amount of data loss measured in time, while RTOs specify the maximum acceptable downtime.

Data Backup Strategies: Implementing robust data backup strategies, including regular backups, off-site storage, and using a combination of full and incremental backups, ensures that data can be restored quickly and efficiently after an incident. The 3-2-1 backup rule—keeping at least three copies of data, on two different media, with one copy off-site—is a widely recommended practice.

Infrastructure Redundancy: Building redundancy into the IT infrastructure, such as having failover systems, mirrored sites, or cloud-based solutions, can provide additional layers of protection, enabling quicker recovery from incidents.

Communication Plan: A well-defined communication plan that outlines how to notify employees, stakeholders, and customers in the event of a disaster is critical. Clear, timely communication can mitigate the impact on reputation and customer trust.

Disaster Recovery Team: Establishing a dedicated disaster recovery team with clearly defined roles and responsibilities ensures that there is a coordinated effort to restore operations following an incident. This team should work closely with the incident response team to ensure a cohesive approach to managing and recovering from incidents.

Considerations in Disaster Recovery Planning

Regular Testing and Drills: Regular testing of the disaster recovery plan through drills and simulations is critical to ensure that the plan is effective and that the disaster recovery team is prepared to execute it under stress.

Plan Maintenance and Updates: The disaster recovery plan should be a living document, regularly reviewed and updated to reflect changes in the business environment, IT infrastructure, and emerging threats.

Vendor and Stakeholder Coordination: Coordination with vendors, service providers, and other external stakeholders is essential for ensuring that all aspects of the disaster recovery plan are feasible and that external dependencies are considered.

Compliance and Legal Requirements: Ensuring that the disaster recovery plan complies with legal, regulatory, and industry-specific requirements is crucial to avoid potential legal issues and fines.

Integration with Business Continuity: The disaster recovery plan should be integrated with the broader business continuity plan, ensuring that the organization can not only restore IT operations but also maintain critical business functions during and after a disaster.

Disaster Recovery Planning is a vital component of the Recovery phase in Incident Response, focusing on the restoration of IT systems and operations to minimize downtime and data loss. Through thorough planning, regular testing, and continuous improvement, organizations can enhance their resilience against cyber and physical disasters, ensuring that they can quickly recover and maintain business continuity in the face of adversity.

Communication:

Effective communication is vital throughout the incident response and recovery process. This includes internal communication within the response team and external communication with stakeholders, customers, and possibly the public. Transparency and timeliness can help manage expectations and mitigate reputational damage.

Communication during the Recovery phase of Incident Response and Recovery is pivotal for managing the aftermath of a cybersecurity incident effectively. Transparent, timely, and accurate communication not only aids in the swift recovery of operations but also plays a crucial role in maintaining stakeholder trust, managing public relations, and fulfilling legal and regulatory obligations. This phase necessitates a strategic approach to communication, ensuring that all stakeholders are appropriately informed about the incident's impact, recovery efforts, and steps taken to prevent future occurrences.

Key Strategies in Communication

Pre-Defined Communication Plan: Having a pre-defined communication plan is crucial. This plan should outline who needs to be communicated with (internal teams, partners, regulators, customers), what information should be communicated, and the channels to be used. The plan should also identify spokespersons authorized to speak on behalf of the organization (Coombs, 2014).

Consistency and Accuracy: Messages should be consistent across all channels and stakeholders to avoid confusion and misinformation. Providing accurate and verified information is critical to maintaining credibility and trust. If certain details are unknown or under investigation, this should be communicated transparently.

Timeliness: Rapid communication is essential, particularly in the early stages of incident discovery and response. Early communication can help manage the narrative and reduce speculation and rumors.

Sensitivity and Empathy: Communications should be crafted with sensitivity to the concerns and anxieties of affected parties. Demonstrating empathy and a commitment to resolving the issue can help preserve relationships and trust.

Legal and Regulatory Compliance: Organizations must be aware of and comply with legal and regulatory requirements related to incident reporting. This includes mandatory reporting to regulatory bodies and notifications to affected individuals, as stipulated by laws such as the General Data Protection Regulation (GDPR) in Europe.

Considerations in Communication

Audience Segmentation: Tailoring the message to different audience segments (e.g., employees, customers, investors) ensures that the information is relevant and understandable to each group. Internal communication might focus on action items and recovery processes, while customer communication might emphasize the impact on services and data protection measures.

Use of Multiple Channels: Utilizing multiple communication channels (e.g., email, press releases, social media, dedicated incident response websites) ensures that the message reaches all stakeholders effectively. The choice of channels should consider the audience's preferences and the nature of the information being communicated.

Monitoring and Feedback: Actively monitoring the public and internal response to communications provides valuable feedback that can guide future messages and actions. This includes monitoring social media, news outlets, and internal communication channels for questions, concerns, and sentiments related to the incident.

Post-Recovery Communication: Communication should not end once operations are restored. Follow-up communication that outlines the lessons learned, improvements made, and steps taken to prevent future incidents is crucial for rebuilding and maintaining trust.

Effective communication during the Recovery phase is vital for managing the aftermath of a cybersecurity incident. A well-executed communication strategy helps mitigate the impact on the organization's reputation, maintains stakeholder trust, and ensures compliance with legal and regulatory obligations. By prioritizing transparency, accuracy, timeliness, and empathy, organizations can navigate the challenges posed by cybersecurity incidents and emerge with their stakeholder relationships intact.

Regulatory Compliance and Legal Issues:

Organizations must consider legal and regulatory requirements related to incident reporting and data breaches. Compliance with laws such as GDPR, HIPAA, or other relevant regulations is crucial to avoid potential fines and legal challenges.

The Recovery phase in Incident Response and Recovery, while primarily focused on restoring operations and systems to normalcy, also necessitates a rigorous examination of regulatory compliance and legal issues arising from the incident. Cybersecurity incidents can have significant legal and regulatory ramifications, including obligations under data protection laws, requirements for breach notification, and potential legal liabilities. Navigating these complexities is crucial for organizations to ensure they meet their legal obligations and protect themselves from further legal risk.

Regulatory Compliance

Data Breach Notification Laws: Many jurisdictions have enacted data breach notification laws that require organizations to notify regulatory bodies and affected individuals about security breaches within a specified timeframe. For example, the General Data Protection Regulation (GDPR) in the European Union mandates notification to the relevant supervisory authority within 72 hours of becoming aware of the data breach, if it poses a risk to individuals' rights and freedoms (European Parliament and Council of the European Union, 2016).

Sector-Specific Regulations: Certain industries may be subject to additional regulatory requirements related to cybersecurity and incident response. For instance, the financial sector and healthcare sector in various countries operate under strict regulatory frameworks that dictate specific cybersecurity practices and incident reporting obligations.

Legal Issues

Liability for Data Breaches: Organizations may face legal liability if a breach occurs due to negligence or failure to adhere to industry-standard cybersecurity practices. Legal actions can arise from affected individuals, business partners, or regulatory bodies.

Contractual Obligations: Organizations must also consider their contractual obligations to business partners and customers. Contracts may specify security standards, incident response requirements, and notification procedures that must be followed in the event of a security incident.

Preservation of Evidence: In the aftermath of a cybersecurity incident, preserving evidence is critical for potential legal proceedings or regulatory investigations. Organizations must ensure that their recovery actions do not compromise the integrity of evidence related to the incident.

Best Practices in Addressing Regulatory Compliance and Legal Issues

Early Engagement of Legal Counsel: Involving legal counsel early in the incident response process can help navigate the complex landscape of legal obligations and protect the organization's interests.

Comprehensive Documentation: Maintaining detailed documentation of the incident response process, decisions made, and actions taken is essential for demonstrating compliance with regulatory requirements and legal obligations.

Communication with Regulators: Proactive and transparent communication with regulatory bodies can help manage regulatory scrutiny and demonstrate the organization's commitment to compliance.

Review and Update Policies: Post-incident reviews should include an assessment of compliance with legal and regulatory obligations. Policies and procedures should be updated based on lessons learned to improve compliance in future incidents.

The Recovery phase's handling of regulatory compliance and legal issues is a critical component of effective incident response. By understanding and adhering to legal and regulatory requirements, preserving evidence, and engaging with legal counsel and regulators proactively, organizations can mitigate legal risks and demonstrate their commitment to responsible cybersecurity practices.

Best Practices in Incident Response and Recovery

Regular Training and Simulations: Conducting regular training sessions and simulated incident response exercises helps prepare the IR team and the broader organization for potential incidents, ensuring that roles and procedures are well-understood.

Continuous Improvement: Incident response and recovery processes should be continuously reviewed and improved based on lessons learned from past incidents and emerging threats. This includes updating IR plans, refining detection mechanisms, and enhancing recovery strategies.

Collaboration with External Partners: Collaborating with external cybersecurity experts, law enforcement, and industry groups can provide additional resources and intelligence, enhancing an organization's ability to respond to and recover from incidents.

Incident Response and Recovery are essential for managing and mitigating the effects of cyberattacks and security breaches. By establishing comprehensive IR plans, conducting regular training, and implementing effective recovery strategies, organizations can reduce the impact of incidents, restore normal operations more quickly, and strengthen their overall cybersecurity posture.

Steps In an Effective Incident Response Plan

An effective Incident Response Plan (IRP) is paramount for organizations to prepare for, respond to, and recover from cybersecurity incidents. The plan outlines the processes and procedures an organization follows when confronted with a cyber incident, ensuring a swift, organized, and effective response. The recovery steps in an IRP are designed to minimize impact, restore normal operations, and prevent future incidents. These steps are critical to mitigating damage, maintaining trust with stakeholders, and ensuring business continuity.

Steps in an Effective Incident Response Plan for Recovery

1. **Assessment and Damage Control**: As soon as an incident is contained and eradicated, an immediate assessment is crucial to understand the full extent of the impact on systems, data, and operations. This step involves identifying which systems were compromised, the type of data accessed or stolen, and the potential business impact.

2. **Prioritization of System Restoration**: Based on the assessment, organizations should prioritize the restoration of affected systems and services. Priority is given to critical systems that are essential for business operations, with a focus on restoring them to full functionality as quickly and securely as possible.

3. **Repair and Restoration**: This involves repairing damaged systems, which may include reconfiguring or reinstalling software, applying patches to fix vulnerabilities, and restoring data from backups. It's crucial that restored systems are thoroughly tested to ensure they are free of any vulnerabilities or remnants of the incident before being brought back online.

4. **Communication**: Effective communication throughout the recovery process is essential. This includes internal communication to keep staff informed about the status of recovery efforts and external communication to stakeholders, customers, and, if necessary, the public. Transparency about the incident and the steps being taken to resolve it can help maintain trust and confidence.

5. **Review and Analysis of the Incident**: Once recovery is underway or completed, conducting a detailed review and analysis of the incident is essential. This includes analyzing how the incident occurred, the effectiveness of the response, and any lessons learned. The goal is to identify any weaknesses in systems,

policies, or procedures that were exploited and to develop recommendations for strengthening them.

6. **Implementation of Improvements**: Based on the review and analysis, organizations should implement improvements to their cybersecurity defenses, IRP, and other relevant policies and procedures. This may involve enhancing security measures, updating incident response strategies, and conducting additional training for staff.

7. **Continuous Monitoring**: Post-recovery, continuous monitoring of systems and networks is critical to detect any signs of resurgence or new threats. Ongoing vigilance helps ensure that the organization remains protected against future incidents.

8. **Legal and Regulatory Compliance**: Throughout the recovery process, organizations must ensure compliance with relevant legal and regulatory requirements, including data breach notification laws. Working closely with legal counsel can help navigate these complexities and fulfill any obligations.

9. **Post-Incident Reporting**: Preparing a comprehensive post-incident report for internal use and, if required, for regulatory bodies, is a crucial final step. The report should document the incident, the response actions taken, the impact, and the improvements implemented to prevent future incidents.

Disaster Recovery:

Disaster Recovery (DR) and Business Continuity Planning (BCP) are integral components of an organization's broader strategy to prepare for, respond to, and recover from disruptive incidents, including cyberattacks, natural disasters, and other emergencies. While closely related, DR focuses on the restoration of IT operations and systems after a disaster, BCP encompasses a wider scope of ensuring the continuation of business operations during and after a disaster. Together, these plans ensure that an organization can quickly recover from an incident, minimizing downtime and mitigating potential financial and reputational damage.

Disaster Recovery Planning

Objective: The primary goal of DR is to restore IT infrastructure and critical systems to operational status after a disruption. This includes recovering data, reinstating network services, and ensuring that applications are back online within a defined time frame.

Key Components:

- **Risk Assessment and Impact Analysis**: Identifying potential risks and assessing their impact on IT systems helps prioritize recovery efforts based on the criticality of different systems and applications.
- **Recovery Strategies**: Developing strategies for recovering hardware, applications, data, and network services. This may involve using off-site backups, cloud services, or redundant systems.
- **Plan Development and Documentation**: Documenting the step-by-step procedures for recovery, including roles and responsibilities, communication protocols, and detailed recovery processes.
- **Regular Testing and Updates**: Conducting regular drills to test the DR plan and updating it based on test results, changes in technology, or shifts in business operations.

Business Continuity Planning

Objective: BCP aims to maintain essential business functions operational during and after a disaster, ensuring that the organization can continue to operate at an acceptable level of efficiency.

Key Components:

- **Business Impact Analysis (BIA)**: Identifying essential business functions and the resources required to support them. BIA helps determine which business units and processes are critical to the organization's survival and thus should be prioritized in the continuity plan.

- **Continuity Strategies**: Developing strategies to maintain operations during disruptions. This may include alternative work arrangements, such as remote work, or establishing manual processes to replace automated ones temporarily.
- **Plan Development and Documentation**: Outlining procedures and policies to sustain business operations, including chain-of-command, communication plans, and emergency response actions.
- **Training and Exercises**: Training staff on their roles in the continuity plan and conducting exercises to ensure they are prepared to implement the plan under actual disaster conditions.

Integration of DR and BCP

Integrating DR and BCP is essential for a holistic approach to organizational resilience. This integration ensures that IT recovery efforts (DR) are aligned with the broader goal of maintaining business operations (BCP), providing a seamless strategy for responding to and recovering from incidents.

Best Practices:

- **Executive Support**: Gaining buy-in from senior management is crucial for ensuring that DR and BCP are given the necessary resources and priority.
- **Cross-Functional Team**: Establishing a cross-functional team involving IT, operations, human resources, and other key departments ensures that both DR and BCP address all aspects of the organization.
- **Communication Plan**: A comprehensive communication plan is essential for keeping employees, customers, and stakeholders informed during and after a disaster.

- **Continuous Improvement**: Regularly reviewing and updating the DR and BCP in response to new threats, technological changes, or shifts in business processes ensures that the plans remain effective and relevant.

Disaster Recovery and Business Continuity Planning are critical for ensuring that an organization can respond to and recover from disruptive events with minimal impact on operations. By carefully planning, regularly testing, and continuously improving DR and BCP, organizations can enhance their resilience, safeguard their assets, and maintain trust with their customers and stakeholders.

Conclusion

The Recovery phase is a critical component of the Incident Response process, focusing on restoring operations, minimizing damage, and preventing future incidents. By following these steps in an effective IRP, organizations can ensure a structured and efficient response to cyber incidents, safeguarding their assets, reputation, and the trust of their stakeholders.

Steps In an Effective Incident Response Plan

An effective Incident Response Plan (IRP) is a crucial component of an organization's cybersecurity posture. It outlines a structured approach for detecting, responding to, and recovering from cybersecurity incidents. This plan minimizes the impact of attacks, ensuring swift restoration of normal operations and maintaining trust with stakeholders. The steps in an IRP are designed to be comprehensive yet flexible, allowing for adaptation to the specific context and needs of the organization.

Steps in an Effective Incident Response Plan

1. **Preparation**:

This foundational step involves establishing an incident response team, developing communication protocols, and setting up detection tools. Organizations must also conduct regular training and simulations to ensure readiness. Critical assets and data flows should be identified to prioritize protection efforts (Cichonski et al., 2012).

2. **Detection and Identification**:

The ability to quickly detect and accurately identify an incident is critical. This involves monitoring systems and networks for signs of unauthorized access, malware infection, or other malicious activities. Effective detection relies on a combination of technological solutions and human expertise.

3. **Containment**:

Once an incident is detected, the immediate priority is to contain it to prevent further spread or damage. This may involve isolating affected systems, blocking malicious network traffic, or temporarily shutting down services. Containment strategies should be flexible to address the diverse nature of cyber threats.

4. **Eradication**:

With the threat contained, the focus shifts to removing it from the organization's systems. This involves identifying and eliminating the root cause of the incident, such as malware, unauthorized access points, or exploited vulnerabilities. Systems should be cleaned and patched to prevent recurrence of the incident.

5. **Recovery**:

Recovery involves restoring affected systems and services to normal operations while ensuring they are not compromised. This step includes validating the integrity of systems and data, monitoring for signs of residual impact, and gradually returning operations to normal. Communication with stakeholders is crucial during recovery to manage expectations and provide assurance.

6. **Lessons Learned**:

After the incident is resolved, conducting a post-incident review is essential. This involves analyzing the incident, the effectiveness of the response, and identifying improvements for the IRP. Lessons learned should be integrated into the organization's security practices to strengthen defenses against future incidents.

Considerations for an Effective IRP

Comprehensive Documentation: Detailed documentation throughout the incident response process is vital for post-incident analysis, legal compliance, and continuous improvement.

Stakeholder Communication: Effective communication with internal stakeholders, customers, and possibly regulators is critical throughout the incident response process. Transparency and timeliness can help mitigate reputational damage.

Legal and Regulatory Compliance: The IRP should consider legal and regulatory requirements related to cybersecurity incidents, including data breach notification laws and industry-specific regulations.

Integration with Business Continuity: The IRP should be integrated with the organization's broader business continuity and disaster recovery plans to ensure cohesive response efforts across all levels of the organization.

Continuous Improvement: The IRP is not static; it should be regularly reviewed and updated based on emerging threats, technological changes, and lessons learned from past incidents.

Conclusion

An effective Incident Response Plan is integral to an organization's ability to manage and recover from cybersecurity incidents. By following these structured steps—Preparation, Detection and Identification, Containment, Eradication, Recovery, and Lessons Learned—organizations can enhance their resilience against cyber threats. Continuous improvement, based on regular reviews and integration of lessons learned, ensures that the IRP evolves in line with the changing cyber threat landscape.

Chapter 9: Legal and Ethical Considerations

Legal and ethical considerations form the cornerstone of cybersecurity practices, guiding how organizations and individuals should responsibly manage and protect information. In the context of cybersecurity, adhering to legal standards and ethical principles is not only about compliance but also about fostering trust, respect for privacy, and the integrity of systems and data. The dynamic nature of cyber threats and the evolving legal landscape necessitate a proactive and informed approach to these considerations.

Legal Considerations in Cybersecurity

<u>Data Protection and Privacy Laws:</u>

Across the globe, various jurisdictions have enacted laws to protect personal data and privacy. The General Data Protection Regulation (GDPR) in the European Union and the California Consumer Privacy Act (CCPA) in the United States are prime examples. These regulations mandate strict data handling procedures, provide individuals with rights over their data, and impose significant penalties for non-compliance (European Parliament and Council of the European Union, 2016; State of California, 2018).

Data protection and privacy laws constitute a significant legal consideration in cybersecurity, shaping how organizations collect, store, process, and share personal data. With the increasing volume and sensitivity of personal information being handled online, these laws aim to safeguard individual privacy rights while setting standards for data security.

Data Protection and Privacy Laws: An Overview

General Data Protection Regulation (GDPR): Implemented in May 2018, the GDPR is a comprehensive data protection regulation that applies to all organizations operating within the European Union (EU) and the European Economic Area (EEA), as well as to organizations outside the EU/EEA that offer goods or services to individuals in the EU/EEA or monitor their behavior. The GDPR emphasizes principles such as lawfulness, fairness, transparency, purpose limitation, data minimization, accuracy, storage limitation, integrity, and confidentiality of personal data. It grants individuals several rights, including the right to access, correct, delete, and port their data. Organizations are required to implement appropriate technical and organizational measures to ensure and demonstrate compliance, including data protection impact assessments, data protection by design and by default, and, in certain cases, the appointment of a Data Protection Officer (DPO) (European Parliament and Council of the European Union, 2016).

California Consumer Privacy Act (CCPA): The CCPA, which took effect in January 2020, grants California residents new rights regarding their personal information and imposes various obligations on businesses that collect, share, or sell Californians' personal information. Similar to the GDPR, the CCPA aims to provide consumers with greater transparency and control over their personal data, including the right to know about data collection practices, the right to delete personal information, the right to opt-out of the sale of personal information, and protection against discrimination for exercising their CCPA rights (State of California, 2018).

Impact on Cybersecurity Practices

Data Protection Measures: Compliance with data protection and privacy laws requires organizations to implement robust cybersecurity measures to protect personal data against unauthorized access, disclosure, alteration, and destruction. This includes encryption, access controls, network security, and incident response mechanisms.

Data Breach Notification: Many privacy laws mandate timely notification to regulatory authorities and affected individuals in the event of a data breach that poses a risk to individuals' rights and freedoms. This requirement emphasizes the need for effective incident detection and response plans.

Data Processing Agreements: Organizations must ensure that data processing agreements with third-party service providers comply with data protection laws, requiring processors to implement adequate security measures and stipulating the purposes for which data can be processed.

International Data Transfers: Laws like the GDPR impose restrictions on the transfer of personal data outside the EU/EEA, requiring adequate protections to be in place. This impacts organizations' choices regarding data storage and processing locations and necessitates adherence to mechanisms like Standard Contractual Clauses (SCCs) or adequacy decisions for international data transfers.

Navigating Compliance Challenges

Regular Training and Awareness: Organizations should conduct regular training for employees on data protection laws and the importance of compliance to ensure everyone understands their role in safeguarding personal data.

Data Protection Impact Assessments (DPIAs): Conducting DPIAs for processing activities that pose high risks to individuals' rights and freedoms can help identify and mitigate data protection risks.

Privacy by Design and by Default: Incorporating data protection considerations into the design of products, services, and business practices from the outset is crucial for compliance and for building trust with users.

Data protection and privacy laws are foundational to legal considerations in cybersecurity, compelling organizations to adopt stringent measures to protect personal data. By understanding and complying with these laws, organizations not only fulfill their legal obligations but also demonstrate their commitment to privacy and data protection, enhancing their reputation and building trust with stakeholders.

Breach Notification Laws:

Many jurisdictions require organizations to notify affected individuals and relevant authorities in the event of a data breach. These laws aim to ensure transparency and allow individuals to take protective measures against potential harm resulting from breaches.

Breach Notification Laws are a critical aspect of the legal landscape in cybersecurity, designed to ensure transparency and accountability when personal data breaches occur. These laws require organizations to notify affected individuals and, in many cases, regulatory authorities, when certain types of personal data are compromised in a security breach. The objective is to enable individuals to take protective actions against potential harm, such as identity theft or fraud, and to reinforce the accountability of organizations in protecting personal data.

Overview of Breach Notification Laws

Breach Notification Laws vary by jurisdiction but generally include requirements for timely notification, the content of the notification, and the conditions under which notification is mandated. For example:

General Data Protection Regulation (GDPR): Under the GDPR, data controllers are required to notify the appropriate supervisory authority of a personal data breach within 72 hours of becoming aware of it, unless the breach is unlikely to result in a risk to the rights and freedoms of natural persons. If the breach poses a high risk to individuals' rights and freedoms, the data controller must also inform the affected individuals without undue delay (European Parliament and Council of the European Union, 2016).

Health Insurance Portability and Accountability Act (HIPAA): In the United States, HIPAA requires covered entities and their business associates to notify affected individuals following a breach of unsecured protected health information. Notifications must be sent without unreasonable delay and in no case later than 60 days following the discovery of the breach. In certain circumstances, notifications to the Secretary of Health and Human Services and the media are also required (U.S. Department of Health & Human Services, n.d.).

California Consumer Privacy Act (CCPA): While the CCPA primarily focuses on privacy rights and consumer protections, it indirectly influences breach notification through its provision allowing consumers to sue businesses for data breaches of nonencrypted and nonredacted personal information due to the business's failure to maintain reasonable security procedures and practices (State of California, 2018).

Impact on Cybersecurity Practices

Incident Response Planning: Organizations must incorporate breach notification requirements into their incident response plans, ensuring they have procedures to quickly assess the scope and impact of a breach and determine their notification obligations.

Data Security Measures: Compliance with breach notification laws also underscores the need for robust data security measures to prevent breaches from occurring in the first place. Implementing security best practices, such as encryption, access controls, and regular security assessments, can mitigate the risk of data breaches.

Stakeholder Communication: Effective communication strategies are essential for managing breach notifications. Organizations must be prepared to clearly and empathetically communicate with affected individuals, providing them with information about the breach and advice on protecting themselves from potential harm.

Legal and Regulatory Compliance: Navigating the complex landscape of breach notification laws requires legal expertise to ensure compliance across different jurisdictions. Organizations may need to consult with legal counsel to understand their notification obligations, particularly if they operate in multiple jurisdictions.

Breach Notification Laws play a crucial role in promoting transparency and protection in the digital realm. By mandating timely notification of data breaches, these laws empower individuals to take protective actions and hold organizations accountable for data security. For organizations, adherence to these laws is not only a legal requirement but also an opportunity to demonstrate their commitment to data protection and to build trust with customers and stakeholders.

<u>Intellectual Property Rights:</u>

Cybersecurity measures intersect with intellectual property rights, particularly in the protection of proprietary information and the legal use of software and digital tools. Ensuring that cybersecurity practices do not infringe on intellectual property rights is a legal imperative.

Intellectual Property Rights (IPR) play a pivotal role in the legal and ethical considerations of cybersecurity, safeguarding the creations of the mind, including inventions, literary and artistic works, designs, symbols, names, and images used in commerce. In the digital realm, where the theft, unauthorized use, or infringement of intellectual property can be facilitated by the anonymity and reach of the internet, understanding and respecting these rights become crucial for organizations and individuals alike.

Understanding Intellectual Property Rights in Cybersecurity Types of Intellectual Property:

- **Copyrights**: Protect literary and artistic works such as writings, software, and multimedia.
- **Patents**: Grant inventors exclusive rights to their inventions, preventing others from making, using, or selling the invention without permission.
- **Trademarks**: Protect symbols, names, and slogans used to identify goods or services.
- **Trade Secrets**: Protect confidential business information that provides a competitive edge, such as formulas, practices, processes, designs, instruments, or patterns.

Cybersecurity and IPR Challenges:

- **Digital Piracy**: The unauthorized copying and distribution of copyrighted digital content, such as software, music, and videos.
- **Counterfeiting**: The production of imitation products typically covered by trademark protection, sold under the brand name without authorization.
- **Cyber Espionage**: The theft of intellectual property, including trade secrets, through cyber means to gain a competitive advantage.
- **Reverse Engineering**: While often legal under certain conditions, reverse engineering can raise ethical and legal questions when it infringes on copyrights or patents.

Legal Frameworks and Agreements

Various international agreements and national laws provide a legal framework for the protection of IPR, including the Agreement on Trade-Related Aspects of Intellectual Property Rights (TRIPS), administered by the World Trade Organization (WTO), and specific laws in individual countries, such as the Copyright Act, the Patent Act, and the Lanham Act in the United States.

Ethical Considerations

Respecting intellectual property rights extends beyond legal compliance; it is also a matter of ethics. Ethical considerations include:

- **Respect for Creativity and Innovation**: Acknowledging and respecting the time, effort, and resources invested in creating and developing new ideas, products, and services.
- **Fair Competition**: Maintaining a level playing field in the marketplace by respecting the intellectual property rights of competitors.
- **Consumer Trust**: Building and maintaining trust with consumers by ensuring that products and services are genuine and legally obtained.

Best Practices for Protecting IPR in Cybersecurity

- **Implementing Robust Security Measures**: Protecting intellectual property from cyber threats requires robust cybersecurity measures, including data encryption, access controls, and regular security audits.
- **IPR Awareness and Training**: Educating employees about the importance of intellectual property rights and the legal and ethical implications of their infringement is critical.
- **Legal Compliance and Monitoring**: Organizations should ensure compliance with applicable IPR laws and monitor the internet and marketplaces for potential infringements of their intellectual property.
- **Collaboration and Sharing of Best Practices**: Engaging with industry groups, law enforcement, and intellectual property organizations can enhance efforts to protect IPR and combat infringement.

Intellectual Property Rights are fundamental in fostering innovation, creativity, and fair competition in the digital age. The protection of these rights involves navigating complex legal landscapes and adhering to ethical standards, underscoring the importance of robust cybersecurity measures, legal compliance, and awareness. By upholding these principles, organizations can safeguard their intellectual assets while contributing to a culture of respect for intellectual property.

International Cybersecurity Standards and Laws:

International cybersecurity standards and laws play a crucial role in shaping the global landscape of cybersecurity practices and legal compliance. As cyber threats increasingly transcend national boundaries, these standards and laws provide a framework for international cooperation, ensuring a consistent approach to cybersecurity across different jurisdictions. They help organizations protect against cyber threats, manage risks, and ensure the privacy and integrity of data across global networks.

International Cybersecurity Standards

ISO/IEC 27001: Developed by the International Organization for Standardization (ISO) and the International Electrotechnical Commission (IEC), ISO/IEC 27001 is the leading international standard for information security management systems (ISMS). It outlines a systematic approach to managing sensitive company information so that it remains secure. It includes people, processes, and IT systems by applying a risk management process (ISO/IEC, 2013).

NIST Cybersecurity Framework: Developed by the National Institute of Standards and Technology (NIST) in the United States, the NIST Cybersecurity Framework has gained international recognition. It provides a policy framework of computer security guidance for how private sector organizations in the US can assess and improve their ability to prevent, detect, and respond to cyber attacks. Its principles and best practices, however, are applicable to organizations worldwide, making it a reference point for international cybersecurity efforts (NIST, 2018).

GDPR - General Data Protection Regulation: Although GDPR is a regulation established by the European Union, its impact is global. It imposes strict data protection and privacy requirements on all entities that process the personal data of EU residents, regardless of where the organization is based. GDPR has set a high standard for data protection and privacy worldwide, influencing many countries to revise or enact new data protection laws (European Parliament and Council of the European Union, 2016).

International Cybersecurity Laws

The legal landscape for cybersecurity is complex and varied across different countries. However, there are initiatives and conventions aimed at fostering international legal cooperation in combating cybercrime:

Budapest Convention on Cybercrime: Also known as the Council of Europe Convention on Cybercrime, it is the first international treaty seeking to address Internet and computer crime by harmonizing national laws, improving investigative techniques, and increasing cooperation among nations. As of now, it remains the most significant multilateral treaty on the subject, with parties including both member states of the Council of Europe and non-member states (Council of Europe, 2001).

United Nations Initiatives: The United Nations has been active in promoting norms, rules, and principles of responsible behavior of states in cyberspace. While not laws in themselves, these initiatives aim to establish a common understanding and framework for international cooperation in ensuring cybersecurity and combating cybercrime at the global level.

Navigating International Standards and Laws

Compliance Challenges: Organizations operating across international borders face the challenge of complying with a myriad of cybersecurity laws and regulations, which may vary significantly from one jurisdiction to another.

Implementing Best Practices: Adhering to internationally recognized cybersecurity standards can help organizations navigate these challenges by implementing best practices that are likely to be compliant with various national regulations.

Legal and Cybersecurity Expertise: Organizations should seek expertise in both cybersecurity and international law to understand their obligations under different jurisdictions and to develop a comprehensive cybersecurity strategy that addresses these requirements.

Cross-Border Cooperation: Engaging in cross-border cooperation through information sharing and collaborative initiatives can enhance an organization's ability to respond to international cyber threats and navigate the complex landscape of international cybersecurity laws.

International cybersecurity standards and laws are critical in establishing a cohesive and effective global response to cyber threats. By understanding and adhering to these standards and laws, organizations can not only ensure compliance but also contribute to a more secure and resilient global cyberspace.

Organizations operating across borders must navigate a complex web of international laws and standards. Compliance with international frameworks, such as the ISO/IEC 27001 series for information security management, is often necessary for global operations.

Ethical Considerations in Cybersecurity

Confidentiality: Maintaining the confidentiality of information is a fundamental ethical duty in cybersecurity. This involves safeguarding sensitive data from unauthorized access or disclosure, respecting the privacy expectations of individuals and organizations.

Integrity: Ethical practices also demand the protection of data integrity, ensuring that information is accurate, reliable, and not subject to unauthorized alterations. This encompasses measures to prevent data tampering, corruption, or loss.

Availability: The ethical principle of availability pertains to ensuring that authorized users have timely and reliable access to information and systems. This includes implementing safeguards against denial-of-service attacks and other disruptions.

Responsible Disclosure: When security vulnerabilities are discovered, ethical considerations dictate responsible disclosure to the affected parties, allowing them to remediate the issue before it is publicly disclosed or exploited.

Respect for User Rights: Ethical cybersecurity practices respect user rights, including the right to be informed about how their data is collected, used, and protected. This also involves providing users with control over their personal information through consent mechanisms and data portability options.

Ethical considerations in cybersecurity are paramount for guiding the conduct of individuals and organizations in the digital realm. These ethical considerations help ensure that actions and policies not only comply with legal requirements but also uphold the principles of fairness, respect, and responsibility. As cybersecurity threats evolve, the ethical landscape becomes increasingly complex, requiring a thoughtful approach to dilemmas such as privacy vs. security, the responsible disclosure of vulnerabilities, and the use of cybersecurity tools and techniques.

Core Ethical Considerations in Cybersecurity

Privacy and Personal Data Protection: Respecting and protecting the privacy of individuals is a fundamental ethical obligation. This involves safeguarding personal data from unauthorized access and ensuring that data collection and processing are transparent, limited to what is necessary, and based on consent or legitimate interest (Floridi, 2014).

Security: Providing a secure digital environment for users, customers, and stakeholders is a key ethical responsibility. This includes implementing appropriate measures to prevent, detect, and respond to cyber threats, as well as ensuring the integrity and availability of data and systems.

Transparency and Accountability: Ethical practices in cybersecurity emphasize transparency in policies, actions, and decision-making processes, particularly when they impact users' privacy and security. Organizations should be accountable for their cybersecurity practices, including how they respond to and communicate about security incidents.

Equity and Access: Ethical considerations extend to ensuring equitable access to cybersecurity resources and protection. This includes addressing the digital divide and ensuring that all users, regardless of their technical expertise or socio-economic status, are informed and protected against cyber threats.

Responsible Disclosure: The discovery of security vulnerabilities presents ethical challenges regarding disclosure. Ethical norms advocate for responsible disclosure, where vulnerabilities are reported to the affected parties and given a reasonable timeframe for remediation before public disclosure, balancing the need for public awareness with the risk of exploitation (Cavusoglu et al., 2008).

Navigating Ethical Dilemmas

Balancing Privacy and Security: One of the most prevalent ethical dilemmas in cybersecurity is balancing individual privacy with the broader need for security. Ethical decision-making requires careful consideration of the impacts on privacy rights and the justification for any intrusion in the name of security.

Use of Cybersecurity Tools: The use of certain cybersecurity tools and techniques, such as penetration testing and network monitoring, raises ethical questions regarding consent, legality, and the potential for abuse. Clear guidelines and ethical standards are essential for governing their use.

Artificial Intelligence and Automation: The increasing use of AI and automation in cybersecurity introduces ethical concerns related to bias, accountability, and the potential for unintended consequences. Ethical AI use in cybersecurity emphasizes transparency, fairness, and human oversight (Taddeo & Floridi, 2018).

Ethical Frameworks and Guidelines

Developing and adhering to ethical frameworks and guidelines is critical for navigating the ethical landscape of cybersecurity. Professional organizations, such as the ACM (Association for Computing Machinery) and the IEEE (Institute of Electrical and Electronics Engineers), provide codes of ethics that outline principles for ethical conduct in the field. Additionally, organizations should develop their own ethical guidelines tailored to their specific context and challenges.

Ethical considerations are integral to responsible cybersecurity practices, ensuring that actions not only comply with legal standards but also uphold moral principles. By prioritizing privacy, security, transparency, and equity, and by navigating ethical dilemmas with careful consideration, individuals and organizations can contribute to a more secure, fair, and trustworthy digital environment.

Navigating Legal and Ethical Considerations

Continuous Education and Awareness: Staying informed about the latest legal developments and ethical standards is essential for cybersecurity professionals. This includes regular training and professional development opportunities.

Legal Consultation and Compliance Programs: Organizations should engage with legal experts to ensure their cybersecurity practices comply with applicable laws and regulations. Implementing comprehensive compliance programs can help manage legal risks.

Ethical Guidelines and Codes of Conduct: Developing and adhering to ethical guidelines and codes of conduct for cybersecurity practices can guide decision-making and foster a culture of integrity and responsibility.

Stakeholder Engagement: Engaging with stakeholders, including employees, customers, and partners, about legal and ethical practices in cybersecurity builds trust and promotes transparency.

Conclusion

Legal and ethical considerations are integral to effective cybersecurity practices. By adhering to applicable laws, respecting privacy and rights, and upholding ethical principles, organizations and individuals can navigate the complexities of the digital world responsibly, ensuring the trust and safety of all stakeholders.

Chapter 10: Emerging Trends in Cybersecurity

Part V: Looking Ahead

Emerging trends in cybersecurity reflect the evolving landscape of digital threats and the innovative approaches to defense that organizations must adopt to protect against increasingly sophisticated cyber attacks. As technology advances, so do the techniques employed by cybercriminals, necessitating continual adaptation and vigilance in cybersecurity practices.

The Rise of Artificial Intelligence and Machine Learning

The application of Artificial Intelligence (AI) and Machine Learning (ML) in cybersecurity represents a significant trend, offering both opportunities and challenges. AI and ML can enhance threat detection and response through the analysis of large datasets to identify patterns and anomalies indicative of cyber threats. These technologies can automate complex processes for faster and more efficient threat response. However, cybercriminals also leverage AI and ML to develop more sophisticated malware and phishing attacks, creating a cyber arms race between attackers and defenders (Taddeo & Floridi, 2018).

Increasing Focus on Cloud Security

With the accelerated adoption of cloud computing, ensuring the security of cloud-based systems and data has become a priority. Organizations are transitioning to a cloud-first strategy, necessitating robust cloud security solutions to protect against data breaches, insecure interfaces, account hijacking, and the unique challenges of multi-cloud and hybrid cloud environments. Cloud security posture management (CSPM) and cloud workload protection platforms (CWPP) are emerging as critical tools in securing cloud environments (Gartner, 2020).

IoT and the Expansion of the Attack Surface

The proliferation of Internet of Things (IoT) devices expands the cybersecurity attack surface, introducing vulnerabilities in a network's security architecture. Many IoT devices lack robust built-in security, making them susceptible to attacks that can compromise not only the device itself but also other connected systems. Securing the IoT ecosystem requires a comprehensive approach, including the development of secure IoT frameworks, adoption of zero trust models, and the implementation of endpoint security solutions (Sicari et al., 2015).

The Evolution of Ransomware Tactics

Ransomware attacks have evolved from opportunistic encryption of systems for ransom to more sophisticated double extortion schemes. Attackers increasingly exfiltrate sensitive data before encryption, threatening to release the data publicly unless additional ransom payments are made. The emergence of Ransomware-as-a-Service (RaaS) further complicates the threat landscape, lowering the barrier to entry for cybercriminals (Coveware, 2020).

The Importance of Cyber Hygiene and User Education

As technical cybersecurity measures advance, the human element remains a critical vulnerability. Phishing attacks, social engineering, and insider threats continue to pose significant risks. Emphasizing cyber hygiene—basic practices like regular software updates, use of strong passwords, and secure Wi-Fi connections—and comprehensive user education programs are essential for mitigating these risks (Hadnagy, 2018).

Regulatory and Legal Developments

The regulatory landscape for cybersecurity is becoming increasingly complex, with new laws and regulations being introduced globally. Organizations must navigate compliance with regulations such as the

GDPR in the European Union, the California Consumer Privacy Act (CCPA) in the United States, and other national and sector-specific regulations. Compliance requires a deep understanding of legal requirements and the implementation of policies and practices to safeguard personal data and ensure privacy (European Parliament and Council of the European Union, 2016).

The Role of Artificial Intelligence and Machine Learning

The role of Artificial Intelligence (AI) and Machine Learning (ML) in cybersecurity represents one of the most transformative emerging trends, profoundly impacting how organizations defend against, detect, and respond to cyber threats. As cyber attackers continually evolve their tactics, AI and ML technologies offer powerful tools to enhance cybersecurity defenses, automating complex processes and enabling more sophisticated threat detection and response mechanisms.

Enhancing Threat Detection with AI and ML

AI and ML algorithms can analyze vast volumes of data at speeds and scales impossible for human analysts, identifying patterns and anomalies that may indicate a cyber threat. By learning from historical data, these algorithms can detect known threats and predict potential future attacks, including zero-day exploits for which no prior signature exists (Apruzzese et al., 2018). This proactive threat detection capability is crucial in an environment where attackers constantly devise new methods to breach defenses.

Automating Incident Response

AI and ML also play a pivotal role in automating incident response activities. By integrating AI-driven decision-making processes, organizations can automate responses to common types of cyber threats, significantly reducing response times. For example, if an intrusion detection system powered by ML algorithms identifies an ongoing phishing attack, it can automatically initiate countermeasures such as isolating affected systems or blocking malicious IP addresses, often before significant damage occurs (Taddeo & Floridi, 2018).

Behavioral Analysis and Anomaly Detection

One of the key advantages of ML in cybersecurity is its ability to conduct behavioral analysis, learning normal network and user behaviors and detecting deviations that may indicate a security incident. This capability is particularly effective against sophisticated threats like Advanced Persistent Threats (APTs) and insider threats, where malicious activities may blend in with legitimate operations. By identifying subtle anomalies, ML algorithms can alert security teams to potential threats that might otherwise go unnoticed (Veeramachaneni et al., 2016).

Challenges and Considerations

While AI and ML hold great promise for cybersecurity, their implementation comes with challenges. The accuracy of AI and ML models depends on the quality and quantity of the training data; models trained on incomplete or biased data may produce inaccurate results or miss certain types of threats. Additionally, there is a concern about the "black box" nature of some AI models, where the decision-making process is not transparent, making it difficult to understand how a model arrived at a particular conclusion.

Cyber attackers are also leveraging AI and ML to develop more sophisticated attack methods, creating a cyber arms race between attackers and defenders. For example, AI can be used to automate the creation of phishing emails that are more convincing and targeted, increasing the likelihood of successful attacks.

Ethical and Privacy Considerations

The use of AI and ML in cybersecurity raises ethical and privacy concerns, particularly regarding the collection and analysis of personal data. Organizations must navigate these challenges carefully, ensuring that their use of AI respects privacy rights and complies with data protection regulations such as the GDPR.

The integration of AI and ML into cybersecurity strategies offers significant advantages in threat detection, incident response, and behavioral analysis. Despite the challenges, the potential of these technologies to improve security posture and resilience against cyber threats is immense. As the cybersecurity landscape continues to evolve, AI and ML will undoubtedly play a crucial role in shaping future defenses.

Future Challenges in Digital Security

Future challenges in digital security are evolving rapidly, driven by technological advancements, changes in cyber threat tactics, and the expanding digital footprint of organizations and individuals. Addressing these challenges requires a forward-looking approach to cybersecurity, encompassing not only technological solutions but also strategic, regulatory, and educational initiatives.

Increasing Complexity of Cyber Attacks

Cyber attackers are continuously refining their techniques, leveraging advanced technologies like artificial intelligence (AI) and machine learning (ML) to automate attacks, improve evasion capabilities, and increase the sophistication of their campaigns. The rise of AI-powered cyber attacks poses significant challenges for traditional defense mechanisms, necessitating the development of AI-enhanced security solutions to detect and counteract these threats (Taddeo & Floridi, 2018).

Expanding Attack Surface

The proliferation of Internet of Things (IoT) devices, cloud computing, and mobile technologies has dramatically expanded the attack surface available to cyber attackers. Securing a growing array of devices and cloud-based systems, each with its unique vulnerabilities, presents a complex challenge for cybersecurity professionals. This expansion requires comprehensive security strategies that go beyond perimeter defenses to include device-level security, secure software development practices, and effective cloud security frameworks (Sicari et al., 2015).

Supply Chain and Third-Party Risks

Cybersecurity is increasingly recognized as a supply chain issue, with attackers targeting less secure elements in the supply chain to gain access to larger, more secure organizations. The SolarWinds attack highlighted the potential for widespread compromise through third-party vendors. Addressing these risks requires enhanced scrutiny of third-party vendors' security practices, implementation of secure software development frameworks, and increased collaboration across the supply chain to identify and mitigate threats (NIST, 2020).

Privacy and Data Protection

With data becoming an increasingly valuable asset, protecting personal and sensitive information is a paramount challenge. Regulations such as the General Data Protection Regulation (GDPR) and the California Consumer Privacy Act (CCPA) have raised the bar for data privacy and protection, imposing strict requirements on organizations that collect and process data. However, ensuring compliance and protecting against data breaches in an environment where data is constantly under threat from cyber attackers is an ongoing challenge (European Parliament and Council of the European Union, 2016; State of California, 2018).

Workforce Shortage

The cybersecurity industry faces a significant workforce shortage, with millions of positions unfilled worldwide. This gap between the demand for skilled cybersecurity professionals and the available talent pool presents a critical challenge for the future of digital security. Addressing this issue requires investment in cybersecurity education and training programs, initiatives to attract a more diverse workforce, and the development of tools and technologies that can augment the capabilities of existing personnel (Morgan, 2017).

Legal and Ethical Considerations

As cybersecurity technologies evolve, so do the legal and ethical considerations surrounding their use. The deployment of offensive cybersecurity measures, the ethical use of AI and ML in security practices, and the balance between security and privacy are just a few of the issues that will continue to challenge policymakers, legal experts, and cybersecurity professionals.

The future challenges in digital security are diverse and complex, reflecting the dynamic nature of the cyber threat landscape and the increasing reliance on digital technologies. Addressing these challenges requires a multifaceted approach that combines technological innovation, strategic planning, regulatory compliance, and a commitment to ethical principles. By staying ahead of emerging threats and fostering a culture of security awareness and collaboration, organizations can navigate the challenges of digital security and protect against the evolving threats of the future.

Conclusion

Emerging trends in cybersecurity underscore the dynamic and multifaceted nature of the field. Organizations must remain vigilant, adopting advanced technologies like AI and ML for defense, securing cloud and IoT environments, countering sophisticated ransomware tactics, emphasizing the importance of cyber hygiene, and ensuring compliance with evolving regulations. Staying ahead of these trends is critical for building resilient cybersecurity defenses in an increasingly interconnected world.

APPENDICES

Glossary:

Definitions Of Technical Terms and Acronyms:

In the field of cybersecurity, understanding technical terms and acronyms is crucial for professionals, students, and individuals seeking to navigate or comprehend the complexities of digital security practices and threats. Here's a glossary of key terms and acronyms that are commonly used in cybersecurity discussions:

1. **Malware (Malicious Software)**

   Malware is any software intentionally designed to cause damage to a computer, server, client, or computer network. Types of malware include viruses, worms, Trojan horses, ransomware, spyware, adware, and scareware.

2. **Phishing**

   A cyber attack that uses disguised email as a weapon. The goal is to trick the email recipient into believing that the message is something they want or need — a request from their bank, for instance, or a note from someone in their company — and to click a link or download an attachment.

3. **Ransomware**

   A type of malicious software designed to block access to a computer system or data until a sum of money is paid. Often, there is a threat that the data will be destroyed or released publicly if the ransom is not paid.

4. **DDoS (Distributed Denial of Service)**

   A cyber attack in which the perpetrator seeks to make a machine or network resource unavailable to its intended users by temporarily or indefinitely disrupting services of a host connected to the Internet.

5. **Zero-Day Exploit**

   A cyber attack that occurs on the same day a weakness is discovered in software. At that point, it is exploited before a fix becomes available from its creator.

6. **Encryption**

   The process of converting information or data into a code, especially to prevent unauthorized access. It is a critical tool for protecting data privacy and securing electronic communications.

7. **Firewall**

   A network security device that monitors incoming and outgoing network traffic and decides whether to allow or block specific traffic based on a defined set of security rules.

8. **VPN (Virtual Private Network)**

   A service that encrypts your internet traffic and protects your online identity by hiding your IP address. VPNs are used to secure data transmissions and to bypass geographic restrictions on websites or streaming audio and video.

9. **IoT (Internet of Things)**

   The network of physical objects — devices, vehicles, buildings, and other items — embedded with sensors, software, and other technologies for the purpose of connecting and exchanging data with other devices and systems over the internet.

10. **SIEM (Security Information and Event Management)**

    A set of tools and services offering a holistic view of an organization's information security. SIEM tools provide real-time analysis of security alerts generated by applications and network hardware.

11. **GDPR (General Data Protection Regulation)**

    A regulation in EU law on data protection and privacy in the European Union and the European Economic Area. It also addresses the transfer of personal data outside the EU and EEA areas.

12. **APT (Advanced Persistent Threat)**

    A prolonged and targeted cyberattack in which an intruder gains access to a network and remains undetected for an extended period of time. The intent is usually to steal data rather than to cause damage to the network or organization.

13. **CISO (Chief Information Security Officer)**

    A senior-level executive responsible for developing and implementing an information security program, which includes procedures and policies designed to protect enterprise communications, systems, and assets from both internal and external threats.

14. **SOC (Security Operations Center)**

    A centralized unit that deals with security issues on an organizational and technical level. An SOC within a building or facility is a central location from where staff supervises the site, using data processing technology.

15. **Penetration Testing**

An authorized simulated cyber attack on a computer system, performed to evaluate the security of the system; not to be confused with a real cyber attack.

This glossary provides a foundation for understanding the key concepts and technologies involved in cybersecurity. Mastery of these terms is essential for effective communication and operation within the field of digital security.

Additional Resources

Appendices in the context of cybersecurity literature, reports, or educational materials serve as a vital component, offering readers additional resources, tools, and references to deepen their understanding, facilitate further research, or implement security measures. These appendices can range from lists of software tools and services, regulatory documents, to comprehensive guides on best practices. Here's an overview of what additional resources might be included in appendices related to cybersecurity:

Appendix A: Cybersecurity Frameworks and Standards

1. **NIST Cybersecurity Framework**: Provides a policy framework of computer security guidance for how private sector organizations in the United States can assess and improve their ability to prevent, detect, and respond to cyber attacks. **2. ISO/IEC 27001**: An international standard on how to manage information security. **3. GDPR Compliance Checklist**: A detailed checklist for organizations to ensure compliance with the EU's General Data Protection Regulation.

Appendix B: Cybersecurity Tools and Software

1. **Security Information and Event Management (SIEM) Tools**: List and comparison of leading SIEM solutions that provide real-time analysis of security alerts generated by applications and network hardware. **2. Antivirus and Anti-malware Software**: A compilation of recommended antivirus and anti-malware tools for different platforms. **3. Network Scanners and Vulnerability Assessment Tools**: Information on tools like Nessus, Nmap, and Wireshark for scanning network vulnerabilities.

Appendix C: Cybersecurity Legal and Regulatory Documents

1. **Text of GDPR**: The full text of the General Data Protection Regulation for reference. **2. HIPAA Compliance Guide**: A guide for organizations to understand and comply with the Health Insurance Portability and Accountability Act in the United States. **3. National Cybersecurity Legislation**: A directory of cybersecurity laws and regulations by country.

Appendix D: Educational and Training Resources

1. **Online Cybersecurity Courses and Certifications**: A list of platforms and institutions offering courses and certifications in cybersecurity, including free and paid options. **2. Cybersecurity Awareness Training Materials**: Resources and materials for conducting cybersecurity awareness training within organizations. **3. Research Papers and Journals**: A bibliography of key research papers, articles, and journals dedicated to cybersecurity topics.

Appendix E: Incident Response and Best Practices Guides

1. **Incident Response Plan Templates**: Sample templates and guides for developing an organization's incident response plan. **2. Best Practices for Data Encryption**: Guidelines and recommendations for implementing data encryption to protect sensitive information. **3. Ransomware Response Checklist**: A step-by-step guide for organizations to respond to and recover from ransomware attacks.

Appendix F: Cybersecurity Organizations and Forums

1. **Information Security Forums and Communities**: A list of online forums, communities, and social media groups where

cybersecurity professionals can share knowledge and discuss trends. **2. Industry Associations and Organizations**: Contact information and descriptions of key cybersecurity industry associations and organizations worldwide. **3. Governmental Cybersecurity Agencies**: Directory of governmental agencies responsible for cybersecurity and cybercrime prevention in different countries.

Appendices provide a treasure trove of additional resources, extending the value of cybersecurity literature by offering practical tools, in-depth information, and avenues for further exploration. Whether for academic, professional development, or operational implementation purposes, these resources can significantly enhance an individual's or organization's cybersecurity posture.

Sources For Further Reading and Research

In the ever-evolving field of cybersecurity, continuous learning and research are essential for staying abreast of the latest threats, technologies, and best practices. Sources for further reading and research range from academic journals and textbooks to online courses, blogs, and forums where cybersecurity professionals share insights and discuss trends. Below is a curated list of sources that can serve as a foundation for further exploration in the realm of cybersecurity.

<u>Academic Journals and Conferences</u>

1. **IEEE Security & Privacy**: A publication offering articles and insights on various aspects of cybersecurity and privacy, from foundational theory to practical applications. **2. ACM Transactions on Privacy and Security (TOPS)**: Publishes scientific articles on a range of topics including, but not limited to, cryptography, security protocols, and systems security. **3. The Annual Computer Security Applications Conference (AC-SAC)**: Provides a platform for exploring cutting-edge security research, with proceedings that are a valuable resource for in-depth studies.

<u>Online Courses and Certifications</u>

1. **Coursera Cybersecurity Specializations**: Offers courses in partnership with universities and cybersecurity organizations, covering topics from cybersecurity basics to advanced network security. **2. (ISC)² Certifications**: Renowned certifications such as Certified Information Systems Security Professional (CISSP) and Certified Cloud Security Professional (CCSP) offer in-depth knowledge and are recognized across the industry. **3. SANS Institute**: Provides a wide range of courses and certifications focusing on different areas of cybersecurity, including incident response, penetration testing, and cyber defense.

Books and Textbooks

1. **"The Art of Invisibility" by Kevin Mitnick**: Offers insights into how to protect privacy in the age of constant digital surveillance. **2. "Applied Cryptography" by Bruce Schneier**: A comprehensive resource on the science of cryptography, covering historical, technical, and practical aspects. **3. "Cybersecurity – Attack and Defense Strategies" by Yuri Diogenes and Erdal Ozkaya**: Provides a holistic view of cybersecurity practices, including how to build a robust defense strategy and understanding the mindset of cyber attackers.

Blogs and Online Forums

1. **Krebs on Security**: Run by journalist Brian Krebs, this blog covers in-depth security news, investigations, and analysis of the latest cyber threats. **2. Schneier on Security**: A blog by security expert Bruce Schneier that discusses security issues, privacy, and government policy. **3. Reddit's r/netsec**: A community forum on Reddit dedicated to discussing network security, latest vulnerabilities, and cybersecurity news.

Government and Industry Reports

1. **National Institute of Standards and Technology (NIST):** Offers a wealth of publications, guidelines, and standards on cybersecurity practices, including the NIST Cybersecurity Framework. **2. The Verizon Data Breach Investigations Report (DBIR):** An annual report that analyzes data breaches and incidents, providing insights into trends and tactics used by cyber attackers. **3. The European Union Agency for Cybersecurity (ENISA) Reports**: Publishes reports and guidelines on various cybersecurity topics, including threat landscapes and best practice recommendations.

Conclusion

The field of cybersecurity is dynamic, with new challenges and solutions emerging constantly. Staying informed and engaged with the latest research, discussions, and best practices is crucial for anyone involved in cybersecurity, whether they are seasoned professionals or newcomers to the field. The sources listed above provide a starting point for further reading and research, offering valuable knowledge and insights to enhance understanding and skills in cybersecurity.

References

Top of Form

Top of Form

Top of Form

Aljawarneh, S., Alawneh, A., & Jararweh, Y. (2020). A survey on security and privacy issues in internet-of-things. IoT in 5G Mobile Technologies, 2020, 693-717.

Alperovitch, D. (2011). Revealed: Operation Shady RAT. McAfee. https://www.mcafee.com/enterprise/en-us/assets/reports/rp-operation-shady-rat.pdf

Anderson, N., et al. (2016). "Future of Cybersecurity: The Role of Artificial Intelligence and Machine Learning." *Technology Innovation Management Review*, 6(4).

Anderson, R., Barton, C., Böhme, R., Clayton, R., Van Eeten, M. J. G., Levi, M., Moore, T., & Savage, S. (2012). Measuring the cost of cybercrime. *The 11th Workshop on the Economics of Information Security*.

April Tanner, & Cam, H. (2018). "Machine Learning and Deep Learning Techniques for Cybersecurity." *IEEE Access*, 6, 35365-35381.

Apruzzese, G., Colajanni, M., Ferretti, L., Guido, A., & Marchetti, M. (2018). On the Effectiveness of Machine and Deep Learning for Cybersecurity. In 10th International Conference on Cyber Conflict (CyCon), 371-390.

Bada, M., Sasse, M. A., & Nurse, J. R. (2019). Cyber security awareness campaigns: Why do they fail to change behaviour? *ArXiv*. https://arxiv.org/abs/1901.02672

Bejtlich, R. (2004). *The Tao of Network Security Monitoring: Beyond Intrusion Detection.* Addison-Wesley.

Bernstein, D. J., & Lange, T. (2017). Post-quantum cryptography. *Nature,* 549(7671), 188-194.

Bilge, L., & Dumitras, T. (2012). Before we knew it: An empirical study of zero-day attacks in the real world. Proceedings of the 2012 ACM Conference on Computer and Communications Security, 833-844.

Bishop, M. (2003). *Computer Security: Art and Science.* Addison-Wesley.

Boneh, D. (1999). Twenty years of attacks on the RSA cryptosystem. *Notices of the AMS,* 46(2), 203-213.

Borger, J., & Hern, A. (2014). Sony Pictures hack: the whole story. The Guardian. https://www.theguardian.com/technology/2014/dec/17/sony-pictures-hack-the-whole-story

Caltagirone, S., Pendergast, A., & Betz, C. (2013). *The Diamond Model of Intrusion Analysis.* Center for Cyber Intelligence Analysis and Threat Research.

Castells, M. (2001). The Internet Galaxy: Reflections on the Internet, Business, and Society. Oxford University Press.

Cavusoglu, H., Mishra, B., & Raghunathan, S. (2008). The Effect of Internet Security Breach Announcements on Market Value: Capital Market Reactions for Breached Firms and Internet Security Developers. International Journal of Electronic Commerce, 9(1), 69-104.

Chen, L., et al. (2016). "Report on Post-Quantum Cryptography." U.S. Department of Commerce, National Institute of Standards and Technology.

Cheswick, W. R., Bellovin, S. M., & Rubin, A. D. (2003). *Firewalls and Internet Security: Repelling the Wily Hacker* (2nd ed.). Addison-Wesley Professional.

Cichonski, P., Millar, T., Grance, T., & Scarfone, K. (2012). *Computer Security Incident Handling Guide.* National Institute of Standards and Technology (NIST), Special Publication 800-61 Rev. 2.

Cichonski, P., Millar, T., Grance, T., & Scarfone, K. (2012). *Computer Security Incident Handling Guide*. National Institute of Standards and

Cohen, F. (1987). Computer Viruses: Theory and Experiments. *Computers & Security*, 6(1), 22-35.

Cohen, F. (2016). *Ransomware: To Pay or Not to Pay?* Computer Fraud & Security, 2016(4), 8-12.

Collins-Sussman, B., Fitzpatrick, B. W., & Pilato, C. M. (2004). *Version Control with Subversion*. O'Reilly Media.

Coombs, W. T. (2014). *Ongoing Crisis Communication: Planning, Managing, and Responding*. SAGE Publications.

Council of Europe. (2001). Budapest Convention on Cybercrime. CETS No.185.

Council of Europe. (2001). Budapest Convention on Cybercrime. Retrieved from https://www.coe.int/en/web/conventions/full-list/-/conventions/treaty/185

Coveware. (2019). *Q4 Ransomware Marketplace report*.

Coveware. (2020). Coveware Quarterly Ransomware Report.

Cyber Threat Alliance. (n.d.). About us. Retrieved from https://www.cyberthreatalliance.org/

Daemen, J., & Rijmen, V. (2002). The design of Rijndael: AES - The Advanced Encryption Standard. Springer.

Denning, P. J. (1987). An Intrusion-Detection Model. *IEEE Transactions on Software Engineering*, SE-13(2), 222-232.

Dhillon, G., & Backhouse, J. (2000). Information system security management in the new millennium. *Communications of the ACM*, 43(7), 125-128.

Dierks, T., & Rescorla, E. (2008). The Transport Layer Security (TLS) Protocol Version 1.2. RFC 5246.

Diffie, W., & Hellman, M. (1976). New directions in cryptography. *IEEE Transactions on Information Theory*, 22(6), 644-654.

Easttom, C. (2016). *Computer Security Fundamentals* (3rd ed.). Pearson IT Certification.

Eichin, M. W., & Rochlis, J. A. (1989). With Microscope and Tweezers: An Analysis of the Internet Virus of November 1988. *Proceedings of the IEEE Symposium on Security and Privacy*, 326-343.

European Parliament and Council of the European Union. (2016). *Regulation (EU) 2016/679 of the European Parliament and of the Council of 27 April 2016 on the Protection of Natural Persons with Regard to the Processing of Personal Data and on the Free Movement of Such Data (General Data Protection Regulation)*. Official Journal of the European Union.

European Union Agency for Network and Information Security (ENISA). (2018). *Introduction to Network Security.*

Farley, T. (2001). Mobile IP Technology and Applications. Cisco Press.

Farwell, J. P., & Rohozinski, R. (2011). Stuxnet and the Future of Cyber War. *Survival*, 53(1), 23-40.

Feng, Q., Zhang, M., & Zhang, Y. (2019). Blockchain for the IoT and industrial IoT: A review. *Internet of Things*, 100129.

Ferraiolo, D. F., Sandhu, R., Gavrila, S., Kuhn, D. R., & Chandramouli, R. (2001). Proposed NIST Standard for Role-Based Access Control. ACM Transactions on Information and System Security, 4(3), 224–274.

Finneran, T. (2007). *The Realities of Securing Virtualized Networks.* Light Reading.

Floridi, L. (2014). The Fourth Revolution: How the Infosphere is Reshaping Human Reality. Oxford University Press.

G Data Software. (1987). G Data Software company history. https://www.gdata-software.com/company

Gartner. (2019). *Magic Quadrant for Endpoint Protection Platforms.*

Gartner. (2020). Innovation Insight for Cloud Security Posture Management.

Gentry, C. (2009). A fully homomorphic encryption scheme. PhD thesis, Stanford University.

Ghosh, A. K., & Schwartzbard, A. (1999). A study in using neural networks for anomaly and misuse detection. *USENIX Security Symposium.*

Global Cyber Alliance. (n.d.). About the Global Cyber Alliance. Retrieved from https://www.globalcyberalliance.org/

Global Cyber Alliance. (n.d.). About us. Retrieved from https://www.globalcyberalliance.org/about-us.html

Gordon, L. A., Loeb, M. P., Lucyshyn, W., & Zhou, L. (2015). Externalities and the magnitude of cybersecurity underinvestment by private sector firms: A modification of the Gordon-Loeb model. *Journal of Information Security*, 6(1), 24-30.

Graves, K. (2007). *CEH: Certified Ethical Hacker Study Guide.* Sybex.

Grimes, R. A. (2012). *Malware: Fighting Malicious Code.* Prentice Hall.

Hadnagy, C. (2010). Social Engineering: The Art of Human Hacking. Wiley.

Hadnagy, C. (2018). *Social Engineering: The Science of Human Hacking* (2nd ed.). Wiley.

Hassan, M. A. (2020). Cyber reconnaissance: Techniques and methods for information gathering. *International Journal of Information Management*, 52, 102059.

Hong, J. (2012). *The State of Phishing Attacks.* Communications of the ACM, 55(1), 74-81.

Howard, M., & LeBlanc, D. (2003). *Writing Secure Code* (2nd ed.). Microsoft Press.

Howard, M., & Lipner, S. (2006). The Security Development Lifecycle. Microsoft Press.

Hypponen, M. (2016). The history of ransomware. *F-Secure.* https://blog.f-secure.com/the-history-of-ransomware/

International Organization for Standardization. (2013). *ISO/IEC 27001:2013 Information technology — Security techniques — Information security management systems — Requirements.* https://www.iso.org/standard/54534.html

ISACA. (2018). *COBIT 2019 Framework: Introduction and Methodology.* https://www.isaca.org/resources/cobit

ISO/IEC. (2013). *ISO/IEC 27001:2013 Information technology — Security techniques — Information security management systems — Requirements.* International Organization for Standardization. https://www.iso.org/standard/54534.html

Jagatic, T. N., Johnson, N. A., Jakobsson, M., & Menczer, F. (2007). Social phishing. *Communications of the ACM, 50*(10), 94-100.

Jain, A. K., Ross, A., & Nandakumar, K. (2016). *Introduction to Biometrics.* Springer.

Jansen, W., & Grance, T. (2011). Guidelines on Security and Privacy in Public Cloud Computing. NIST Special Publication 800-144. DOI: 10.6028/NIST.SP.800-144.

Kahn, D. (1967). *The Codebreakers: The Comprehensive History of Secret Communication from Ancient Times to the Internet.* Macmillan.

Kaspersky. (2017). *What is the WannaCry Ransomware?* Kaspersky Daily.

Kaspersky. (2021). *A brief history of cybersecurity.* Retrieved from https://www.kaspersky.com

Kaspersky. (n.d.). The History of Antivirus Software. Retrieved from https://www.kaspersky.com/resource-center/threats/the-history-of-antivirus-software

Kent, K., & Souppaya, M. (2006). *Guide to Computer Security Log Management.* National Institute of Standards and Technology (NIST), Special Publication 800-92.

Kharraz, A., Robertson, W., Balzarotti, D., Bilge, L., & Kirda, E. (2015). Cutting the Gordian Knot: A Look Under the Hood of Ransomware Attacks. In *DIMVA 2015: Detection of Intrusions and Malware, and Vulnerability Assessment.*

Killcrece, G., Kossakowski, K.-P., Ruefle, R., & Zajicek, M. (2003). Organizational Models for Computer Security Incident Response

Teams (CSIRTs). Carnegie Mellon University, Software Engineering Institute.

Kim, P. (2014). *The Hacker Playbook: Practical Guide to Penetration Testing*. Secure Planet LLC.

Koomey, J. (2017). *A Simple Model for Determining True Total Cost of Ownership for Data Centers*. Uptime Institute White Paper.

Krsul, I., Spafford, E. H., & Tripunitara, M. (1998). Computer Vulnerability Analysis. Purdue University.

Langner, R. (2011). Stuxnet: Dissecting a cyberwarfare weapon. *IEEE Security & Privacy*, 9(3), 49-51.

Leiner, B. M., Cerf, V. G., Clark, D. D., Kahn, R. E., Kleinrock, L., Lynch, D. C., ... & Wolff, S. (2009). A brief history of the Internet. *ACM SIGCOMM Computer Communication Review, 39*(5), 22-31.

Manky, D. (2013). The evolution of botnets. *Fortinet Blog.* https://www.fortinet.com/blog/threat-research/the-evolution-of-botnets.html

MasterCard & Visa. (1997). Secure Electronic Transaction (SET) Specification.

Menezes, A. J., van Oorschot, P. C., & Vanstone, S. A. (1996). *Handbook of Applied Cryptography*. CRC Press.

Mirkovic, J., & Reiher, P. (2004). A taxonomy of DDoS attack and DDoS defense mechanisms. *ACM SIGCOMM Computer Communication Review*, 34(2), 39-53.

Mitnick, K. D., & Simon, W. L. (2002). *The Art of Deception: Controlling the Human Element of Security*. Wiley.

Mohurle, S., & Patil, M. (2017). A brief study of Wannacry Threat: Ransomware Attack 2017. International Journal of Advanced Research in Computer Science, 8(5).

Moore, D., Shannon, C., & Brown, J. (2002). *Code-Red: a case study on the spread and victims of an Internet worm*. Proceedings of the 2nd ACM SIGCOMM Workshop on Internet measurment.

Morgan, S. (2017). Cybersecurity Jobs Report: A Special Report from the Editors at Cybersecurity Ventures. Cybersecurity Ventures.

Morgan, S. (2020). Cybersecurity spending to exceed $1 trillion from 2017 to 2021. *Cybercrime Magazine.* https://cybersecurityventures.com/cybersecurity-market-report/

Myers, M. (2007). *Social Media Communication: Concepts, Practices, Data, Law and Ethics.* Routledge.

Nachenberg, C. (1997). Computer Virus-antivirus Coevolution. *Communications of the ACM,* 40(1), 46-51.

Narayanan, A., Bonneau, J., Felten, E., Miller, A., & Goldfeder, S. (2016). *Bitcoin and Cryptocurrency Technologies: A Comprehensive Introduction.* Princeton University Press.

National Institute of Standards and Technology (NIST). (2018). Framework for Improving Critical Infrastructure Cybersecurity, Version 1.1.

National Institute of Standards and Technology (NIST). (2020). SolarWinds Cybersecurity Incident.

National Institute of Standards and Technology. (2001). Data Encryption Standard (DES). FIPS PUB 46-3.

National Institute of Standards and Technology. (2015). SHA-3 Standard: Permutation-Based Hash and Extendable-Output Functions. FIPS PUB 202.

National Institute of Standards and Technology. (2018). Framework for Improving Critical Infrastructure Cybersecurity, Version 1.1. Retrieved from https://nvlpubs.nist.gov/nistpubs/CSWP/NIST.CSWP.04162018.pdf

NIST. (2018). *Framework for Improving Critical Infrastructure Cybersecurity, Version 1.1.* National Institute of Standards and Technology. https://nvlpubs.nist.gov/nistpubs/CSWP/NIST.CSWP.04162018.pdf

O'Gorman, L. (2013). Comparing Passwords, Tokens, and Biometrics for User Authentication. *Proceedings of the IEEE,* 91(12), 2021-2040.

OWASP. (2021). *OWASP Top Ten Web Application Security Risks.* Open Web Application Security Project.

Ozment, A., & Schechter, S. E. (2011). Bootstrapping the adoption of internet security protocols. *IEEE Security & Privacy*, 9(3), 24-33.

Palo Alto Networks. (2014). *Next-Generation Firewalls For Dummies*, Special Edition. John Wiley & Sons.

Patterson, D. A., Gibson, G., & Katz, R. H. (1988). A Case for Redundant Arrays of Inexpensive Disks (RAID). *Proceedings of the 1988 ACM SIGMOD International Conference on Management of Data*, 109-116.

PCI Security Standards Council. (2018). *Payment Card Industry (PCI) Data Security Standard.* https://www.pcisecuritystandards.org/document_library

Peltier, T. R. (2005). Information Security Policies, Procedures, and Standards: Guidelines for Effective Information Security Management. Auerbach Publications.

Perkins, C. (2017). *Practical Malware Analysis: The Hands-On Guide to Dissecting Malicious Software.* No Starch Press. Cova, M., Egele, M., Kruegel, C., & Vigna, G. (2010). Detection and analysis of drive-by-download attacks and malicious JavaScript code. Proceedings of the 19th International Conference on World Wide Web, 281-290.

Pfleeger, C. P., & Pfleeger, S. L. (2012). *Security in Computing* (4th ed.). Prentice Hall.

Post, G., & Kagan, A. (2015). Evaluation of the strength of least privilege in Windows Vista for securing desktop applications. Computers & Security, 48, 58-71.

Provos, N., McNamee, D., Mavrommatis, P., Wang, K., & Modadugu, N. (2007). The ghost in the browser: Analysis of web-based malware. Proceedings of the first conference on First Workshop on Hot Topics in Understanding Botnets, 4-4.

Reddy, P. (2017). Penetration Testing and Network Defense. Cisco Press.

Rivest, R. L., Shamir, A., & Adleman, L. M. (1978). A Method for Obtaining Digital Signatures and Public-Key Cryptosystems. Communications of the ACM, 21(2), 120-126.

Rose, S., Borchert, O., Mitchell, S., & Connelly, S. (2020). Zero Trust Architecture. NIST Special Publication 800-207. National Institute of Standards and Technology. https://nvlpubs.nist.gov/nistpubs/SpecialPublications/NIST.SP.800-207.pdf

Rosenberg, J. (2012). *Securing the Network from Malicious Code: A Complete Guide to Defending Against Viruses, Worms, and Trojans.* Wiley.

Sahai, A., & Waters, B. (2005). Fuzzy identity-based encryption. In *Advances in Cryptology – EUROCRYPT 2005* (pp. 457-473). Springer.

Sandhu, R. S., & Samarati, P. (1994). Access Control: Principle and Practice. *IEEE Communications Magazine, 32*(9), 40-48.

SANS Institute. (2019). *Securing The Human: A Review of Issues of Human Computer Interaction and Cybersecurity Awareness.*

Scarfone, K., & Mell, P. (2007). Guide to Intrusion Detection and Prevention Systems (IDPS). *National Institute of Standards and Technology Special Publication* 800-94.

Scarfone, K., & Mell, P. (2007). Guide to Intrusion Detection and Prevention Systems (IDPS). NIST Special Publication 800-94. National Institute of Standards and Technology.

Scarfone, K., & Mell, P. (2007). *Guide to Intrusion Detection and Prevention Systems (IDPS).* NIST Special Publication 800-94.

Scarfone, K., & Mell, P. (2009). *Guide to Intrusion Detection and Prevention Systems (IDPS).* NIST Special Publication 800-94.

Scarfone, K., Souppaya, M., & Cody, A. (2008). Guide to Enterprise Patch Management Technologies. NIST Special Publication 800-40 Version 2.

Schneier, B. (2000). Secrets and Lies: Digital Security in a Networked World. Wiley.

Schneier, B. (2015). *Data and Goliath: The Hidden Battles to Collect Your Data and Control Your World.* W. W. Norton & Company.

Sebag-Monteriore, H. (2000). *Enigma: The Battle for the Code.* Wiley.

Sicari, S., Rizzardi, A., Grieco, L. A., & Coen-Porisini, A. (2015). Security, privacy and trust in Internet of Things: The road ahead. Computer Networks, 76, 146-164.

Sicari, S., Rizzardi, A., Grieco, L. A., & Coen-Porisini, A. (2015). Security, privacy and trust in Internet of Things: The road ahead. Computer Networks, 76, 146-164.

Singh, S. (1999). *The Code Book: The Science of Secrecy from Ancient Egypt to Quantum Cryptography.* Doubleday.

Singh, S. (1999). *The Code Book: The Science of Secrecy from Ancient Egypt to Quantum Cryptography.* Doubleday.

Skoudis, E., & Zeltser, L. (2019). *Counter Hack Reloaded: A Step-by-Step Guide to Computer Attacks and Effective Defenses* (2nd ed.). Prentice Hall.

Solove, D. J., & Schwartz, P. M. (2015). *Information Privacy Law* (5th ed.). Wolters Kluwer Law & Business.

Spafford, E. H. (1989). The Internet Worm Program: An Analysis. *ACM SIGCOMM Computer Communication Review, 19*(1), 17-57.

Spring, J. (2017). Towards improving CVSS-based vulnerability prioritization and response with software properties. Software Quality Journal, 25(3), 893-917.

Stallings, W. (1995). Network and Internetwork Security: Principles and Practice. *Prentice Hall.*

Stallings, W. (2005). *Cryptography and Network Security: Principles and Practices* (4th ed.). Pearson.

Stallings, W. (2017). Cryptography and Network Security: Principles and Practice (7th ed.). Pearson.

Stallings, W., & Brown, L. (2012). *Computer Security: Principles and Practice* (2nd ed.). Pearson.

State of California Department of Justice. (n.d.). California Consumer Privacy Act (CCPA). https://oag.ca.gov/privacy/ccpa

State of California. (2018). California Consumer Privacy Act (CCPA). https://oag.ca.gov/privacy/ccpa

Stobert, E., & Biddle, R. (2014). The password life cycle: user behaviour in managing passwords. SOUPS 2014, 243-255.

Stobert, E., & Biddle, R. (2014). The Password Life Cycle: User Behaviour in Managing Passwords. *SOUPS 2014.*

Stouffer, K., Pillitteri, V., Lightman, S., Abrams, M., & Hahn, A. (2015). Guide to Industrial Control Systems (ICS) Security. NIST Special Publication 800-82 Rev. 2.

Stuttard, D., & Pinto, M. (2011). *The Web Application Hacker's Handbook: Finding and Exploiting Security Flaws* (2nd ed.). Wiley.

Symantec. (2018). *Internet Security Threat Report.*

Symantec. (2019). *Internet Security Threat Report.*

Szor, P. (2005). *The Art of Computer Virus Research and Defense.* Pearson Education.

Taddeo, M., & Floridi, L. (2018). "Regulate artificial intelligence to avert cyber arms race." *Nature,* 556, 296-298.

Tankard, C. (2011). Advanced persistent threats and how to monitor and deter them. *Network Security,* 2011(8), 16-19.

Thomas, D. (2003). *Creeper and Reaper: The first virus and the first antivirus.* The Hacker Quarterly. Retrieved from http://www.foo.be/docs-free/mirror/www.textfiles.com/magazines/HCK/1986-10.txt

U.S. Congress. (2015). Cybersecurity Information Sharing Act of 2015. https://www.congress.gov/bill/114th-congress/senate-bill/754

U.S. Department of Homeland Security. (2018). Cybersecurity and Infrastructure Security Agency Act of 2018. https://www.dhs.gov/CISA

United States Congress. (2002). Sarbanes-Oxley Act of 2002. Public Law 107-204.

United States Department of Health and Human Services. (n.d.). Health Insurance Portability and Accountability Act of 1996 (HIPAA). https://www.hhs.gov/hipaa/index.html

United States Department of Justice. (n.d.). Computer Fraud and Abuse Act (CFAA). Retrieved from https://www.justice.gov

United States v. Morris, 928 F.2d 504 (2d Cir. 1991).

Veeramachaneni, K., Arnaldo, I., Korrapati, V., Bassias, C., & Li, K. (2016). AI²: Training a big data machine to defend. In 2016 IEEE International Conference on Big Data Security on Cloud (BigDataSecurity), IEEE International Conference on High Performance and Smart Computing, (HPSC) and IEEE International Conference on Intelligent Data and Security (IDS), 49-54.

Voigt, P., & Von dem Bussche, A. (2017). *The EU General Data Protection Regulation (GDPR): A Practical Guide.* Springer International Publishing.

von Solms, R., & van Niekerk, J. (2013). From information security to cyber security. *Computers & Security*, 38, 97-102.

Wallace, M., & Webber, L. (2017). *The Disaster Recovery Handbook: A Step-by-Step Plan to Ensure Business Continuity and Protect Vital Operations, Facilities, and Assets.* AMACOM.

Weidman, G. (2014). *Penetration Testing: A Hands-On Introduction to Hacking.* No Starch Press.

West-Brown, M. J., Stikvoort, D., Kossakowski, K.-P., Killcrece, G., Ruefle, R., & Zajicek, M. (2003). Handbook for Computer Security Incident Response Teams (CSIRTs). *Carnegie Mellon University, Software Engineering Institute.* Retrieved from https://resources.sei.cmu.edu

Whitfield Diffie. (2018). *Cryptography's Role in Securing the Information Society.* National Academies Press.

Whitman, M. E., & Mattord, H. J. (2013). *Principles of Information Security.* Cengage Learning.

Zetter, K. (2014). Countdown to Zero Day: Stuxnet and the Launch of the World's First Digital Weapon. Crown.

Zhou, J., Gollmann, D., & Mitchell, C. (Eds.). (2013). *Information Security and Privacy: 18th Australasian Conference, ACISP 2013, Brisbane, Australia, July 1-3, 2013, Proceedings.* Springer.

Zimmermann, P. R. (1995). *The Official PGP User's Guide.* MIT Press.

Zurko, M. E., & Simon, R. T. (1996). User-Centered Security. *New Security Paradigms Workshop.* DOI: 10.1145/304851.304912

Zwicky, E. D., Cooper, S., & Chapman, D. B. (2000). *Building Internet Firewalls* (2nd ed.). O'Reilly Media.